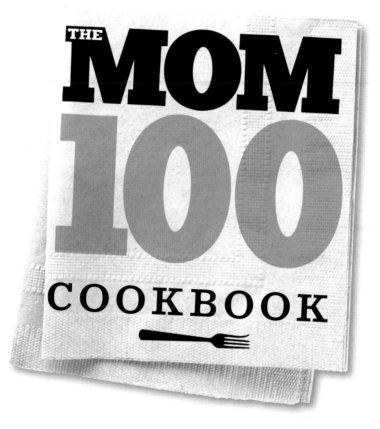

THE MOM 100 COOKBOOK

KATIE WORKMAN

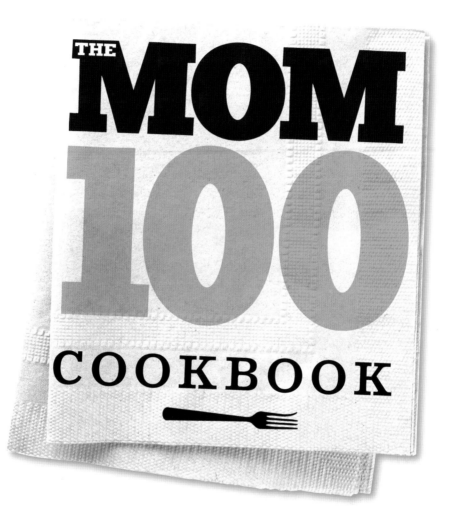

THE MOM 100 COOKBOOK

100 Recipes Every Mom Needs in Her Back Pocket

Photographs by Todd Coleman

WORKMAN PUBLISHING
NEW YORK

Library of Congress Cataloging-in-Publication Data is available.
ISBN 978-0-7611-6603-0

Cover and interior design by Raquel Jaramillo
Cover and interior photographs by Todd Coleman
Additional photography: p. xxiv: left © Nattika/Shutterstock; right © Photolinc/Shutterstock

Workman books are available at special discounts when purchased in bulk for premiums and sales promotions as well as for fund-raising or educational use. Special editions or book excerpts can also be created to specification. For details, contact the Special Sales Director at the address below, or send an e-mail to specialmarkets@workman.com.

Workman Publishing Company, Inc.
225 Varick Street
New York, NY 10014-4381
www.workman.com

Printed in the United States of America
First printing March 2012

10 9 8 7 6 5 4 3

For Jack and Charlie and Gary, my loves

Acknowledgments

Lucky, lucky, lucky. The "acknowledgments" are my absolute favorite part of the book to write.

Suzanne Rafer is my brilliant and amazing editor. When I was growing up, loving cookbooks, reading them at bedtime, it was Suzanne's cookbooks that were stacked up on my night table. I taught myself how to cook from the Silver Palate cookbooks, and admired everything about anything her hands touched from stem to stern. When she said to me a couple of years ago, "I think you should write a cookbook," my heart nearly busted. I might not have done this if it weren't for her, and she certainly made it better and also made it fun. Erin Klabunde, her assistant, was a lovely, bright note punctuating the whole process.

Raquel Jaramillo, who designed this book, is an extraordinary and talented person in every way, and if I could thank her in song I would, but that would suck because I can't sing.

The people at Workman could have their own page of acknowledgments. I worked in publishing for years (and at Workman for several years), so I know exactly what all of these excellent people are doing behind the scenes, and they need to all come out and take a bow: Selina Meere and Rebecca Carlisle, for being the wind beneath my publicity wings; David Schiller, for being brilliant and insightful in many capacities; the lovely Anne Kerman, for orchestrating the photography; Jessica Wiener, marketing smartypants; and Marissa Hussey, Internet whisperer. The unsung heroes who make sure the t's are crossed, the i's dotted, and that "acknowledgments" is spelled correctly are Barbara Mateer and Beth Levy, with the aid of Barbara Peragine and Jarrod Dyer in the type department. And the way the book looks and feels in your hands is due to the production skill of Julie Primavera.

Admiration and appreciation also go to core members of the Workman team, Jenny Mandel, Pat Upton, Walter Weintz, Suzie Bolotin, Bob Miller, Page Edmunds, and the entire sales and marketing teams.

I e-mailed the skilled food editor and photographer of *Saveur* magazine, Todd Coleman, for thoughts on who might shoot this book. He e-mailed back, "I'll shoot your book." I e-mailed "What? Really?" And shoot the book he did, with the extraordinary help of Ben Mims, Hilary Merzbacher, Judy Haubert, Monica Floirendo, Lauren Utvitch, Alex Saggiomo, and Maxime Iattoni, led by the wonderful and organized *Saveur* kitchen director, Kellie Evans. I will remember the crazy-fun days of our shoot for the rest of my life. Who knew there was such a thing as "shoot beers"?

A huge thank you to the smart cookies at Bullfrog & Baum, in particular Pamela Spiegel.

We all have people who influence our lives, and sometimes believe in us more than we believe in ourselves. Pam Krauss was my first boss, and to this day someone whose friendship, ideas, and opinions mean more to me than I can say. Jennifer Baum was there during every major life decision, and said, "Do it, I'll be there for you." Dana Cowin made and makes me feel like anything is possible. Catherine Skobe would not only buy ice from me in Alaska, but would also get fifty of her friends to do the same. If I were a drug addict, but love and support were my drug, then Chris Styler would be my dealer. And Joe Seone would wash our vials.

Gail Silverton, the kids' (okay, our family's) longtime caregiver, minced more things and washed more dishes for this book than most people do in a lifetime. She believed in everything, and to her we all owe so much. She almost never swore, so when she tasted something and said "Damn!" I knew it was a keeper.

I wrote a bunch of this book in the middle school library of my kids' school (Quiet! Peaceful!) and librarians Joe Quain and Roxanne Feldman could not have been more welcoming hosts, or better companions when I needed a break.

Jean Witter, Abby Rothschild, Rebecca Stettner, and Robin Easton—just thank you for everything. When your kids' friends' parents become your own great friends . . . well, that's just stupendously lucky. (Hey, can you pick up my kids on Friday?)

Many thanks to the following always, always supportive people: My awesome sister, Lizzie Workman, and her husband Mark Williams. The Freilich clan: Arnie, Sandy, Jeff, Silvina, Andy, Lisa, and Adam—thank you all. And thanks to Ted and Donna Bocuzzi, Alison and Bryan Dunn, the Rosenblatts, Kelly Hoey, Charlie Masson, Alexis Romer and Kevin Verronneau, Karen Kreitsek, Sharon Almog, Eugenia Bone, Pam Horn, Kate Tyler, Rob Easton, David Erlanger, Mark and Maryanne Alonso, Amy and Debby Ziff, Leigh Galione, Dave Barry, Carla Sinatra, Gijs Van Thiel, Amy

Wilton, Andrea Szasz, Katie Chin, and Stephanie Testa. And many thanks to the inimitable Christopher Idone, who always reminds me what real food and real cooking are all about, and to Will Schwalbe, who thinks big, and to the postive force that is Abby Schneiderman.

Special thanks to Marion Wilton, who shared some of her treasures for the photo shoots, and Laurie Griffith, who professionally tested a bunch of these recipes. Barbara Goldstein loaned us her kitchen for the cover shoot, and then came up with the very funny line, "Does my kitchen look thin in the photo?"

And to all the kid testers, who sat at the table again and again, giving me feedback (you honest little people you) and reality checks, especially Aaron Erlanger, Jack Stettner, Beau Radomisli, Ryan McCormick, Ryan Easton, Aidan and Ethan Dunn, Grant Gordon, and Ben Rothschild. Ben, thanks for liking the cod.

Finally, finally . . . my parents' opinions matter more to me than anyone else's, with the exception of my husband's (see Gary; below). I don't think it's always healthy, but it's just true. My mom is a very good intuitive cook, and from her all things sprung. She is clever, funny, giving, complicated, and often inappropriate. All qualities to which I aspire, and emulate. My dad is annoyingly smart and inspiringly generous. His last name is on the spine of this book (he's the Workman who is in fact Workman), but he stood back from this project because he wanted it to be what it was going to be. That, and I think he was a little scared, like the time I got a nose ring.

To my kids: Every day, every day, I love you so much. You are extraordinary and brave and fun and smart and you make me want to be all of those things, too.

To Cooper: You are a dog. I did not want you at first. I was wrong. I love you. You need a bath more often. I am glad you like the food. I will snuggle you tonight.

To my husband: Gary. You are amazing. It's rare to find unconditional love amidst all the knots and craziness. You always wanted me to figure it out, and have fun (and keep cooking). I love you so much. And thank you.

Contents

What You May Be Looking For 334
Need a dish you can cook in under 30 minutes?
Wondering how many dishes in the book are
vegetarian? Curious to see which dishes call
for chicken? Check out the useful lists in this
section.

Introduction

How to Pick Your Battles and Find Happiness in the Kitchen

There was a bizarre perfume commercial that ran on TV throughout the late seventies and eighties that must have made many women cringe. The ad presented its own view of the liberated woman: She was someone who was not only able to bring home the bacon, but also able to fry it up in a pan, all the while never, never letting her partner "forget he's a man." It popped into my mind as I was scraping cheese off the bottom of the toaster oven. And, while the stunning, multi-tasking woman who stars in the ad does make reference to having children (the singing voice-over boasts that she can make the kids breakfast and still be at work at 5 minutes to 9:00) there is simply no evidence of kids at all. This über-every-woman may be holding a frying pan, but frankly it's empty and I think the price sticker is still on it. There are no sticky-fingered children clinging to her shapely legs, pinching each other, getting maple syrup on her brand-new stockings. I don't think her perfume is the solution I'm looking for.

Well, happily that's over, those crazy high expectations that a mom can do it all, with only the help of a perfume.

Oh, wait . . . what? It's not over? We still need to do that whole thing with the bacon and the kids and the work and the man (or at least the kids and the work)? Oh.

May I make a suggestion? Let's stop acting as if life isn't messy and complicated and highly inconvenient at times. Let's not even acknowledge the imagined platonic ideal of the woman who can breastfeed a baby while beating eggs for a soufflé and at the same time tally up the P&L spread-sheets for Huge Important Company, Inc. Let's ignore her completely (since she's not real, we're not hurting anyone's feelings).

One of the commonest denominators in the lives of all moms is the often anxiety-inducing need to feed our families. Like, every day! Really, just completely non-negotiable. And I don't think you need to hear another diatribe about how we're not making enough time to be a family at the dinner table, and how packaged foods and take-out are ruining our health, and how hard you have to fight to keep your kids from turning into French fry–munching, video game–loving, sugar-addicted zombies. You already know all that. You're sufficiently concerned. You're a good mom. Okay, we're all on the same page . . . but now what do we do?

100 Answers to the 20 Most Common Feeding-Kids Dilemmas

This book is simply a collection of one hundred straightforward and imminently usable recipes that address a dilemma, a predicament, a head-scratcher that we moms face day in and day out. "How can I get my kids to try fish?" "How can I broaden my kids' white food horizons?" "What was I thinking when I invited everyone over after the school play?" "Why are you telling me at 8:30 tonight that you signed me up to make muffins for tomorrow morning's Corn Festival?"

The one hundred solutions are great-tasting recipes that every mom can rely on, share, and feel good about. They are that stockpile of foolproof, crowd-pleasing, familiar (but not boring) recipes you've been wishing you had at your fingertips. Here you will find recipes for weekday breakfasts, weeknight dinners, bake sales, potlucks, and white and nonwhite foods that kids will embrace. Unfussy recipes, reliable recipes, but recipes that may surprise you a little bit, in terms of what you and your family can enjoy together.

Why These 100?

There are a number of fairly consistent cooking situations we moms find ourselves in. Weeknight dinners is a biggie. Then there are lunches, potluck school events, bake sales, easy family entertaining, vegetables sides. We need meals to make ahead, meals for vegetarians, meals with different levels of spiciness. You will find answers here, recipes that you'll want to go to again and again and again. You will still use and love other cookbooks. You will still use and be grateful for recipes on the Internet. But when you need a simple mom-and-family-friendly recipe, and don't have the time or energy to sift through dozens of sources, you should find just what you are looking for right here.

And There's More: Extra Helpful Elements

Where relevant, each recipe has notes on these topics to provide more information.

Make Ahead: Tips on how the dish, or parts of it, can be made in advance.

Cooking Tips: Miscellaneous bits of advice, clarifications, shortcuts, and other info about preparing the recipe.

Vegetarian Notes: If a non-vegetarian recipe can be made into a vegetarian version, here's where you'll find out how to do it.

Fork in the Road (see page xvi)

What the Kids Can Do: There's no guarantee on this, but it's often the case that when your kids help prepare something, they're more likely to try it. With that in mind, each recipe is accompanied by tips on what your kids can do, though of course you'll have to make the determination based on their age and ability.

Variations: There are so many ways to tweak a recipe, and lots of them are presented throughout. But don't hesitate to come up with some of your own to best suit your family's tastes: switch in a favorite vegetable, change up the spices, make the recipes your own.

Fork in the Road

Throughout the book you will notice a number of dishes are marked as Fork in the Road recipes. This addresses the need to adapt a recipe to suit the needs of a family where picky palates are prevalent. Basically a recipe is made, fairly simply, up to a certain point. Then, some of the dish is removed (think plain pasta sauce, pita chips, simple sautéed chicken cutlets), and set aside for the kids or for those with milder palates. Then, you continue on with the rest of the dish, adding some additional ingredients and flavors for those with more adventurous palates. The result is that you get to make one dish for the whole family, everyone is sharing the same meal, but the grown-ups are eating something with more interest, more sophistication, while the kids are eating a great meal that doesn't push them past their limits.

This solves a couple of issues:

1. It allows you all to share the same dinner. You won't be making several different things for dinner as if you were a short-order cook, or resorting to frozen chicken nuggets or plain pasta for the kids just because you want to eat something interesting and they don't.

2. Without "dumbing down" food for your kids, or conversely sweating over a meal that your kids and their friends will refuse to eat (usually while guests are over, it seems), you will be able to introduce different flavors to your dinner table. If you think the more flavored version of a dish will be a stretch for your kids, keep their portions simple, and let them try yours. Maybe next time you'll be making the whole recipe with more complex flavors.

Cut Yourself Some Slack

To be a good mom, you do not have to cook every meal, or make everything from scratch, or know the provenance of every morsel of food your children eat. Give yourself a break. This cooking thing should be a little bit fun. Wow, we've really gotten to a point where food has become serious. We're either ankle deep in news about hormones in our meat, or trying to pronounce thiamin mononitrate, or hearing about kids with weight issues, or trying to remember which red dye number is going to kill us fastest, or just looking at the stove at the end of the day like it's our arch enemy. We need to figure out how to capture some joy in the kitchen, because guess what? We get to make dinner just about every night! And we can approach this task as though we are being asked to regrout our bathtub nightly, or approach it with a certain amount of *joie de vivre*. We might as well pick that *joie* thing, because (as I mentioned possibly twice already) *we have to do it anyway*.

Also, while there is plenty of good food-oriented television programming and interesting writing about food, there is also a lot that is . . . well . . . kind of ridiculous and/or kind of intimidating. Certainly we should all be aware of where our food comes from, and pick up a thing or two about sustainability, eating locally, and the like. But when too much information gets in the way of our getting dinner on the table, it's time to tell the food police to take their thesis about the care and propagation of endangered heirloom potatoes and play somewhere else. You, my friend . . . you have dinner to make.

A Word About Picky Eaters

No one is enchanted by people who say, "My kids are such wonderful eaters, they eat everything." The only responses are, "Wow! Good for you, and good for them!" or "Liar, liar, pants on fire." Some kids eat a lot of different foods, and some don't. I do feel glad/lucky that my own kids are pretty darn good eaters. However, they don't eat everything. Who eats

everything? And why does eating everything make you such a spectacular human being?

If you have kids who *do* eat pretty much everything, then you are one lucky duck. But a gentle reminder—this information isn't as enthralling to others as it is to you. If it secretly makes you feel better, you can hold your head a little higher at the PTA meeting and think to yourself, "I see you over there, Claire, bragging about your little Donny, and how well he did at the chess tournament. Well, good for you, miss missy; my Brian eats Brussels sprouts. Checkmate, baby." And you can rest assured that your mother-in-law is sharing the good news with her mah-jongg friends.

Cooking for kids is not always the most gratifying experience, I'm the first to admit. And when someone I'd like to impress, just a little bit, is sitting at the

5 Basic Tips for Getting Your Kids to Eat More Things

1. Sorry for the all caps but DO NOT OFFER YOUR KID SOMETHING TO TRY WHILE SIMULTANEOUSLY SAYING, "I DON'T THINK YOU'RE GOING TO LIKE THIS." We all catch ourselves doing this occasionally, and realize, just after the words have escaped and it's too late, Oops. Now what are the odds that your child will turn around and say, "No, Mom, you're wrong; this 8-bean soup is fantastic!"

2. Realize that your kids probably think they *are* going to hate most new things, and that it is your job to basically ignore that fact, and keep moving forward, like a shark. Otherwise in fifty years we are going to be looking at senior communities filled with people nibbling on chicken nuggets and debating the merits of honey-mustard vs. barbecue sauce, both of which will probably give them all heartburn.

3. Start with small portions. This is mentioned a couple of times in the book, especially when it comes to things like fish or anything kids look at suspiciously. A big slab or bowl of something they are skeptical of may result in a stonewall, while a little

table, one of my kids usually picks that moment to say, "Ew, Mom are those capers?! I'm not eating that." To which I usually respond, smiling with gently clenched teeth and stiff cheeks, "Honey, you ate that last month, and you loved it. Really, you loved it. You asked for seconds. No big deal, it's just so funny that you don't remember!" It's so FUNNY!

And as the old song goes (yes, Kenny Rogers) "You got to know when to walk away, know when to run." On some family trips to a certain kind of destination, there are chicken nuggets as far as the eye can see, and you have to give in to the moment, Zen nugget–like. Serenity now.

two-bite experiment is much more likely to be acceptable.

4. Keep a bit of a poker face. In other words, as hard as it is (and it is hard) don't beg (except for fish, where begging is sometimes acceptable; see pages 139 to 151). If your kids know you really want them to like something, they may resist it more. This isn't total control-freakism on their part, just a little.

5. Employ peer pressure (the good kind). Make an effort to eat with other kids (often bigger kids) who have broader palates than your children do. Your picky eater may be willing to give something a shot in the name of being perceived as cool or more grown up. In summary, my children would probably not have ingested such large portions of Thai-flavored carrot coconut milk bisque at a friend's house recently without three super cool, unflappable high schoolers at the table.

17 Amazing Ingredients

Everyone won't find all seventeen of these ingredients amazing, but here is a list of items that I love and use all the time.

1. **Olive oil:** For most savory food, except for Asian food, this is the kind of oil I use. It's smart and economical to have two kinds of olive oil. You can use the less-expensive pure olive oil for cooking, saving the more pricey extra-virgin for uncooked dishes, like salad dressings or tomato bruschetta and the like. There are tons of brands out there, and you should try a variety since some have a much more pronounced flavor, some are fruitier than others, and so on, and find ones that you really like.

2. **Kosher or coarse salt:** All of the recipes, whether savory or sweet, call for this kind of salt, or coarse salt. Any kind is fine; I use Morton's Coarse Kosher Salt most often; it's just the right texture. You should avoid salt that is *too* coarse, or you'll be crunching chunks, which is not so pleasant.

   You also may want to experiment with some other fancy salts, like fleur de sel, Maldon Sea Salt (it's flaky), or some of the Hawaiian varieties, but make sure to save those for sprinkling on at the end of a dish. They are expensive, so you'll want to use them sparingly, and their subtle flavors will get lost if you use them in cooking.

3. **Onion and its family:** The onion family includes garlic, leeks, onions, shallots, and scallions, and practically

every non-sweet recipe in the book includes one or more of these. In short, the onion family, whether cooked or raw, provides a flavor base for almost any kind of savory dish, no matter what the ethnic orientation. When raw the flavor is sharper, when cooked it becomes more mellow and sweet, but it's hard to think of any other ingredient that has a place in so many dishes and cultures.

Store onions, shallots, and garlic in a cool, dry place. Scallions should be stored in the fridge.

4. **Dijon mustard:** A little bit in everything, from salad dressing to tuna fish to macaroni and cheese, turns things from blah to not blah very quickly. Dijon mustard also includes wine or vinegar or both for that identifiable tang, and is the mustard I use most in cooking. Even if your family is not a mustard family, when used as an ingredient in various dishes it elevates the flavor much like salt or pepper or soy sauce. Speaking of which . . .

5. **Soy sauce:** Indispensible in all things Asian (and kids on the whole seem to really like the basic flavors of Asian food), but also interesting as an ingredient in recipes that aren't particularly Asian in tone. If you think of soy sauce like salt, and use small amounts judiciously, it can add a different note to a lot of savory dishes.

I usually use low-sodium soy sauce. If you have regular soy sauce, but want to dilute it for a lower sodium content, you can add water to regular soy sauce (to make 1 cup low-sodium soy sauce, use ¾ cup regular soy sauce mixed with ¼ cup water, so a 3 to 1 ratio).

6. **Chipotle peppers in adobo sauce:** Spicy? In large amounts, sure. And lots of kids aren't nuts about very spicy. But if you add a little to various dishes (chili, stews, soups, and dips) it will add a smoky, warm quality that brings a great deal of interest and depth to your cooking.

Chipotles in adobo sauce are smoked jalapeño peppers that have been stewed in a sauce with tomatoes, garlic, vinegar, salt, and various spices such as cumin, oregano, and paprika. Imagine doing all that yourself! Now imagine pureeing a little 7-ounce can of the peppers and sauce, transferring it to a plastic container, putting it in the fridge, and scooping out teaspoons whenever you need it for a couple of months worth of cooking. When it's all gone, you do it again. It lasts for weeks upon weeks, and you will fall in love with its smoky, sultry taste. To summarize: A little bit of puree equals nice flavor, not so much heat; a lot of puree equals a lot of flavor *and* heat. It is sold in the Hispanic/Mexican sections of most supermarkets.

7. **Fresh ginger:** Another ingredient often associated with Asian food, and rightly so, ginger adds wonderful aroma and flavor to lots of dishes. Ginger is sharply spicy when raw, but mellows with cooking, and it can be used in sweet dishes and baking, as well as savory dishes. You'll find it in the produce sections of most supermarkets.

   Buy small branches, amounts you'll use in a week or two if possible. The best way to store fresh ginger is in a zipper-top bag, with all of the air pressed out, in the crisper drawer in your fridge. It should last for up to two months that way.

8. **Fresh Parmesan cheese:** The real stuff puts anything you buy in a can to shame. Freshly grated Parmesan is a central ingredient in dishes such as macaroni and cheese or risotto, but a little bit sprinkled on a salad or a soup or a grilled pizza or mashed potatoes offers an extra hit of flavor and a bit of saltiness. In a perfect world, you'll buy a nice big block and grate it yourself as needed. In a more real world, you

FOOD ALLERGIES

Lots of kids have food allergies, and if you think that they seem much more prevelant than when you were a kid, you're right. Twelve million people in the U.S., have them according to the Food Allergies and Anaphylaxis Network. People can be allergic to anything, but the most common food allergies are to tree nuts, peanuts, dairy, eggs, wheat (gluten), fish and shellfish, and seeds.

Why allergies are on the rise is unclear, though there are several factors many researchers believe are contributing to their increase. One strongly held theory is known as "hygiene hypothesis," which contends that people in industrialized countries are living in increasingly sterile environments, and our immune systems don't get challenged as often, and therefore become hypersensitive. In other words, because our immune systems have less to challenge them, they over-react to things that are not inherently harmful, like certain foods. Eating more processed foods and eating out in restaurants also poses increased risk for people who do have allergies, so reactions are on the rise as well.

Allergic reactions can range from mild rashes and itchiness to anaphylactic shock. New treatments are being developed as we speak, but if your child has food allergies, your family knows how scary and frustrating living with them can be. I have had severe allergies since I was a baby. It sucks, there's no two ways about it.

Severe food allergies can be overwhelming, and it takes some effort not to let them dictate too much of how you live your life. While being immensely careful, and never taking preventable chances, it is a good thing if you can help your kid see his or her allergies as just a small part of who they are, not a defining part. It's important for them to learn to watch out for themselves, and ask the right questions and recognize any symptoms, but it's also important to be able to feel good about food, and not have it feel like the obstacle course at the center of their existence.

might buy the pre-grated Parmesan, but even if you do, go for the good stuff at the cheese counter or a specialty store.

Parmesan is a hard granular cheese, made from raw cow's milk, and the authentic stuff, Parmegiano-Reggiano, is produced in the Emilia-Romagna region of Italy. The name Parmesan is also used for cheeses that imitate Parmigiano-Reggiano, since the use of the actual words are protected by Italian and European law to designate cheese made specifically in that region. The closest legitimate Italian cheese to Parmigiano-Reggiano is Grana Padano, which can be slightly less sharp and nutty. There are also good domestic versions of Parmesan.

One good way to store a chunk of Parm is to moisten a piece of cheesecloth or a paper towel and wrap it around the cheese, then wrap the whole thing in aluminum foil and store it in the crisper drawer of your refrigerator. The foil allows just the right amount of air to circulate around the cheese, and it should keep for months.

9. **Sriracha sauce:** This is just a type of hot sauce that my family loves. Originally from Thailand (though some contend Vietnam), it includes a bit of garlic and vinegar along with the chili pepper paste. You can absolutely use Tabasco sauce or any other hot sauce in place of sriracha when you are looking to add a bit of heat. Again, don't think of this only as a way of making things spicy; in the same way that black pepper is used, a small amount elevates flavors, while a larger amount will definitely make things hot. It is available at most supermarkets, sometimes in the Asian section, sometimes with the hot sauces.

10. **Canned tomatoes:** These are available in many varieties, whole (in puree or juice), crushed (in puree or juice), pureed, diced, as sauce, and more. You can buy them whole and cut them up yourself, or go for the pre-pureed/diced/crushed versions to save time. Tuttorosso makes a good crushed tomato in puree, and other brands to look for include Muir Glen and Pomi.

You may have heard about San Marzano tomatoes, which are from Italy, and extremely flavorful because of the unique soil and environment they are grown in. They are pretty fantastic, and so are other tomatoes that are grown in nearby regions (but can't be called San Marzano because they aren't grown in that exact region. Francesconi is one brand someone in the know turned me on to. If you find them, buy lots). San Marzanos are more expensive than your everyday canned tomato, but worth the splurge when you are making something for a special occasion. They usually come whole, so you have to do any crushing or dicing or pureeing yourself.

11. **Pasta:** This is sort of a "no, duh" thing to include, but it is, in fact, one of those life-saving items to always, always have in the house. If you have a box of pasta, you will almost definitely be able to get dinner on the table from whatever you have in the fridge or in your pantry. And pasta also equals casseroles, macaroni and cheese, skillet meals, and so forth.

12. **Canned beans:** Garbanzos, kidneys, black beans, pintos, cannellini, navy beans . . . whichever you use the most are the ones you should stock up on.

Beans are a low fat, vegetarian protein that stores well for years, can be used in so many different ways and in so many different cuisines, and is very economical on top of all that. Dried beans also last for a long time, and are even cheaper, but in most cases you do have to plan ahead because they need to be soaked and cooked before you use them in recipes, so they are less of a last-minute help.

Beans have significant amounts of fiber and soluble fiber, with one cup of cooked beans providing between nine and thirteen grams of fiber. Soluble fiber is believed to help lower blood cholesterol. Beans are also high in complex carbohydrates, folate, and iron.

13. **Butter:** Usually unsalted is the way to go, whether you are baking or using it in savory dishes. That way, you can add salt to your liking, without taking into account the salt that's already in the butter. If you want to treat yourself, buy one of the slightly more expensive European butters, or another brand with a high butterfat content. Less moisture in the butter yields a richer texture and flavor.

14. Eggs: Always have eggs on hand. Large is the size called for in all of the recipes in the book, though if you use extra-large you won't mess anything up. Eggs are used in almost all baking, and allow you to get a quick protein-filled breakfast together. They also make a great lunch or super-fast dinner, whether plainly scrambled, or in a fancier form, like a frittata (page 279).

15. Canned or boxed broth: Chicken, beef, or vegetable broth are very helpful pantry staples (just vegetable if you are a vegetarian, of course), and you'll find them called for frequently. Choose low-sodium, if you can, since the regular varieties tend to have a high sodium content. Play around with the brands to find your favorite, and buy different sizes so you'll have a small can available when you need just a bit, and a bigger box or two when you are making a substantial pot of soup.

16. Lemons and limes: Citrus adds such a great burst of flavor to all sorts of recipes. The juice is great, and the zest (the thin colored outer skin of the fruit—avoid the bitter tasting white pith underneath) also gives a refreshing hit of flavor. Keep lemons and limes in the fridge, and before using, give them a firm roll on the counter with your hand pressing down on the fruit; this will make them easier to juice.

17. Vinegars: How many vinegars are there? Lots. Here are some of the ones available in supermarkets and speciaty food stores, not to mention online: white wine vinegar, red wine vinegar, Port wine vinegar, Sherry vinegar, Champagne vinegar, balsamic vinegar, rice vinegar (seasoned and unseasoned—unseasoned is best for dressings), black rice vinegar, apple cider vinegar, fruit vinegars (such as raspberry, blackberry, or blueberry), malt vinegar, and flavored vinegar (such as fig, herbed, spiced, and citrus)

4 Handy Kitchen Tricks

1. Put leftover tomato paste into freezer-safe zip-top bags, flatten, and freeze (see the sidebar on page 196 for more information).

2. Substitute ketchup for tomato paste, in equal amounts.

3. Bake your bacon instead of frying it: If you lay the strips of bacon on a wire rack placed on a rimmed baking sheet and bake them in a preheated 400°F oven for 20 minutes you'll get nice crisp flat strips of bacon, and save yourself cleaning a oil-splattered stovetop. Drain on paper towels.

4. Use freezer-safe zip-top bags to store food in the freezer. Fill the bag—about two inches shy of the top—with the food (this works especially well with stews and soups), zip the bag almost completely closed, leaving a small enough opening to press the air out of the bag without squirting food all over the place. Then seal completely. These can then be placed flat in the freezer.

• Freeze foods in the sizes you will likely want to defrost. In other words, use a quart container (or zip-top bag) vs. a gallon size if you think that's the right amount for the next meal. It's easier to

defrost four quart containers than one gallon anyway, and you have the option of using the smaller amount, if that's a better amount.

• Label all foods with the name of the dish and the date you froze it. Use a permanent marker, either writing on the container itself or a piece of tape. I can't tell you how many times I've thought, "Oh, I'll know what that is," only to find later that I defrosted pasta sauce instead of chili, or vice versa.

If you take a bit of time during the week, maybe Sunday evening, to mince and chop a bunch of veggies you will thank yourself all week long. Pour a glass of wine or make yourself a mug of tea, put on some music, and pay it forward.

Here are some suggestions, but you'll determine the ingredients you most often use. If you have a food processor you can just pulse everything up, one at a time, and have yourself an arsenal of prepped ingredients at the ready. Keep all of these things in tightly sealed containers in the fridge.

- minced garlic (cover with a bit of extra virgin olive oil to help it stay fresh for a week)
- minced shallots (up to 5 days)
- chopped onions (up to 4 days)
- carrots peeled and cut into sticks—which means you can munch on them or have them easily cut-able into smaller pieces (up to a week)
- freshly squeezed lemon juice (up to 5 days)
- broccoli florets (up to a week)
- chopped parsley (up to 4 days)
- cooked crumbled bacon (up to 4 days)

8 Cooking Tips:

1. Taste as you go.

2. Experiment in a comfortable way. If you're interested in trying a new spice, add it to some of the roasted potatoes you're making. This way you'll see if you like it without jeopardizing all the potatoes or a more involved main course, if it turns out the flavor is not your thing.

3. Make the Fork in the Road concept your own. If you're making a dish, any dish, and don't know if your kids will like it fully seasoned, see if you can separate some out before you keep going, then fully season the rest.

4. Don't be scared of heat. For instance, when you put a piece of meat into a pan, make sure that the pan is hot, and resist the urge to start moving it around or flipping it repeatedly. In fact, turn the meat as few times as you can. This will allow it to sear properly, and create great flavors that develop when meat, or other foods, meet high heat and their natural sugars caramelize. (Make sure the meat is dry before browning it—it won't get a nice sear or color if it's wet.)

5. Learn how to make a pan sauce. The most basic technique is this: Heat some oil or butter in a pan, add a boneless piece of meat, chicken, or fish and sauté it. When it's cooked through, or almost cooked through, take it out and set it aside. In the same pan, add some seasonings—anything from spices to chopped onion/shallots/garlic to chopped carrots or other veggies. Sauté them for a bit until softened, then deglaze the pan with the liquid of your choice (this means to add some liquid to the pan and allow the heat and the liquid to loosen up all of the bits and pieces that are getting nicely browned on the bottom of the skillet). You can add other flavors at this time, and maybe some more liquid if you're looking for more copious amounts of

sauce. Then you can pour this pan sauce over the meat, or return the meat back to the pan for a last bit of cooking. And that's that. If you wish to keep a piece or two of meat plain, then you can devise endless Fork in the Road meals of your own.

6. Cook in big batches. There is little point to making a small batch of tomato or meat sauce, most soups, chilies, and stews. Making a big batch, or doubling a recipe, usually takes only a small amount of additional time, and then you can freeze enough for another meal (or two!) and give yourself the gift of a dinner waiting in the freezer. Also, leftovers rule.

7. Most soups and stews and chilies are better if you can make them the day before and reheat them. It also allows any fat to congeal on top, which makes it easier to remove.

8. Get your ingredients organized! In restaurants and in professional cooking situations they call this *mise en place,* which translates to "everything in its place." It sounds fancy but it really means "take a minute to make sure you have everything prepped and ready for the dish you're making. That way, you aren't freaking out as you watch the garlic burn while you frantically mince ginger."

The Big Shop

Many people are quite intimidated by the idea of a big weekly shop. Getting that organized feels way too daunting. I get that. But here are a few things to keep in mind:

• Take a bit of time to get your pantry into shape. A bit of groundwork really pays off in terms of being well stocked and knowing what you have and what you need . . . not to mention the peace of mind it brings.

- Getting more purchased in one big swell foop is just an easier way to get through the week. Yes, you will probably have to go to the market again, for milk and the forgotten jar of oregano. It's okay. This is not a perfect science.

  But ultimately, stopping by the market every night for a can of crushed tomatoes and some boneless skinless chicken breasts is no fun at all. I mean it's not like you're wandering the outdoor markets in Provence, sampling the local chevre—you're dashing up aisle 13 for chicken broth while Kenny Rogers sings "Lady" over the speakers and the fluorescent lights beat down on you like a . . . see? See how not fun that is?

- Give yourself time to get into the rhythm of it. If you can embrace the idea of keeping lists, and checking your pantry before you do your weekly big shop, then you will save money, save time, and give yourself (I don't want to oversell this) a Supermom-ish post-shop high that may not last long, but sure feels great.

- Back to that saving money thing. Organizing your pantry, and knowing what basics you like to have around allows you to be more adept on shopping the sales at the markets. If you know that chicken broth and chickpeas are items you turn to over and over again, when they are on sale, buy lots. This works less well with things like heavy cream.

In Closing

Is cooking a homemade dinner more work than heating up a frozen dinner or grabbing take-out? Yes it is. But this can't be an argument against cooking. Almost everything that is worth doing takes some time and effort. Imagine if instead of presents, Santa left envelopes with twenty dollar bills under the tree. Ridiculous examples aside, there aren't a whole lot of things that are more important in the stunningly endless sphere of parenting than feeding your family. And by the way, even those of us who like to cook sometimes feel like throwing a spoonful of peas at our kids when they are being cranky about dinner.

P.S. Okay, I know I'm obsessing a bit here, but I need to reference that perfume ad one more time. There's actually a slightly later version—I think it was on air in 1980—where the whole concept is essentially the same (she works, she is a stellar mother, she makes her husband feel like a real man, yadda yadda). But in this version she is demonstrating how she reads to her children (in full makeup, hair blown out), and in the midst of that a deep voice (presumably her husband) says, "Honey, tonight I'm gonna cook for the kids." She glances sideways and smiles with smug satisfaction at the camera.

HAHAHAHA. I don't mean to laugh. Oh wait, yes I do: HAHAHAHAHAHA.

Now, in some households the guy is the cook. I know it's true, I have seen some of them with my very own eyes. And maybe some of those dad-cooks will use this book, ignoring the title, which will surely be irritating to them, and just focus on the recipes. However, in most houses (including mine), the mom is the cook, and that's why the book is called what it is.

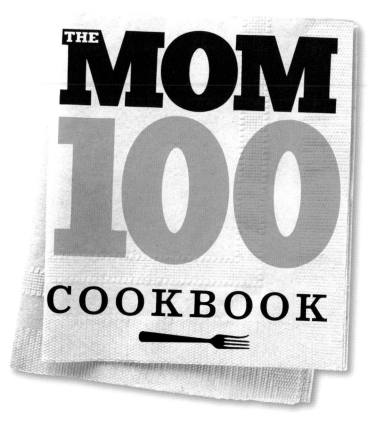

THE **MOM** 100 COOKBOOK

Oatmeal
Your Way
(page 16)

Chapter 1

Quick and Easy Breakfasts

The first sentence out of both my boys' mouths on a typical school morning is "Can-I-have-a-cut-up-apple-and-a-bowl-of-Cinnamon-Life-with-milk." It's not an actual sentence so much as a drowsy run-on phrase, mumbled by my half-asleep children into their folded arms as they slump onto the breakfast table. Other mornings, when there's something vigorous on the day's agenda, like a test or a flag football practice, we're all looking for something that gives our young warriors a bit more protein and substance in their bellies.

> ### THE DILEMMA
>
> *Getting the kids fed and out the door.*

Scrambled eggs can be made as naked as you like or gussied up in dozens of ways. Manhole Eggs turn fried egg and toast into an event. And serving up pizza for breakfast will earn you newfound admiration in the eyes of your offspring. Homemade granola can be made in big batches, though likely not on the actual weekday morning that you are serving it. Finally, oatmeal really is a champion breakfast, filling you up and offering formidable nutritional bang for the buck while at the same time being infinitely customizable.

Other breakfast items in the book are Fruit Salad Kebabs (page 295) and Berries with Sweetened Yogurt (page 296). If you have more time, check out Vegetable Frittata (page 279), Lazy Oven French Toast (which is made the night before; page 274), You-Are-the-Best-Mom-in-the-World Pancakes (page 276), and Moist Banana Muffins (page 284).

Imagine scrambled eggs as the base for all kinds of add-ins, and think about eggs in terms of lunch or dinner, too.

Scrambled Eggs, Many Ways

Serves 2 to 4
Vegetarian, if you want them to be

Most kids like eggs, which is a big relief in the breakfast protein department. If your kids do like scrambled eggs, you should also think of them as your ticket to introducing new flavors and ingredients. Just like chicken, eggs are a great blank protein slate; guess it's not so surprising, since they're related. This is a great opportunity to let your kids get creative, too, in terms of making up their own recipes.

Scrambled eggs are a quasi Fork in the Road dish since it's not much trouble to stir up a few little bowls of eggs with the ingredients of each person's choice. There is that small matter of the first batch of eggs getting cool while the other batches cook, but you can either use two pans or not worry about it too much.

If you already make perfectly fine scrambled eggs then skip along to the suggested add-ins. If you would like a refresher course on successful scrambling, read on.

CHARLIE'S OLIVE PERCENTER

As your kids hit upon their perfect scrambled egg add-ins, let them name their creations, perhaps after themselves. When Charlie was three years old he created what has been and forever will be known in our house as Charlie's Olive Percenter. It's scrambled eggs with sliced green pimiento-stuffed olives mixed in, and after they are cooked and put on the plate, the eggs are covered with thinly sliced cool fresh cucumbers. Don't knock it; the whole thing is a great medley of salty-refreshing, hot-cold, and we eat it all the time.

Charlie picked the name because he said it was "100 percent good." He earnestly dictated the recipe to me, then brought it to a neighborhood restaurant and asked the owner if he would offer them for breakfast. The owner promised that as soon as his restaurant (a fried seafood self-serve place) was open for breakfast, he would do just that.

6 large eggs

Kosher or coarse salt and freshly ground black pepper (optional)

Nonstick cooking spray (optional)

2 teaspoons unsalted butter

1. Crack the eggs into a medium-size bowl, season them with salt and pepper, if using, to taste, and blend well with a fork or a whisk.

2. Spray a medium-size skillet with nonstick cooking spray, or use a nonstick pan if you have one. Melt the butter in the skillet over medium-high heat. Pour in the eggs and let them cook until the bottom starts to set slightly, about 1 minute. Then, using a spatula or wooden spoon, keep scraping the bottom of the skillet, pausing for 20 seconds or so after every few pushes to let the eggs set again. Break apart any very large pieces and keep moving the eggs around so that the runny parts hit the skillet. Stop just as the eggs are done to your liking and scoop them onto plates. Season the eggs with more salt and pepper, if desired.

Cooking Tip: If you want to be ultracautious, cracking the eggs one at a time into a small cup and then adding each to the bowl ensures that one not-so-fresh egg won't spoil the whole bowl (you'll know a bad egg when you see/smell it). The best way to pick out random pieces of eggshell is to use a half of an eggshell as a scoop to fish them out.

Variations

Egg Scrambles

So, now you have the basic recipe down. What can you add? Here are some ideas. The amounts are for six eggs, which usually feed two to four people. Because you're making scrambled eggs, and not an omelet, feel free to stir ingredients right into the beaten eggs before adding them to the pan.

Don't hesitate to mix and match the ingredients. The fun is in creating your own masterpiece, and your kids will soon be ordering up or cooking their very own "eggs of the house" with a side of pride of ownership. These suggestions and combos are just ideas to help you and your kids think about the possibilities.

Cheese scramble: Add 2 to 3 tablespoons of shredded or crumbled cheese, such as mozzarella, cheddar, Monterey Jack, goat cheese, feta, even American—just about all cheese works beautifully with eggs.

Fresh herb scramble: Stir in about 1 teaspoon of minced fresh herbs. This version is especially great if you grow herbs in your home or garden; let the kids pick a sprig of the one that smells the best, and show them how to pick off the tiny leaves. A little bit will add a lot of flavor.

Dried herb scramble: Mix in ¼ to ½ teaspoon of dried herbs, such as oregano, thyme, marjoram, and basil.

Meat scramble: Add ¼ cup of crumbled cooked bacon or sausage (you may need to add less salt to the eggs if you use one of these salty meats).

Vegetable scramble: Mix in ¼ to ½ cup chopped or shredded vegetables, such as chopped tomato, zucchini, summer squash, or shredded carrot. Vegetables like broccoli or asparagus should be lightly cooked first. A variety of veggies makes a colorful medley, and if you play with the name (Breakfast Garden or Confetti Eggs, for example), you may find that your kids are quite game to try some new vegetables.

Mexican scramble: Try a medley of cheeses, a pinch of chili powder, slivered scallions, maybe a couple of tablespoons of kidney or black beans, and a bit of cooked corn. Top the cooked eggs with a spoonful of salsa and sour cream. You might even wrap the whole thing up in a flour tortilla and create a breakfast burrito—kids love the idea of picking up scrambled eggs with their hands.

Italian scramble: Beat in a couple of slivered fresh basil leaves (or ¼ teaspoon of dried basil), 2 tablespoons of shredded mozzarella and/or Parmesan cheese, and maybe a teaspoon or two of some chopped fresh or sun-dried tomatoes. You can serve a dollop of pasta sauce on the side if you like.

Indian scramble: A pinch of curry powder and cumin are very interesting in eggs. Serve the scrambled eggs with a spoonful of chutney and plain yogurt or sour cream (or stir some grated cucumber into the yogurt or sour cream).

All-American scramble: Add some slivered ham, some shredded cheddar, and for those who like their eggs old-school diner style, some ketchup on the side.

Green Eggs: If your kids are Dr. Seuss fans, they may be very open to the addition of some chopped cooked broccoli or spinach in their eggs, about ¼ cup for every 3 eggs. If you want to get really silly, let the kids add a couple of drops of green food coloring to the eggs before you beat them. It won't affect the taste, and they really will be green eggs. You're on your own with the ham.

What the Kids Can Do:
Kids of all ages can crack the eggs (yes, it can be messy, but it's a messy childhood rite of passage). They can stir them up and mix in any add-ins they like. Older kids can be supervised at the stove while they stir. It's a great first stovetop cooking lesson, since eggs require nothing more than some attention as they cook.

Manhole Eggs

Serves 1, can be multiplied as desired
Vegetarian

An egg fried in a hole cut into a piece of bread is not a new invention at all. It has been called by a whole bunch of names: egg in the basket, egg-in-the-hole, bird's nest, gashouse eggs, one-eyed monster, cowboy egg, and sometimes erroneously toad-in-the-hole, which is actually a dish that involves sausage. You simply cut out a circular hole in a piece of bread with a cookie cutter (ha! keep reading) and fry the bread up in a pan with some butter and an egg cracked into the hole. The "ha!" part comes from the fact that if you think I can find my circular cookie cutter at 7 A.M. you clearly have not been to my house for breakfast on a weekday. If I did happen to dredge up a cookie cutter it would probably be one shaped like a dreidel or an autumn leaf or a seahorse, and the egg would be squished into an uncomfortable shape and the yolk wouldn't stand a chance and the children would be perplexed.

So I grab a glass or the cap from the nonstick cooking spray or a largish votive candleholder or anything else I have lying around that has a two- to three-inch diameter, and I punch a hole in the bread and make the magic happen. Also, since you may be wondering about the name here, it's because we live in New York City and even though the term manhole is kind of old-timey and slightly misogynistic it makes sense to us.

> 1 large slice bread, such as sourdough, challah, country, or whole wheat (firmer bread is good), about ½-inch thick
>
> 1½ teaspoons unsalted butter
>
> Nonstick cooking spray (optional)
>
> 1 large egg
>
> Kosher or coarse salt and freshly ground black pepper

Cooking Tip: The way the egg yolk runs into the toast that it was cooked with is a pleasure for many of us, but if your kids don't love a runny yolk, just cook the whole thing for a little longer and you'll have a quasi hard-boiled egg nestled in the bread. Either way your kids will be impressed that you have managed to make two breakfast items become one.

If you use a bigger pan you can make two or three of these at one time. Also, if you want, you can buy small eggs, cut smaller holes in the bread, and put two eggs in a piece of toast so they look like eyes staring out at you. Or that might scare your children, so your call.

What the Kids Can Do: Kids can cut the hole in the bread, and if they are old enough, with supervision they can crack the egg into the hole.

1. Using a cookie cutter or the rim of a glass or whatever works, cut a 2- to 3-inch circle in the middle of the slice of bread. Set aside the cutout piece of bread.

2. Melt the butter in a small nonstick skillet with a lid, or a small skillet sprayed liberally with nonstick cooking spray, over medium heat. Place the slice of bread in the skillet with the cutout piece next to it and lightly toast them, about 2 minutes. Flip the toast and circle with a spatula. Crack the egg into the hole in the bread and season it with salt and pepper to taste. Cook until the bottom of the egg is set, about 2 minutes, then cover the pan with the lid for about 1 to 3 more minutes, peeking to see that the top of the egg firms up as you like it.

3. Using the spatula, transfer the egg in the toast to a plate and top it with the toasted bread circle (the manhole cover), which you can use for dipping into the yolk. Repeat as needed.

Do you ever feel like you're being watched?

English Muffin Pizzas

Serves 2 to 4
A Fork in the Road Recipe
Vegetarian

Tomorrow morning, when your sleepy, groggy, possibly grumpy kids drag their butts to breakfast and mumble incoherent complaints, try saying this: "Who wants pizza for breakfast?" Their little necks will snap up so fast they may pull something.

Somewhere along the way, certain foods were identified as breakfast foods, and most of us are content to face a plate of eggs, some fruit, or perhaps some oatmeal in the morning. But sometimes it's nice to shake it up (and by the way, you will likely get a similar reaction if you offer up pancakes for dinner every once in a while). The main point of breakfast, the piously anointed "most important meal of the day," is to give you energy to go forth and conquer. Or at least go forth and do well on the spelling quiz. So, pretty much any food that sounds good at 7 A.M. and isn't riddled with sugar is fair game. Charlie in particular is often delighted to encounter things like a bowl of vegetable soup or leftover meatballs or chicken piccata first thing in the morning, as am I, which some people find irresistible and others just find weird and confusing.

English Muffin Pizzas come together in the same amount of time it takes to make hot cereal or scramble some eggs. Follow these up with some fruit, or just serve them with a glass of OJ, and all of the consecrated food groups are present. Think of these for an afterschool snack, too, not to mention lunch.

What the Kids Can Do:
Spoon the sauce on the English muffins and lay on the cheese—although on a weekday morning your kids may well be too busy trying to find their shoes or indignantly informing you of a test they forgot to study for and why it isn't their fault.

This will get their attention first thing in the morning.

2 English muffins, preferably whole grain (see Note), split

I cup store-bought or homemade tomato sauce (see page 174)

4 slices (¼ inch thick) mozzarella, preferably fresh

1. Preheat a toaster oven or standard oven to 350°F.

2. Toast the English muffin halves until very lightly brown, 3 to 4 minutes. Spoon ¼ cup of the tomato sauce evenly over each English muffin half. You can continue with Step 3 or go directly to Step 4.

3. See the Fork in the Road suggestions on this page for optional toppings.

4. Top each English muffin with a slice of mozzarella.

5. Bake or toast the pizzas until the cheese is melted and a bit bubbly, about 4 minutes. Serve, making sure your kids know that the pizzas are hot!

Note: I have yet to find an English muffin that beats Thomas'. They just know their nooks and crannies.

Fork in the Road

Once you spoon on the tomato sauce, you can add anything to the pizza that you would use to top a regular pizza: slivered cooked onions or peppers, sliced olives, chopped cooked broccoli, and so on. My gang finds plain works just fine first thing in the morning, but yours might appreciate a nonvegetarian addition like bacon crumbled between the sauce and cheese.

Crunchy Chewy Granola

Makes 6 to 7 cups
Vegetarian

Granola is so customizable that once you start playing around with it, making granola can become almost as addictive as the granola itself. Although you will not actually be making the granola on a weekday morning, unless you plan to get up extra early, it will become a fantastic breakfast staple in your home.

You've probably read all about how most store-bought granolas have so much fat and sugar in them that you'd be better off eating a slab of French toast drizzled with syrup atop a plate of eggs Benedict for breakfast. And let's face it, that's why those granolas taste so decadent. You will notice that this recipe also has a bit of fat and sweetening in it, because otherwise the granola would in fact not taste so great (and it does taste great), but it is a much more tolerable amount than what you will find in most of the stuff you can buy. The granola keeps well, so feel free to double or triple the recipe.

For breakfast with milk, delicious, but if you are a granola person, relegating granola to breakfast simply will not do. You will start to look for opportunities to work granola into different corners of the day. Here are some ideas to get you started.

Use granola as a topping for yogurt, plain or flavored, and maybe some fresh fruit, too, layered up all parfaitlike; on ice cream; on oatmeal for some nice contrasting texture (see page 16 for an oatmeal recipe); in a little cup, as a dip for a banana—dip, bite, repeat; as a topping for a fruit crisp—sprinkle it on, dot it with tiny pieces of butter, and bake.

Keep this in a glass jar so you can admire it.

¼ cup honey

¼ cup pure maple syrup

2 large egg whites

⅓ cup vegetable oil, plus oil for the baking sheet (optional)

1 teaspoon pure vanilla extract

1 teaspoon ground cinnamon

1 teaspoon kosher or coarse salt

½ teaspoon grated orange zest (optional)

4 cups old-fashioned oats (not quick-cooking)

1 cup chopped unsalted nuts, such as walnuts, pecans, pistachios, cashews, or almonds (optional)

2 cups mixed chopped dried fruit, such as apricots or prunes, and/ or dried cherries, blueberries, cranberries, and raisins

Nonstick cooking spray (optional)

1. Preheat the oven to 275°F.

2. Place the honey, maple syrup, egg whites, oil, vanilla, cinnamon, salt, and orange zest, if using, in a large bowl and mix until well blended. Set ½ cup of the honey mixture aside in a medium-size bowl. Add the oats and nuts, if using, to the large bowl and mix with a spoon or your hands until everything is well combined and coated.

3. Add the dried fruit to the reserved ½ cup of the honey mixture and stir to combine. Set the dried fruit mixture aside.

4. Spray a rimmed baking sheet with nonstick cooking spray, or coat it lightly with oil, or line it with parchment paper. Spread the oat mixture out on the prepared baking sheet in a thin, even layer. Bake the oat mixture for 30 minutes.

5. Add the dried fruit mixture to the oat mixture and stir well with a spoon or spatula to combine. Spread the granola out again in an even layer. Bake the granola until the oats are golden brown and crunchy, 40 to 45 minutes, stirring it once more halfway through the baking time but leave some clumps! Let the granola cool on the baking sheet on a wire rack.

Cooking Tip: The granola bakes first without the dried fruit because the fruit doesn't need as much time to get just the right amount of done. Trial and error confirmed that cooking the fruit for the whole 1¼ hours made it too tough and slightly burned tasting, while about 45 minutes was just enough to make it chewy and incorporated into the mix.

Make Ahead: You betcha; this granola keeps for three weeks in a cool place, well sealed.

What the Kids Can Do: Measure and mix and spread everything out on the baking sheet. With supervision regarding the hot baking sheet, they can gently stir the granola during baking.

The best way: by the handful straight out of the container.

Oatmeal Your Way

Serves 4
Vegetarian

Brown sugar, pecans, and cream

Dried apricots

The very definition of "rib sticking," of sustaining, of nourishing: During the coldest months, my kids ask for oatmeal most mornings. Cooking it always tests my self-control; you add an improbably small amount of oats to what seems like way too much liquid and stir, and wait. "This will never thicken properly," you think. "This can't possibly come together and look like anything resembling oatmeal—this is oatmeal soup, at best." You will want to add some more oats; you must resist. Even after five minutes it will still look a bit thin, and then, lo and behold, after cooling for just one or two minutes, in the pot or in individual bowls, it's oatmeal. Having succumbed many times to this "must add more oats" temptation I have found myself with a pot of glue at the end. My family does like it a bit on the thinner side; use the smaller amount of water for a thicker oatmeal.

This recipe calls for half milk, half water, which seems to be a good balance, but you can also use all milk, all water, or any combo of the two. A mere tablespoon of brown sugar provides just the right level of sweetness, and then you can let folks finish off their bowls with other toppings as they see fit.

FOR THE OATMEAL

1¾ cups milk

¼ teaspoon kosher or
  coarse salt

2 cups old-fashioned oats
  (not quick-cooking)

4 teaspoons light or
  dark brown sugar

FOR THE TOPPINGS, OPTIONAL

Butter

Additional brown sugar

Raisins or other chopped
  dried fruit

Chopped nuts

Maple syrup

Milk, half-and-half, or cream

Dried cherries

1. Combine the milk and 1½ to 1¾ cups water in a small saucepan; the amount of water you use depends on how thick you like your oatmeal. Let come to a simmer over medium-high heat. Don't wander too far; the liquid has a tendency to bubble up and over the side of the pan. Stir in the salt and oats. Reduce the heat to medium-low and cook, stirring occasionally, until thickened, about 5 minutes. Stir in the brown sugar. Still stay close and don't be tempted to add more oats; it will thicken up quite a bit at the end.

2. Scoop the oatmeal into four bowls. Then top each serving with a pat of butter, some extra brown sugar, dried fruit, and/or chopped nuts, and a drizzling of maple syrup and/or milk, half-and-half, or cream, as desired.

What the Kids Can Do:
Top their oatmeal as they wish.

Chapter 2

Lunch to Stay or to Go

Lunch can be tricky for us moms. It's hard not to get stuck in a rut, no matter how much we'd like to broaden our midday meal horizons. When the kids are at school, there's that weird unease of not knowing what they are eating, and if they actually *are* eating (not that we mothers have control issues or anything). Even if we pack the world's most delectable, nutritionally balanced lunch, that's no guarantee they're going to consume it.

At home, for my family, leftovers are usually the answer. For lunches on the go the versatile sandwich often does the trick, and in this chapter you'll find the self-effacingly titled The World's Best Tuna Fish Sandwich, several recipes for wraps (plus a guide to creating your own inspired wraps), and a serious Italian sub.

> ### THE DILEMMA
>
> *Making lunches that won't get tossed or returned.*

Basically all sandwiches are Fork in the Road recipes, because even though you may be making grilled cheese sandwiches for everyone in the house, yours might have tomato and bacon in it, one of your kids might have a different cheese, your other kids might have a different bread, and so on.

Some kids are also happy to see soup in a thermos, and so the soup chapter (pages 65 to 81) may hold some more lunch options. You can also check out the list of portable dishes on pages 338 to 339 and see if any of them will be a welcome sight in your kids' lunch bags (knowing that reheating is probably not an option).

The Great Grilled Cheese Sandwich

Makes 2 sandwiches
A Fork in the Road Recipe

There are more than a few ways to make a good grilled cheese sandwich. For the more straightforward and less decadent version, you can use a toaster oven, the regular oven, or the broiler. But the best grilled cheese is made on a griddle or in a skillet.

Laura Werlin, author of many books on cheese, suggests covering the skillet at the beginning of the cooking process so that the cheese melts all the way through and then finishing the sandwiches with the skillet uncovered so that the outside of the bread gets nice and crisp. This tip has changed my grilled cheese sandwich making. Try it and never again will any of you suffer the disappointment of unmelted cheese in the middle of your sandwich or overcooked toast at the expense of perfectly melted cheese.

These sandwiches are best hot from the pan, so they are definitely an excellent at-home lunch choice. My kids actually like them at room temperature, too, so they find their way into their lunch bags often, but that's a very personal predilection.

> 4 slices bread of your choice
>
> 1 tablespoon unsalted butter, at room temperature
>
> 6 thin slices or 1⅓ cups grated or crumbled cheese
> (see Fork in the Road, this page)
>
> Nonstick cooking spray (optional)

1. Spread one side of each slice of bread with the butter, dividing it equally. Place 2 slices on a cutting board, butter side down (a bit messy, yes), and layer 3 slices of cheese or sprinkle ⅔ cup of grated cheese on each slice of bread.

Fork in the Road

What kind of cheese? This is where the fun starts. This recipe is a blueprint, and the sandwich that results is your creation and yours alone. Intermingling different kinds of cheese results in some very special combinations. If you use a stronger flavored cheese, like Stilton for instance, you may want to cut the flavor with a slice of milder cheese like muenster, so the sandwich isn't too intense.

Some cheese options to mix and match: American cheese • blue cheese • Brie or a double cream cheese, trimmed of any thick rind • cheddar • feta • fontina • goat cheese (chèvre) • Gruyère • Jarlsberg • Monterey Jack • muenster • pepper Jack • Provolone • Swiss cheese.

And everyone can pick the add-ins for the grilled cheese of their dreams. Some ideas: spread of tapenade (olive paste), sun-dried tomato paste, or pesto; a thin slice of ham or prosciutto; slices of cooked bacon, crumbled or whole; thin slices of tomato; sautéed onions; and roasted bell pepper.

My boys got a little carried away with their cheese selection.

If you are using more than one kind of cheese, divide the different kinds as you like between the sandwiches. Top the sandwiches with the remaining 2 slices of bread, butter side up.

2. Heat a large skillet, either a nonstick skillet or one that has been sprayed with nonstick cooking spray, over medium heat. Carefully place the sandwiches in the skillet, cover it, and cook the sandwiches until the bottoms start to turn golden brown, about 2 minutes. Uncover the skillet and, using a spatula, turn the sandwiches over (be careful if you've used grated cheese to make sure the filling stays put). Press down on the sandwiches a bit with the spatula and cook them uncovered until the second side is golden brown and crisp, about 3 minutes. Turn the sandwiches one more time and cook them until the bottom is fully golden brown and crispy, 1 to 2 minutes longer.

3. Transfer the sandwiches to the cutting board, let them sit for 2 minutes for the cheese to firm back up a bit, then cut the sandwiches in half and serve.

What the Kids Can Do:
Pick their favorite cheese, choose any add-ins they like, and layer up their sandwiches.

Lunchbox Wraps

Each recipe makes **2** wraps

There is little debate that the sandwich is the mainstay of most kids' lunches; two slices of bread with anything that kids might consume layered in between. Wraps have definitely taken their rightful place in the pantheon of sandwich possibilities, and sometimes the mere novelty of a rolled up sandwich instead of a square one might entice kids to try something, just for the surprise factor.

You can leave the wraps whole, in one big tubelike piece; slice them in half on the diagonal; or slice them into several one- or two-inch pieces, providing that eye-catching, bite-size, "nosh-esque" quality.

A wrap might make an old favorite new again.

Maple Turkey and Bacon Wrap

Kind of like a club sandwich in a wrap.

- 2 large (10-inch) wraps or tortillas
- 4 to 6 thin slices honey or maple roasted turkey breast
- 2 slices cooked bacon
- 4 slices avocado (optional)
- 2 slices Swiss or cheddar cheese
- 2 large leaves romaine lettuce, torn into pieces
- Honey mustard

1. Place the wraps or tortillas on a work surface. Layer half of the slices of turkey on top of each, leaving bare about one quarter of the wrap on the side farthest away from you. Arrange 1 slice of bacon and 2 slices of avocado, if using, on top of the turkey, parallel to the bare quarter of each wrap. Cover each with a slice of cheese and top the cheese with the lettuce. Drizzle a bit of honey mustard over the lettuce, making sure to put a smear of the mustard right at the edge of the bare portion of the wraps.

2. Roll each wrap up toward the bare portion, using the mustard to seal the wraps. Cut the wraps as desired before serving.

What the Kids Can Do:
Talk about a great way to get your kids engaged in thinking about new things to eat for lunch! Lay a wrap on the table, open up the fridge door, and let the kids get creative (see pages 24 to 25).

Chicken Caesar Wrap

You can also add thin slices of peeled cucumber or chopped tomato.

2 large (10-inch) wraps or tortillas

1½ cups Caesar salad (page 89), without the croutons, or
    1½ cups shredded romaine lettuce tossed with ¼ cup Caesar salad
    dressing, homemade (page 90) or store-bought

1 cup shredded cooked chicken (about 1 large chicken breast)

2 teaspoons mayonnaise, or 2 teaspoons more Caesar salad dressing

1. Place the wraps or tortillas on a work surface. Spread half of the Caesar salad over each wrap, leaving bare about one quarter of the wrap on the side farthest away from you. Spoon ½ cup of the shredded chicken over the salad on each wrap. Using a knife, smear 1 teaspoon of the mayonnaise along the edge of the bare portion of each of the wraps.

2. Roll each wrap up toward the bare portion, using the mayonnaise to seal the wraps. Cut the wraps as desired before serving.

Jack and Charlie's "Sub" Sandwich

When we make a pit stop at the sandwich shop chain, my boys usually get the same sandwich. This is the wrap version.

2 large (10-inch) wraps or tortillas

Spicy brown mustard (optional)

A little bit of mayonnaise

6 large thin slices roasted turkey

Shredded romaine or iceberg lettuce

Sliced pickles

Sliced black olives

Side of jalapeños (optional)

1. Place the wraps or tortillas on a work surface. Squiggle some mustard, if using, over each wrap and spread on a bit of mayonnaise, making sure to smear some on the edge of the wrap farthest away from you. Layer 3 slices of the turkey on top of each wrap, leaving about one quarter of the wrap on the side farthest away from you bare. Distribute the lettuce, pickles, and olives over the turkey.

2. Roll each wrap up toward the bare portion, using the mayonnaise to seal the wrap. Cut the wraps as desired before serving. Jack just eats the jalapeños on the side, because he is a little crazy.

WRAP-WORTHY LEFTOVERS

Here are some other recipes that lend themselves to wraps: Soy-Ginger Flank Steak, page 120—thinly slice it • Asian Salmon, page 144—break it into chunks • Apple Glazed Pork Chops, page 134—cut the meat into thin slices • Flaky Fish with Balsamic Glaze, page 142—break it into chunks • Black Beans and Rice, page 196—heat the beans and rice first, then wrap them up with some guacamole (see page 54), shredded cheddar, and maybe a dollop of sour cream. Fold the ends of the tortilla in, more burrito-style, so that the filling doesn't fall out. You may want a knife and fork for this one • Teriyaki Chicken and Beef Skewers, page 230—without the skewers, of course • Simplest Chicken or Shrimp Kebabs, page 237—dice them • Roast Chicken, Several Ways, page 98, with any of the rubs, or Honey Ginger Soy Chicken, page 208—shred or thinly slice it • Pulled Pork, page 213—with or without the barbecue sauce • Honey-Hoisin Tofu, page 192—cut it into cubes.

A BLUEPRINT FOR WRAPS

SOME BASIC GUIDELINES.

1. Pick a wrap.

2. Pick a filling such as cold cuts, cheeses, smoked salmon, beans, or tuna fish (see page 28 for The World's Best Tuna Fish Sandwich filling). Leftovers are very fair game: steak, chicken, pork, fish, shrimp, tofu—whatever you have that can be sliced or chopped into a rollable sandwich filling (see Wrap-Worthy Leftovers (page 23).

3. Pick a spread or condiment that will go with your main filling. Mayo, mustards, chutneys, relishes, jams, hummus, barbecue sauce, hoisin sauce, plain Greek yogurt, salsa, and pestos of all flavors are all good. Maybe there's even a leftover dip or crostini spread lurking in the fridge that will appeal.

4. Add the extras: shredded lettuce or cabbage, chopped tomatoes, sliced olives and pickles, jalapeños, fresh herbs, slivered onions or bell peppers, sprouts, thinly sliced cucumbers or mushrooms. In some cases fruit is also welcome, such as thinly sliced or chopped apples or pears or maybe some chopped dried fruit. Shelled sunflower seeds, pumpkin seeds, nuts, and granola are also ideas. Don't forget salt and pepper, or another seasoning if it makes sense.

5. Do not overfill your wrap or you won't be able to get it closed. It's better to layer everything on about three quarters of the wrap, leaving a little space around the edge for things to squish outward when you roll it up. And then on the edge of the one quarter that has no filling, put a smear of the condiment of your choice, like mustard or mayo. As you roll up the wrap, starting with the filled side closest to you and rolling toward the barer edge, the filling will slide into the bare space a bit, ideally leaving you with enough room so that the condiment at the edge will help seal up the wrap as you finish rolling. You'll find this explanation sounds much more complicated than the actual rolling, of course.

TUNA, LETTUC

PB + J (W/BANANA + GRANOLA)

HAM, SWISS + PICKLES

TURKEY, CHEDDAR, JALAPENO + SALSA

OMATO

YOGURT, CUCUMBER, TOMATO,
OLIVES + FETA

TURKEY, BACON + HONEY MUSTARD

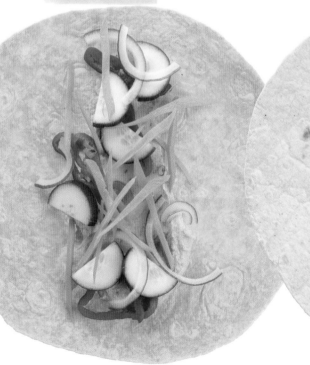

HUMMUS, CUCUMBER, CARROT,

ONION, ROASTED PEPPER, CARROTS

SLICED CHICKEN, PROVOLONE + PESTO

Creamy Tahini, Tofu, and Avocado Pitas

Makes **2** sandwiches
Vegetarian

Tahini is a protein packed, nutty-tasting paste made from sesame seeds, and so these sandwiches are especially good for vegetarians and those who are allergic to peanut butter. The flavor combination is delicate and addictive at the same time. Leave out any of the veggies that won't fly with your kids or add in others that will. Slivered red onions are also a good addition.

Have lots of napkins at the ready— delicious, yes. Neat and tidy, no.

FOR THE CREAMY TAHINI SAUCE

½ cup Greek yogurt (see My Less Fat Greek Dressing, page 85)

2 tablespoons tahini (sesame paste)

1 teaspoon fresh lemon juice

½ teaspoon ground cumin (optional)

Kosher or coarse salt and freshly ground black pepper

FOR THE SANDWICHES

2 whole wheat or white pita breads

½ package (about 8 ounces) firm tofu, pressed and drained (see Pressing Tofu, page 195)

⅓ cup diced tomato (½-inch dice)

½ cup shredded romaine lettuce

½ avocado, sliced

1. Make the creamy tahini sauce: Place the yogurt, tahini, lemon juice, and cumin, if using, in a medium-size bowl and stir to mix. Season the tahini sauce with salt and pepper to taste. The tahini sauce will keep for up to 3 days in the refrigerator.

2. Make the sandwiches: Cut a 1-inch slice from the edge of each pita bread and, using your fingers, open the pocket.

3. Cut the tofu into ¼ inch–wide slices and then slice those crosswise into ¼ inch–thick slices so you have thin sticks of tofu. Add the tofu sticks and the tomato to the tahini sauce and toss gently to combine (the tofu sticks will break up a bit; that's okay).

4. Carefully fill the pocket of each pita with half of the tofu and tomato mixture. Insert half of the lettuce and the avocado slices into each pita so that they are distributed over the tofu filling. Cut the pitas in half or serve them whole, which is a bit less messy.

Cooking Tip: You can also make this into a wrap (see page 24 for wrapping directions).

Make Ahead: These sandwiches should be made right before serving as they will get soggy quickly. If you want to make them to go, put the tofu filling in a container, packing the pitas, lettuce, and avocado separately (toss the sliced avocado with an extra squeeze of lemon juice to prevent browning). Assemble the sandwiches when it's time to eat.

What the Kids Can Do: Make the tahini sauce, slice the tofu, and toss the tofu with the sauce. Kids can also slice the tomatoes, lettuce, and avocado with an age-appropriate knife, and open the pitas and stuff them with the fillings. If you send a container of the tofu filling and separately wrapped pitas to school, this last task is built right in.

The World's Best Tuna Fish Sandwich

Makes 4 hefty sandwiches

For an extra three minutes of your time you can elevate the acceptable but uninspiring combo of tuna and mayonnaise to something significantly more delicious. My older son Jack would eat this until his mercury levels made him glow in the dark. The relish adds a sweet brininess that puts this tuna in a class by itself, and the Dijon mustard gives it a tiny kick. The celery is optional because a very few people in this world (my editor, Suzanne, included) can't stand it. The other 99.7 percent of us think it adds a welcome, refreshing crunch. The onion is optional just because you might not feel like mincing a tablespoon of onion, and who could blame you.

This is the kind of tuna salad you find in the best diners.)

This tuna salad is a great way to locate a new taste bud or two on your kid's tongue: the tuna is a little tangy, a little sweet, with a hint of heat. This is the gateway salad to new flavors. It's also great in the form of a wrap, scooped onto a crunchy green salad, or served with crackers. Wheat Thins in particular are a perfect match for this tuna. And a pickle or two on the side or a handful of chips would not be out of place.

- 2 cans (5 ounces each) solid white tuna fish, drained
- 2 cans (5 ounces each) light tuna fish, drained
- 1/3 cup mayonnaise, preferably Hellmann's, or more, to taste
- I heaping tablespoon sweet relish
- I heaping teaspoon Dijon mustard
- 2 tablespoons chopped celery (optional)
- I heaping tablespoon minced onion (optional)
- Kosher or coarse salt and freshly ground black pepper
- 8 slices whole wheat bread
- Lettuce leaves and sliced tomato (optional)

1. Place the tuna, mayonnaise, relish, mustard, celery, and onion, if using, in a medium-size bowl and blend well. Season with salt and pepper to taste.

2. Evenly spread the tuna salad over 4 slices of bread. Top the tuna salad with lettuce and/or tomato, if desired, and then top each sandwich with another slice of bread.

Variation

Tuna Melt

To make a tuna melt, lightly toast all of the slices of bread in a toaster oven or under the broiler. Place half of the slices on a work surface and top them with the tuna. Arrange a slice of cheddar, Swiss, or muenster cheese over the tuna and toast or broil the open-faced sandwiches until the cheese is melted. Top them with the remaining toasted bread and serve them warm. You can skip the top slice of bread and serve these as open-faced sandwiches. English muffins are particularly good for those.

Cooking Tip: Using all solid white tuna results in a salad that can be too dry, unless you add an unconscionable amount of mayonnaise, and using all light tuna can be perceived by kids (and adults) as too fishy. The fifty-fifty combo results in a tuna fish filling that is nicely in the middle. You might find a different balance to your taste, maybe one can of light tuna to three cans of white. I usually use tuna in water, although if you prefer tuna in oil, you can definitely use that, or mix and match.

What the Kids Can Do: Kids can stir the tuna fish salad all up, and assemble the sandwiches.

Classic Italian Deli Sandwich

Makes 2 sandwiches

These are not wimpy sandwiches, but many kids are drawn to the pungent, salty flavors of the world of the Italian deli. Lots of them love pepperoni pizza and salami and pickles, right? Be warned that your kid may have some overpowering breath after devouring this one.

FOR THE VINAIGRETTE

2 teaspoons red or white wine vinegar

3 teaspoons extra-virgin olive oil

¼ teaspoon dried oregano

1 teaspoon Dijon mustard (optional)

FOR THE SANDWICHES

½ cup slivered homemade (facing page) or store-bought roasted red bell peppers, or pickled peppers (optional)

2 fat sandwich rolls (often called kaiser or bulkie rolls), sliced in half

4 thin slices ham or prosciutto

4 thin slices salami

4 thin slices Provolone cheese

4 slices tomato

⅔ cup shredded iceberg or romaine lettuce

1. Make the vinaigrette: Place the wine vinegar, olive oil, oregano, and mustard, if using (see the Cooking Tip), in a small container with a lid and shake to mix.

2. Make the sandwiches: Arrange ¼ cup of the bell peppers, if using, over the bottom of each roll. Top each with 2 slices of ham, salami, Provolone, and tomato. Distribute the shredded lettuce evenly over the fillings, then drizzle the vinaigrette evenly on top. Cover the sandwiches with the tops of the rolls, pressing down on them so that the filling holds together nicely. Cut the sandwiches in half and serve.

Cooking Tip: Usually a vinaigrette is seasoned with salt and pepper, but in this case there is more than enough salt and pepperiness going on in the meat and cheese. If you or your kids really like things pungent, add a teaspoon of Dijon mustard to the vinaigrette.

What the Kids Can Do: Make the sandwiches!

You can use roasted or pickled peppers (or skip them altogether).

Variations

Sandwich Options

If you or your kids like different cold cuts, feel free to substitute them for what's listed. *Salumi* is the category of good-quality cured meats that includes salami, prosciutto, and many other types, most containing some amount of pork. Other possible classic Italian *salumi* choices are *soppressata, coppa, speck, capocollo,* and *bresaola* (this last one is made from beef). Of course there are many kinds of salami with many different seasonings from subtle to intense. Provolone can be replaced with anything from fontina to mild mozzarella to non-Italian cheeses like cheddar or gentle muenster.

Have a little fun at the deli counter and ask to try some samples; most deli people are happy to see kids trying new things. And remember that you can buy a quarter of a pound of lots of different things and keep switching up your deli sandwiches.

ROASTING PEPPERS

Bell peppers are easy to roast: Preheat the broiler or a grill. Take a whole bell pepper and place it under the broiler or on the grill. As the side facing the heat bubbles and starts to blacken, turn the pepper to the next side. After about four turns, and eight minutes, the whole pepper should be blackened and blistered. Put the pepper in a bowl, cover it with a dish towel, and let it steam. After about five minutes take off the dish towel and, when the pepper is cool enough to handle, peel off the skin and pull the pepper apart so you can remove the seeds and core. (Don't rinse it under water!) If you are using the pepper in a recipe where a bit of extra liquid is welcome, save as much of the flavorful juice from the pepper as you can.

Chapter 3

A Handful of Snacks

"**H**e/she started it." "I didn't do it." "I didn't hear you." "I left it at school." "Can I have a snack?" For most of us it wouldn't be a normal day without hearing each of these sentences at least once.

All of the snacks in this chapter—Edamame Several Ways, Chickpea Poppers, House Pumpkin Seeds, Baked Pita Chips, and Old-Fashioned Stovetop Popcorn—are wholesome, munchable, and happen to be vegetarian. And none of them would be out of place as an appetizer.

There were a couple of great articles in *The New York Times* some time back about how essentially every single activity in our kids' lives has become cause for a snack. Of course

> ## THE DILEMMA
>
> *Finding healthy snacks that don't come in a crinkly bag.*

our growing children need frequent fueling up, and things like soccer practice and plain old hunger absolutely warrant snacks. But we all do reach a moment where we are faced with the possibility that the reason we can't get our kids to eat a decent meal is because they've just had their fourth snack of the day twenty minutes prior.

Wow! Did you see how close I came to sliding into a sermon on snacks? If this book were going to contain a self-righteous diatribe, I think this is where it would probably go. I will simply say that I wish my kids didn't come home from afterschool activities with neon-orange lips or chocolate mustaches so often (or, at the very least, that they would learn to wipe their mouths better).

The toasty sesame version.

Edamame Several Ways

Makes 2 cups edamame
A Fork in the Road Recipe
Vegetarian

Even in our most sanctimonious moments we can certainly admit there aren't tons of food that are (a) good for you, (b) delicious, (c) kid-friendly, and (d) fun to eat. If there were then we wouldn't be having any of these discussions, not to mention all the dinnertime negotiation.

Edamame should have their own theme song, that's how spectacular they are. When I tell you we eat a couple of bags of these a week, this is not exaggerated for dramatic effect. Edamame are simply soybeans, which are available frozen either in or out of the shell (see The World's Most Perfect Snack, page 36). In the shell is more interactive, and out is more convenient if you want to use them in various recipes, for example in the Shrimp Stir-Fried Rice on page 150.

I tablespoon kosher or coarse salt, plus 2 teaspoons more salt if you are making plain edamame

I package about (14 ounces) frozen edamame, in the pod

1. Bring a large pot of water to a boil and add the 1 tablespoon of salt. Add the frozen edamame pods, let the water return to a boil, and boil the edamame, uncovered, until they are tender but still firm, 2 to 3 minutes (scoop one pod out with a spoon, rinse it with cold water, pop out the beans, and eat them to check).

2. Drain the edamame, shaking off as much water as you can. You can continue with Step 3 or go directly to Step 4.

3. See the Fork in the Road suggestions for seasoning the edamame on this page.

4. If you are serving the edamame pods plain, toss them with the 2 teaspoons of salt. Serve the edamame pods warm or at room temperature.

Fork in the Road

Separate the drained edamame pods into two batches. Salt one batch with a teaspoon of salt and toss the remaining batch with one of the variations on page 36. Each of these recipes makes enough seasoning for a half pound (half a package) of edamame. Make sure to encourage your kids to try one of the more seasoned beans and maybe the next go-round they'll ask you to season the whole bag (just double the seasoning amounts).

What the Kids Can Do:

Let the kids salt the edamame, mix up any of the seasoning blends, and toss the edamame with the seasonings.

Spicy Edamame

Mexican meets Japanese.

¼ teaspoon chili powder

⅛ teaspoon red pepper flakes

¼ teaspoon dried oregano

¾ teaspoon kosher or coarse salt

Heat a small skillet over medium heat (do not use a nonstick skillet for this). Add the chili powder and red pepper flakes and cook, stirring, until you can really smell the spices, 1 to 2 minutes. Remove the skillet from the heat and stir in the oregano and salt. Toss the spice mixture with the cooked and drained edamame pods.

Sesame Edamame

Nutty and addictive; serve these edamame with napkins as they are a bit slippery.

½ teaspoon Asian (dark) sesame oil

¾ teaspoon kosher or coarse salt

1½ teaspoons toasted sesame seeds
   (optional; see Toasted Sesame Seeds, page 231)

Toss the cooked and drained edamame pods with the sesame oil and then the salt and toasted sesame seeds, if using. Serve the Sesame Edamame warm.

Lemony Edamame

The addition of lemon juice provides a very simple zing to the edamame.

Juice of ½ lemon, strained (about 1 tablespoon)

1 teaspoon kosher or coarse salt

After the edamame pods are cooked and drained give them a rinse with cold water to lock in their bright green color. Drain the edamame well and sprinkle them with the lemon juice before tossing them with the salt. Lemon juice can make the edamame pods turn brownish but rinsing them first with cold water helps prevent that and sprinkling them with the lemon juice and salt right before serving also helps. Serve Lemony Edamame cool.

THE WORLD'S MOST PERFECT SNACK

They are rich in protein, vitamins, calcium, folic acid, and fiber. They are low in calories. They are a perfect snack, they are a great predinner nibble with drinks (alcoholic or no), they pack beautifully in lunch boxes. They are great to bring to sporty kinds of things because they are a very good energy food. They are fun to eat: You serve them in the pod and everyone pops out the beans. They are also available shelled, convenient for cooking and adding to salads. I know that I sound like a zealoty nut job when I talk about edamame, so I'll stop here and simply say that I think edamame are really, really awesome.

You can buy edamame in the frozen food section of many supermarkets, or at an Asian or specialty food store, or a natural foods sort of place. They usually come in one-pound bags, and you can keep them in the freezer until you are ready to cook them. I have even seen them at a Costco or two in larger-size bags, and my level of excitement caused people to put gentle but protective arms across their children's shoulders.

Baked Pita Chips

Makes 36 pita triangles
A Fork in the Road Recipe
Vegetarian

Another almost-not-a-recipe recipe, but that's not the point. The point is that these pita chips taste great, you can play around with all kinds of seasonings if you like, and you can make them with whole wheat pitas (even if you have a white bread kind of kid, once they're toasted your kid might not notice). If you like crunchier chips you can split the pitas crosswise before baking. Split pitas crisp up faster, so keep an eye on them so they don't get too hard or burn.

Eat the pita chips on their own, or serve them with whatever dips you like. They are also great with salsa or guacamole (page 54) and make a lovely date for a bowl of soup.

⅓ cup olive oil

I small clove garlic (optional), very finely minced or pressed through a garlic press

6 pitas (6 inches each)

Kosher or coarse salt

1. Preheat the oven to 350°F.

2. Place the olive oil in a small bowl. Add the garlic, if using, and stir to mix well. Brush the plain olive oil or the mixture on the pitas, arrange them in a single layer on a baking sheet, and sprinkle them with salt. You can continue with Step 3 or go directly to Step 4.

3. ━━◄ See the Fork in the Road suggestions for seasoning the pitas on page 38.

4. Bake the pitas until they are as crisp as you like them, 5 to 7 minutes (they will get a little crisper as they cool).

5. Cut each pita into 6 triangles. Serve the baked pitas warm or at room temperature.

Cooking Tip #1: You do not have to use extra-virgin olive oil here. In fact, in general, when you are cooking with heat, using pure olive oil is absolutely fine (save the pricier extra-virgin for salad dressings and other uncooked preparations). Also, pure olive oil has a higher smoke point than extra-virgin olive oil, which is just a fancy way of saying it won't burn as quickly when you use it for sautéing.

Cooking Tip #2: A cheap kitchen tool you will be very happy to own is a silicone basting brush. The "bristles" are made from a heat-proof and durable synthetic material. The brush is dishwasher safe, easy to clean, and unlike regular brushes, the bristles won't get all sticky and absorb whatever it is you're brushing on whatever you're making. In other words, you won't catch a whiff of old garlic oil the next time you pull out the basting brush.

Make Ahead: Store a package of pitas in the freezer for making chips. Once toasted, you can keep the chips in a sealed plastic container or zipper-top plastic bag for up to a week.

What the Kids Can Do: Ask the kids to brush the pita chips with the olive oil and sprinkle them with salt and any other seasonings they like.

Separate the oiled (and garlicked, if you've used it) pita chips into two batches on the baking sheet. Keep the chips on one side as is, and in addition to the salt, season the other half with a sprinkling of any of the following seasonings before baking. Just make sure if you are going to be pairing the triangles with dips that the seasoning flavors you choose don't compete or become too repetitive with the dip or spread you're serving. The seasonings and measurements listed here are just a starting point; feel free to use whatever else strikes your—or your kids'—fancy.

For three pitas: 1 tablespoon finely freshly grated Parmesan cheese • a mixture of 1/2 teaspoon garlic powder, 1/2 teaspoon dried oregano, and 2 teaspoons freshly grated Parmesan cheese • a mixture of 1/2 teaspoon ground cumin and 1/2 teaspoon garlic powder • a mixture of 1/4 teaspoon ground cumin, 1/4 teaspoon garlic powder, 1/4 teaspoon ground coriander, and 1/4 teaspoon cayenne pepper • a mixture of 1/2 teaspoon dried oregano and 1/2 teaspoon chili powder • 1 teaspoon *za'atar* (a tangy, nutty, herby Middle Eastern spice blend).

CHILI POWDER

CORIANDER

GARLIC POWDER, OREGANO + PARMESAN

ZA'ATAR

ZA'ATAR

PLAIN

GARLIC POWDER

CAYENNE PEPPER

CUMIN

This is one of the easiest ways to introduce new spices into your family's world.

House Pumpkin Seeds

Makes 2 cups
A Fork in the Road Recipe
Vegetarian

Crunchy, salty, and very satisfying—but now you get to make sure the oil and the salt remain within reason. And you get to make your kids aware that not all snacks come in brightly colored bags; sometimes they come in a pumpkin. (You can also find raw pumpkin seeds at health food stores and they are available online; see Resources, page 343.)

Some recipes call for hulling pumpkin seeds (which means cracking off the outer shell and just using the smaller kernel inside) but few of us have the time or the patience for such things. You can order them hulled, but if you are using them from a fresh pumpkin, go ahead and use the whole seed. The shells are perfectly edible, if not exactly tender, and it's really all about the roasting and the salt anyway. And it can also be about the seasonings, if you choose.

2 cups rinsed and dried raw pumpkin seeds (see Note)

1 tablespoon vegetable or canola oil

Kosher or coarse salt to taste

1. Preheat the oven to 350°F.

2. Dump the pumpkin seeds onto a rimmed baking sheet and drizzle the oil over them. Sprinkle the seeds with salt to taste. Use your hand or a wooden spoon to really mix everything up so the seeds are well coated with the oil and salt. Spread the seeds out in a single layer. You can continue with Step 3 or go directly to Step 4.

3. See the Fork in the Road suggestions for seasoning the pumpkin seeds on this page.

Fork in the Road

Separate the oiled and salted pumpkin seeds into two batches on the baking sheet. Keep the pumpkin seeds on one side as is. Season the other half with a sprinkling of any of the following spices or a combination of all of them:

- ½ teaspoon ground cumin
- ½ teaspoon chili powder
- ½ teaspoon garlic powder
- ½ teaspoon onion powder

Make Ahead: The roasted pumpkin seeds can be stored in an airtight container for up to a week.

What the Kids Can Do: Your little chefs can investigate the spice drawer and come up with their own brand of "house" pumpkin seeds. If your kids unscrew the lids of the cumin and chili powder jars, and do the sprinkling themselves, it's a good bet that they will both give those pumpkin seeds a try and not be so stunned to encounter these flavors in next week's turkey chili (see page 215). Kids can also help clean the pumpkin seeds and then toss them with the oil, salt, and seasonings.

4. Bake the pumpkin seeds until they are golden brown and fragrant, 20 to 25 minutes. Give the baking sheet a shake once or twice as the seeds bake to move them around. Let the seeds cool right on the baking sheet.

Note: For 2 cups of pumpkin seeds, you'll need a very large pumpkin. To get to the seeds, cut a "lid" around the top of the pumpkin with a sharp knife. Remove the top and scoop out all of the guts and seeds from the pumpkin. Put the seeds in a colander and rinse away as much of the extra glop as possible. Spread the seeds on a dish towel or paper towels to dry thoroughly, about 20 minutes (you can speed this up by blotting them with another dish towel or a few paper towels).

SAVORY

SWEET

These also add a nice crunch to salads.

Variation

You can also use 1 tablespoon melted butter, 1 teaspoon sugar (white or brown), and ½ teaspoon ground cinnamon for a sweeter version.

Chickpea Poppers

Makes 3¹/₂ cups
A Fork in the Road Recipe
Vegetarian

Naturally your kids like chips. Of course they do. And of course they'd like it if you sat them down with a big bowl of potato chips every day and said, "Hey, Johnny (or Wendy), go ahead, munch up!" Frankly, when my kids whine about not being allowed to eat chips with impunity, I feel like shouting, "Don't you think I want to eat chips all day long, too?" Chips are fantastic, however, the ramifications of lots of chips are not fantastic (I've grown weary of the word *moderation,* though of course it's all true, what they say).

So, what to give your kids to snack on that you can feel good about? I'm not talking about veggies—as Charlie said the other day, after I handed him a bowl of carrot sticks, looking at me unsettlingly with that level gaze, "Mom, this wasn't exactly what I had in mind when I asked for a snack."

Chickpeas! Not straight from the can, but toasted in the oven, with just the right amount of salt and possibly some light seasonings. In fact, chickpeas can be an interesting and smart way to wiggle a touch of a new spice onto your kids' palates. High in fiber, full of protein, low in fat, a little chewy, a little crispy, this is a snack that a mother could love. And forget the kids for a minute—these make the most killer nibble with cocktails for entertaining or just for you and your other half to nosh.

Nonstick cooking spray

2 cans (15 ounces each) chickpeas, rinsed and drained

2 tablespoons olive oil

1½ teaspoons kosher or coarse salt, or more to taste

Make Ahead: You can store the chickpeas in a tightly sealed container for up to five days, although if you use fresh garlic you'll need to keep them in the refrigerator.

What the Kids Can Do: Let the kids toss the chickpeas with the olive oil and salt along with any of the Fork in the Road seasonings.

Rosemary and garlic in front, plain in back.

1. Preheat the oven to 375°F. Lightly spray a rimmed baking sheet with nonstick cooking spray.

2. Pat the chickpeas dry with a clean dish towel or a few paper towels. Toss the chickpeas on the baking sheet with the olive oil and salt. You can continue with Step 3 or go directly to Step 4.

3. See the Fork in the Road suggestions for seasoning the chickpeas on this page.

4. Bake the chickpeas until they have turned golden brown and shrink slightly, 35 to 40 minutes. They will harden slightly and crisp up as they cool, so do not overbake them or they will get too tough and hard. Taste for seasoning, adding more salt as necessary. Serve the chickpeas warm or at room temperature.

Fork in the Road

Here are two seasoning combos. These make enough for one 15-ounce can of chickpeas. When you want to use one of the seasonings, separate the oiled and salted chickpeas into two batches on the baking sheet. You can keep the chickpeas on one side as is and toss those on the other side with your choice of seasoning. Double the amounts if you want to season the full recipe.

- a mixture of ¼ teaspoon chili powder and ¼ teaspoon ground cumin

- a mixture of I teaspoon minced fresh rosemary and ½ teaspoon finely minced garlic

You can also experiment with the optional seasonings in the Baked Pita Chips recipe (page 37), or the House Pumpkin Seeds recipe (page 40).

Old-Fashioned Stovetop Popcorn

Makes 8 to 9 cups; serves 4 to 6 normal people, or me and Charlie Vegetarian

Popcorn is a bona fide food group in our family, if not a flat out addiction. We pop it on the stovetop, with just a moderate amount of vegetable oil, and lightly salt it at the end. It's pretty healthy, and thank God for that, because if you actually saw the amount that we eat, you might catch your breath. It's also one of the three dishes (the others being oatmeal and coffee) that my husband can make with his eyes shut, because it's that important to the ecosystem of our family.

This popcorn is so much better tasting and better for you than the microwave varieties, although I have to confess, as with so many things, sometimes my kids do clamor for the stuff in a microwave bag. I usually yell, "I can't hear you over the sound of the popcorn popping," and by the time a big bowl of this hits the table they stop whining.

First there's the classic, plain stovetop version. The melted butter at the end is not at all necessary because since the kernels have been popped in oil they already have a "buttery" flavor, but sometimes we all need our lilies gilded.

Then there's a variation for when you might be having a grown-up popcorn night, or if you want to put out a couple of bowls for movie night and see if some of the more intensely flavored popcorn hits a note with your kids. Seriously, just start flinging herbs and spices that you like into the popcorn pot. It's fun, it's cheap, and it usually is delicious.

2 tablespoons canola or vegetable oil

½ cup popcorn kernels

2 tablespoons (¼ stick) unsalted butter (optional), melted

Kosher or coarse salt

If my family had a coat of arms, a bowl of this popcorn would be on it.

What the Kids Can Do:
The kids can concoct seasoning blends and sprinkle the popcorn with salt at the end—otherwise it's up to you to determine how close your kids should get to a hot pot with oil in it.

1. Heat the oil in a large pot over medium-high heat. Add the popcorn and shake it all about. Cover the pot and cook the popcorn until the popping starts, shaking it every once in a while (hold down the lid). Take the pot off the stove just when the popping quiets down to almost nothing, about 4 minutes.

2. Drizzle the butter, if using, over the popcorn, replace the lid and give the pot a few more shakes to evenly distribute the butter. Sprinkle the popcorn with salt to taste, cover the pot again, and shake it once more. Pour the popcorn into a bowl, and eat warm.

Variation

Seasoned Popcorn

Aside from the combination of popcorn seasonings here, you should feel free to experiment with other spices and seasonings. Aim for 1 to 1½ teaspoons total seasonings.

> 2 tablespoons canola or vegetable oil
>
> ½ cup popcorn kernels
>
> ½ teaspoon garlic powder
>
> ½ teaspoon dried oregano
>
> ½ teaspoon chili powder
>
> 2 tablespoons (¼ stick) unsalted butter (optional), melted
>
> Kosher or coarse salt
>
> ½ cup finely grated fresh Parmesan (optional)

1. Heat the oil in a large pot over medium-high heat. Add the popcorn, garlic powder, oregano, and chili powder, and shake it all about. Cover the pot and cook the popcorn until the popping starts, shaking it every once in a while (hold down the lid). Take the pot off the stove just when the popping quiets down to almost nothing, about 4 minutes.

2. Drizzle the butter, if using, over the popcorn, replace the lid and give the pot a few more shakes to evenly distribute the butter. Sprinkle the popcorn with salt to taste and the Parmesan, if using, cover the pot again, and shake it once more. Pour the popcorn into a bowl and eat warm.

NOTHING SAYS HAPPY HOLIDAYS LIKE A DRUGSTORE TIN OF POPCORN

Here's something else that is delicious and goes against the overall raison d'être of this book. You know those big tins that appear in drugstores, supermarkets, big box stores, and ultimately our homes and offices during the holiday season? The ones with three triangular sections of popcorn: yellow ("butter"), orange ("cheese"), and shiny brown ("caramel")? Well, my family loves those tins, we love them so much. We grab handfuls of popcorn, admiring the way the different flavors commingle in exciting ways ("have you tried the caramel mixed with the cheese?"), we speculate about the hard-to-identify, lingering aftertaste. Our neighbor showed up last Christmas with the most beautiful homemade hand-carved salad servers for a gift and also a tin of this popcorn. It was all we could do to pay proper homage to the thoughtful hand-crafted gift before we wrestled that unbelievably sticky piece of tape off the lid of the tin (why does the tape have to be that sticky?) and ripped into the popcorn.

But after a tin or two has been inhaled, and you are trying to brush the viscous colorful residue off your tongue, it is time to return to the healthier, and in fact more delicious, pleasures of simple stovetop popped popcorn. In eleven months the tins will return, and we'll be happy to see them again.

Tomato Bruschetta
(page 52)

Chapter 4

Appetizers? Really? Really.

On the average weeknight in the homes of most people with children the mere thought of an appetizer is ridiculous. At best it consists of a parent plunking a bowl of baby carrots in front of the kids, while saying, "No-you-cannot-have-cookies-dinner-will-be-ready-soon-no-you-cannot-have-a-marshmallow-just-be-a-little-patient-no-you-cannot-have-pretzels-I-know-you-are-starving-if-you-are-so-hungry-then-eat-the-carrots-would-you-please-stop-whining-for-ten-minutes-so-I-can-finish-making-dinner?"

However, sometimes you will have people over to your home and, after you pour everyone a beverage, they may look pointedly at your empty cocktail table. While a bowl of fresh veggies is always a good idea (try them with the ranch dip on page 85), and olives and cheese and crackers are also a solid option, you may want to go the extra step and make a real hors d'oeuvre or two. Or you may say to a friend who's invited your gang to dinner "What can I bring?" and the answer may be an appetizer. Most people recognize that it's rude to ask guests to bring the main course.

Here are five simple but varied appetizers. Most can be made ahead, and many are portable. Crostini can be made simply or with some zing. Bruschetta with tomato is like being smacked with summer, and guacamole comes with tortilla chips (enough said). Pigs in a Blanket and Shrimp Cocktail are simply the most popular appetizers in the world, greeted with great delight by kids and "foodies" alike (whether they admit it or not).

> **THE OBLIGATION**
>
> *Offering the requisite dinner party predinner nibble.*

Poke around in the fridge and pantry for topping inspiration.

Two Crostini—Plain, and Herb and Honey

Makes about 30 crostini
Vegetarian

Crostini are simply slices of bread that have been brushed with olive oil and toasted (if you are up for a debate, see What Is the Difference Between Bruschetta and Crostini? on page 53). Crostini are delicious to munch on all by their lonesome and make a great base for all kinds of toppings; you'll find suggestions on this page. You can rub the toasted slices of bread with cloves of garlic, something technically more associated with bruschetta, or leave them perfectly plain. You can also divide the crostini into two batches, leaving one batch plain and making the other the Herb and Honey variation on page 50. If you do, use only half the ingredients listed below, saving the remaining baguette half for the variation.

> I long baguette, sliced ⅓ to ½ inch thick (about 30 slices; see Note)
>
> About ½ cup olive oil
>
> Kosher or coarse salt
>
> 2 cloves garlic, cut in half (optional)

1. Preheat the oven to 350°F. Line a baking sheet with parchment paper or aluminum foil.

2. Lightly brush each of the baguette slices with olive oil and arrange them on the prepared baking sheet (they can be touching, but not overlapping; you may need to bake the crostini in two batches). Sprinkle the bread with salt.

3. Bake the crostini until lightly browned, 4 to 7 minutes. The bread slices will harden as they cool, so take them out before they get too crisp. If desired, lightly rub the flat side of the garlic halves over the tops before serving.

Note: If your baguette is thin, try slicing the bread on the diagonal. You'll get cooler-looking slices, with more surface area.

CROSTINI TOPPINGS

Other than cheese, some of the toppings listed here might be a stretch for some kids to try, but this book is not just for your kids, it's for you, too. And crostini are a fantastic way to introduce some new flavors in a low-pressure, petitely portioned way. In a partyish setting, your kids may well forget how many things they don't like and be inclined to pick up a crostini that their cool older cousin seems to be enjoying, and off they go. All of the toppings go on the crostini once the bread comes out of the oven.

Cheeses of all kinds • pesto • tapenade (olive paste) • fresh tomatoes and basil (see Tomato Bruschetta on page 52) • roasted bell peppers, with or without chopped capers; try mixing several colors of peppers for a pretty presentation • hummus or white bean spread • thinly sliced ham or prosciutto, or other cured meats.

Herb and Honey Crostini

When you are having company over, you can easily make half a batch of plain crostini and half a batch of Herb and Honey Crostini. The herb and honey version is crostini on steroids—crostini that are so crazy good on their own that they almost dare anything to top them, although a smear of soft tangy sheep or goat cheese throws that dare back in the crostini's face. The concept comes from my food-writer friend Amanda Hesser's Web and book project, food52.com, where she and her partner, Merrill, invite talented home cooks to submit recipes and the rest of the world votes for their favorite dishes. I fell in love with an herb and honey pita chip recipe from a cook whose handle is "machef" and turned it into crostini. These crostini are a bit sweet, which means some kids will like them, though they are also a bit herby, so not all kids will. For half a baguette's worth of crostini, mix up the following.

3 tablespoons unsalted butter, at room temperature

2 tablespoons honey

½ teaspoon kosher or coarse salt, plus salt for sprinkling

½ teaspoon dried thyme

½ teaspoon crushed dried rosemary

½ long baguette, sliced ⅓- to ½-inch thick
   (about 15 slices; see the Note on page 49)

1. Preheat the oven to 350°F. Line a baking sheet with parchment paper or aluminum foil.

2. Place the butter, honey, salt, thyme, and rosemary in a small bowl and stir to mix well.

3. Lightly spread each of the baguette slices with some of the honey-butter mixture and arrange them side by side on the prepared baking sheet.

4. Bake the crostini until the edges are lightly browned, 5 to 8 minutes. Remember the bread slices will harden as they cool, so take them out before they get too crisp. Sprinkle the crostini lightly with additional salt and serve.

Cooking Tip: If you are making the Herb and Honey Crostini you can use only thyme or rosemary instead of combining the two of them. Just double the amount of whichever herb you choose. Play around with the cooking time—if you like your crostini crisp, bake them a bit longer; if you like them with a bit of chewy "give" in the middle, bake them for less time. And if you're firing up the grill, instead of baking them, by all means grill the baguette slices for a couple of minutes on each side for an even more amazing flavor (this is technically how bruschetta was originally made, over coals).

What the Kids Can Do: Brush the bread with olive oil or spread the honey-butter mixture on top. Sprinkle the slices of baguette with salt, and rub the toasted slices with the garlic clove halves, if you like.

Make Ahead: The crostini can be kept in a tightly sealed container for up to 3 days.

The herb and honey crostini are even great naked.

Tomato Bruschetta

Makes about 30 bruschetta
Vegetarian

Throughout the months of August and September we eat this as often as humanly possible. There is that moment where the tables at the farmers' markets are piled high with all kinds of crazy looking tomatoes with funny names: Green Zebra, Brandywine, Lillian's Yellow Heirloom, Mortgage Lifter, Black Krim, and Purple Calabash, to name just a few. This is a great opportunity to let the kids have at it, picking the weirdest looking tomatoes they can find. Then when you get home, and are wondering what to do with all of these gorgeous specimens (other than slice them onto a platter, drizzle them lightly with olive oil, and sprinkle them with coarse salt, which is another option), make this bruschetta. The only key is to use perfectly ripe tomatoes, even if they don't have goofy names.

Cooking Tip: You can make a double batch of the tomato mixture, cook up a pound of pasta, and toss everything together for an amazing late-summer pasta dish. You'll probably want to add an extra splash of olive oil, as well as a ladle of the starchy water you cooked the pasta in to help form a sauce. A sprinkling of freshly grated Parmesan or crumbled goat cheese or a small handful of slivered fresh mozzarella on top of each portion of pasta is excellent.

What the Kids Can Do: Kids who are old enough to handle a serrated knife can help slice the tomatoes. And of course, the kids can stir everything together and help heap the tomato mixture on the toasted bread.

For the love of God, do not refrigerate your tomatoes.

5 cups cored, seeded, and diced ripe tomatoes (about 4 large
   tomatoes; you can use any mixture of tomatoes)

⅓ cup extra-virgin olive oil

⅓ cup slivered fresh basil leaves (see Note)

1 teaspoon minced garlic

1½ teaspoons kosher or coarse salt, or more to taste

Freshly ground black pepper

1 batch crostini (see page 49), with or without the garlic rub

1. Combine the tomatoes, olive oil, basil, garlic, and salt in a
   medium-size bowl. Taste for seasoning, adding pepper to
   taste and more salt as necessary. You can let the tomato
   mixture sit at room temperature for up to an hour before
   topping the crostini.

2. Arrange the crostini on a serving tray and top each with a
   spoonful of the tomato mixture or simply serve the tomato
   mixture in a bowl with the crostini on the side. When you
   scoop the tomatoes onto the bread, use a slotted spoon,
   or tilt the spoon a bit, to allow the liquid to drain off, or
   use your clean hands. If you are topping all the crostini
   yourself, do it right before serving or the bread will become
   soggy.

Note: To sliver, or julienne, fresh basil, simply stack a bunch
of the leaves one on top of the other, roll them up in any
direction into a short little tube, and slice the cylinder into
the thinnest slices you can manage.

WHAT IS THE DIFFERENCE BETWEEN BRUSCHETTA AND CROSTINI?

This discussion can get a little murky, since there are Italian purist definitions, and then there are definitions that have become more commonly associated with each word. Since this isn't the kind of book for lengthy academic classifications, here's my short version.

Crostini translates as little toasts, and generally means plain, thin slices of bread brushed with olive oil and toasted. They may or may not be topped with different things. Bruschetta also means toasted bread, authentically toasted on a grill over coals. Bruschetta are usually thicker and larger than crostini and are often eaten with a knife and fork. They are sometimes rubbed with a garlic clove. Technically it's the toast itself that is actually the bruschetta, which may or may not have toppings. These can be more rugged and messier than crostini toppings so bruschetta are usually served on a plate. Chopped fresh tomato is the most common topping for bruschetta.

Holy Guacamole

Makes about 2 cups; serves 4 to 6
A Fork in the Road Recipe
Vegetarian

My kids started out not liking guacamole but were still ecstatic to see it come out of the kitchen because that meant the basket of tortilla chips wasn't far behind. Eventually they tentatively dipped a chip—just a corner—into the green creaminess. It was deemed "not bad." (Stop, stop you're embarrassing me.) A bolder dip, a dunk, a scoop followed. It's not like the chips aren't still a big draw, but guacamole is now a most-requested appetizer.

2 ripe avocados, preferably Hass

⅓ cup minced onion

1 medium-size ripe tomato, cored, seeded, and chopped (about ⅔ cup)

Kosher or coarse salt and freshly ground black pepper

2 teaspoons fresh lime juice

½ to 1 teaspoon chopped seeded jalapeño pepper (optional)

½ to 1 teaspoon chopped fresh cilantro (optional)

Lots of tortilla chips, for serving

1. Cut the avocados in half, remove the pits, and use a knife to cut the avocado flesh into chunks right in the skin, cutting one direction and then crosswise in a gridlike fashion. Use a spoon to scoop out all of the flesh into a medium-size bowl.

2. Add the onion, tomato, ½ teaspoon of salt, and a few grinds of black pepper. Use a fork or a potato masher to combine the ingredients and mush up the avocado, leaving it as chunky or as blended as you like. Stir in the lime juice, then adjust the seasonings.

3. ◀═ You can serve the guacamole as is with tortilla chips or see the Fork in the Road suggestions for adding other seasonings on this page.

◀═ Fork in the Road

Jalapeños are hot, and cilantro is a serious love-hate herb (for more on this, see Nobody's Neutral on Cilantro on page 185). As with many of the recipes in this book, you can make the guacamole without those seasonings, then divide the mixture into two bowls. Leave one batch plain and spike the other with the more strongly flavored ingredients. Make sure to label the bowls if you do this.

Make Ahead: You want to make the guacamole only an hour or two ahead of time, if possible. Press plastic wrap directly onto the surface of the guacamole, store it in the refrigerator, and stir before serving.

What the Kids Can Do:

They can cut the crosshatches in the avocados, which does not have to be done neatly, nor does it require a sharp knife. You could let littler kids scoop out chunks of the avocado with a spoon instead. And mash away.

DON'T BE LURED IN BY THOSE OVERSIZE AVOCADOS

Hass avocados are smaller, darker green, and bumpier than other varieties of avocados, and in general have a deeper, richer flavor, with denser flesh. They are nutrient rich and have a nice amount of various essential vitamins and minerals. The fat they contain is understood by health experts to be the "good" fat, monounsaturated fat, which, when consumed in moderation and eaten in place of saturated or trans fat, can help reduce blood cholesterol levels and decrease risk of heart disease.

You really need perfectly ripe avocados to make good guacamole; don't bother if your avocados aren't nicely soft to the touch. Make edamame (see page 35) or something else.

You can dial the spiciness up or down as you like.

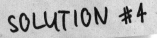

Pigs in a Blanket

Makes not enough (okay, makes about 30)

Do not even think of sneering or rolling your eyes. If you, or anyone in your family, has the internal fortitude to turn up a nose at a platter of darling little hot dogs snuggled into their flaky little dough pashminas, then you are more evolved than anyone in my family. If, however, like most every other mortal on this earth, your heart beats a little faster when you get a glimpse of these happy little morsels, and you lose your ability to concentrate on . . . oh, look there's a butterfly. And here's a sexist comment, I guess, but I'm willing to own it. Men, in particular, get a euphoric glazed look when pigs in a blanket make an appearance. I'll leave it to the social anthropologists to determine why this is.

Making pigs in a blanket is not rocket science, nor innovative cuisine, nor health food (see A Word About Nitrites and Sulfites and Sodium, Oh My on page 59), but you were promised one hundred great mom recipes, by golly, and if this doesn't qualify, well, I don't know what does. If you want to gild the lily a bit, shove a few slivers of cheese into a slit in the hot dogs before rolling them up in the puff pastry. Make more than you think you'll need and serve these babies with spicy brown mustard and ketchup. Maybe honey mustard. Save the Dijon for another day.

A WORD ABOUT APPROPRIATE TIMES TO EAT PIGS IN A BLANKET

In our family, pigs in a blanket are synonymous with New Year's Eve. I don't know about you, but my New Year's Eves have morphed from sequins and clubs (not really . . . maybe the sequins part) to letting the kids stay up until midnight and attempting to do the same myself. On this evening, based on sheer volume consumed, pigs in a blanket transition from an appetizer to an entrée. Other good occasions for eating pigs in a blanket: Super Bowl and sports parties, birthdays, cocktail parties, lengthy study sessions, Tuesdays.

If you're too sophisticated for Pigs in a Blanket, then something has gone awry.

Nonstick cooking spray (optional)

I pound (about 30) mini hot dogs

⅓ cup slivered cheddar cheese (optional)

About 3 tablespoons all-purpose flour, for rolling out the puff pastry

I sheet frozen puff pastry (half of a 17.3 ounce or so package), thawed according to package directions

I large egg

Finely grated fresh Parmesan cheese, or poppy or sesame seeds (optional), for sprinkling

Brown spicy mustard and ketchup, for serving

1. Preheat the oven to 400°F. Line a baking sheet with parchment paper or spray it with nonstick cooking spray and set it aside.

2. If you are using the cheese, make a slit down the middle of each hot dog, being careful not to cut all the way through. Tuck a few pieces of cheese into each hot dog.

3. Lightly flour a work surface and place the thawed puff pastry on top. Most puff pastry comes folded in thirds, which is very helpful; cut it down the seams or, if there are no seams, cut it crosswise into 3 equal pieces. Roll each piece out until it is a bit thinner, trying to maintain the squared off lines of the rectangle. Cut each piece of puff pastry into strips about 1 inch by 3 inches.

4. Beat the egg and 2 teaspoons of water in a small bowl.

5. Place a mini hot dog on the narrow end of one puff pastry strip. Roll it up, pressing on the puff pastry so that it seals itself. Place the pig in a blanket on the prepared baking sheet, seam side down. Repeat with the remaining hot dogs and puff pastry strips, arranging the pigs in blankets on the baking sheet at least 1 inch apart. Brush the tops of the pigs in blankets with the egg wash and sprinkle them with Parmesan or poppy or sesame seeds, if using. At this point it is helpful (but not necessary) to place the baking sheet in the fridge and let chill for 15 to 30 minutes so the pastry will puff up a bit more when it bakes.

6. Bake the pigs in blankets until they are puffed and golden brown, about 20 minutes. Let cool briefly before serving with mustard and ketchup.

Cooking Tip: Pepperidge Farm puff pastry, which I often use, comes in packages with two sheets. This recipe calls for one of the sheets, and you can defrost it and tuck the other back in the freezer for another day, but you can of course double the whole thing if you are cooking for a crowd.

What the Kids Can Do: Pigs in a Blanket are fun for the kids to make because no matter how strangely patched together the puff pastry might look before the hot dogs go into the oven, when they come out, the frozen puff pastry, that miracle of miracles, has magically formed itself into an attractive fluffy, puffy wrapper. The kids can also help sprinkle grated Parmesan or some poppy or sesame seeds over the little wrapped dogs before you pop them into the oven, or over half of them if you want to hedge your bets.

Puff pastry is pretty forgiving as far as doughs go.

COCKTAIL SAUCE

CHIPOTLE SAUCE

REMOULADE

Shrimp Cocktail

Serves 8 to 10
A Fork in the Road Recipe

My husband, Gary, does a great impression of someone pretending to notice the shrimp platter being passed at a cocktail party for the first time. "Oh, look, shrimp!" he exclaims heartily, with his eyebrows raised in simulated surprise. He does this repeatedly until whoever is serving the shrimp starts to sigh audibly. I, however, still find it kind of funny. A fact: No matter how elaborate the array of hors d'oeuvres, the two things that will cause the most people to crowd the buffet or rush the server are shrimp cocktail and Pigs in a Blanket (see page 56). The comment "Oh, look, pigs in a blanket!" repeated over and over also works for these.

This classic Shrimp Cocktail recipe is simple and straightforward and delicious. Having said that, if you want to advance things to a slightly more kicked-up level, there are a few easy ways to take that shrimp cocktail to the next plane without alienating the less intrepid shrimp-o-philes in your brood; see A Word About Cooking Perfect Shrimp on this page.

The cocktail sauce is ultrasimple, but a couple of other dipping sauce recipes also follow in case you're going all out for a party or want a change of pace.

The main point of Shrimp Cocktail is to make everyone happy, yessir.

What the Kids Can Do:
Kids can help with the ice water bath, peel the shrimp, measure and stir the dipping sauce ingredients, and be the arbiters of spiciness.

A WORD ABOUT COOKING PERFECT SHRIMP

The only important things to remember when cooking shrimp are keeping an eye on them so they don't overcook and having a bowl filled with ice water ready so you can plunge the shrimp in to stop the cooking just as they hit the cooked-through, tender-crisp stage. This is the very best way to ensure that the shrimp are not overboiled, ending up with a rubbery consistency.

If you want to add a bit more flavor to the shrimp as they are cooking, once you bring the water to a boil you can add some other ingredients along with the salt: a few peppercorns, a couple of bay leaves, a few slices of onion, a smashed peeled garlic clove or two, a healthy squeeze of fresh lemon juice, or a tablespoon of white wine vinegar. You can also skip the lemon juice or vinegar and add a few glugs of white wine if you have an open bottle. Or not. You can stick with salted water and call it a day and not one person will say anything other than "You are the best and we love you very very much." If anyone in your family says, "These shrimp could have used a bay leaf," you can send them to me and I will handle them.

Ice

Kosher or coarse salt

2 pounds extra-large (21 to 25) or jumbo (16 to 20) shrimp in the shell; basically the biggest you feel like splurging for (see Frozen vs. "Fresh" Shrimp, this page)

¾ cup ketchup, preferably Heinz

½ cup Heinz chili sauce (optional; see Note)

1 to 3 tablespoons prepared horseradish

¼ teaspoon Worcestershire sauce

2 teaspoons fresh lemon juice

1. Fill a large bowl with several cups of ice and add enough cold water to fill it almost to the top. Set the bowl aside.

2. Bring a large pot of water to a boil. Add 1 tablespoon of salt (and anything else you want to add; see A Word About Cooking Perfect Shrimp, page 61).

3. Add the shrimp, stir, and cook the shrimp until just cooked through; they will be opaque throughout, 3 to 5 minutes (the water may not reach a full simmer again during this time). Immediately drain the shrimp and submerge them in the ice water bath for 10 minutes. Drain, peel, and devein the shrimp (leave the tails on for handles). Cover the shrimp and refrigerate them until ready to serve.

4. ✦═ Before making the sauce, see the Fork in the Road suggestions for tips on seasoning on this page.

5. To make the sauce, combine the ketchup, chili sauce, if using, horseradish (start with 1 tablespoon and add more to taste), Worcestershire sauce, and lemon juice in a medium-size bowl. Season with salt to taste.

6. Place the bowl of cocktail sauce in the middle of a large platter and arrange the shrimp around it.

Note: Rarely do I call for a specific brand, but in this case, do try to find Heinz, especially for the chili sauce, which is not overly spicy and has a kid-friendly blend of seasonings. If you use another chili sauce, know that it might well be much, much hotter, and add it very slowly. And if you want to skip the chili sauce, you'll still get a great cocktail sauce with the other ingredients on their own (be generous with the horseradish).

✦═ Fork in the Road

For the cocktail sauce, add the horseradish and the chili sauce slowly, tasting as you go. You may very well want to do a Fork in the Road maneuver here and stop at a certain level of spiciness, separate half of the sauce out into a small bowl for the kids, then continue spiking the grown-up portion with more horseradish, pepper, and lemon juice, until you're happy. If you have sauces with two levels of spiciness, put them in different colored bowls and let the kids know which is which.

FROZEN VS. "FRESH" SHRIMP

It's just fine to use frozen shrimp; the reality is that almost all shrimp has been frozen and thawed before it hits our kitchens, even if you buy it at a fish counter. Just make sure that for safety you thaw shrimp in your refrigerator, not on the counter, You can also thaw shrimp by placing them in a colander and running cold water over them.

Frozen shrimp that have been split and deveined are wonderful; it should be clearly stated on the packaging that the shrimp have been prepared this way. Once you cook them and remove the shells, there's no pesky cleaning involved.

Chipotle Mayonnaise

Makes about 1 cup

Whenever I make this I end up sending guests home with a container of it. It keeps well for at least a couple of weeks. It's a bit hot, a bit smoky, with a creamy consistency. Also use it as a sandwich spread, a dip for crudités, a sauce for poached chicken or fish; spread it on crostini and top them with roasted peppers . . . the mayonnaise's uses are numerous and wonderful.

- I teaspoon very finely minced garlic
- I teaspoon chipotle puree (see Chipotle Peppers, page xx)
- I cup mayonnaise, preferably Hellmann's
- I teaspoon fresh lime juice
- Kosher or coarse salt and freshly ground black pepper

Whisk together the garlic, chipotle puree, mayonnaise, and lime juice in a small bowl. Season with salt and pepper to taste. The mayonnaise can be refrigerated for up to 2 weeks.

"Fresh" Shrimp Rémoulade

Makes 1 generous cup

Rémoulade is a condiment that is kind of like a French-inspired Russian dressing. There are lots of different versions, but this one is a simple combo of mayo, ketchup, a bit of brown mustard, and some straightforward seasonings. Rémoulade is often served with seafood dishes, and it is more tangy than spicy.

- ¾ cup mayonnaise, preferably Hellmann's
- 3 tablespoons ketchup
- I tablespoon brown mustard
- 3 tablespoons finely chopped celery
- I½ tablespoons finely chopped fresh Italian (flat-leaf) parsley
- 2 teaspoons finely chopped scallion, both white and light green parts
- Kosher or coarse salt and freshly ground black pepper

Blend together the mayonnaise, ketchup, mustard, celery, parsley, and scallion in a medium-size bowl. Season with salt and pepper to taste. The rémoulade can be refrigerated, covered, for up to 4 days. Stir it again before serving.

CHIPOTLE SAUCE

RÉMOULADE

COCKTAIL SAUCE

The mother
of all soups.

Chapter 5

Souped Up

Do you know what I like? An oversimplification with a bunch of qualifiers. Here's an example: There seem to be certain categories of food that divide kids into camps pretty readily. Soup is one of them. There are soup kids and there are not-soup kids. My younger kid is a soup kid, ready to slurp down a bowl of almost anything—chunky, smooth, veggie filled, noodley, slightly spicy, creamy . . . "I smell soup!" he yells, bursting into the house. My older son is more along the lines of an "Is that soup?" kid, peering suspiciously into the pot that's simmering cheerfully away on the stove. "What kind? What's in it? What's that?" said while pointing disdainfully at a chickpea innocently bobbing away on the surface. However, he has come a long way, and soup is now entering his repertoire, although he doesn't often ask for seconds. Unless it's chicken noodle matzoh ball soup; then he asks for seconds, and thirds.

THE DILEMMA

Broadening your family's soup horizons.

The soups in this chapter represent a nice range of flavors and consistencies, and they have all passed muster within my kids' circle of friends (except for the really picky ones, and we simply have to be patient about this). The cauliflower soup may come as a bit of a surprise, but if you have a kid who gravitates toward white foods, this is a good opportunity to introduce a non-carb white food; also, the cheese in it doesn't hurt.

Three take-them-or-leave-them soup thoughts:

1. Start off by serving a new soup to your kids in a very small bowl or in a ramekin; try a dish that holds about five spoonfuls. You wouldn't throw first timers a big slab of pork loin on their plates—all new foods seem more

approachable when they are served in a size proportionate to the diminutive and discriminating diner.

2. Soup is one of the most forgiving, versatile, and flexible foods out there. The recipe for Vegetable Bin Stone Soup is a full-blown example of how just about anything can become soup. And soup is a very smart way to get your kids involved in the kitchen without butter and sugar always being the starring ingredients. Realizing that many recipes can be endlessly adapted to your likes and tastes is one of the best cooking lessons all of us—and "us" includes our kids—can internalize. Liberating, practically therapy, but so much cheaper as well as being delicious.

3. Add-ins at the end can make a big difference in terms of what soups appeal to which members of your family. A plain minestrone, for instance, may work just fine for most kids, but a sprinkling of Parmesan and a shot of Sriracha hot sauce may really make it happen for the more seasoned palates in the house. The category of cheese is vast all on its own, and a crumble or sprinkle of any of a number of kinds can transform something simple into something fabulous (see Ideas for Topping a Bowl of Soup, opposite page).

When it comes to doctoring up a bowl of soup, this is where I like to peer at the no-man's-land otherwise known as the refrigerator door shelves. Sure, you've got your mustard and your ketchup there, and maybe some soy sauce, but you probably also have that eclectic collection of condiments that have accumulated over time in your fridge, which you've been waiting to find something to do with. Soup is your big chance! And of course there are the pantry, the vegetable bins, and the way, way back of the fridge, where mysterious things lurk, mysterious things that may inspire you and open the door to your inner chef. Or mysterious things that you should probably throw away.

Plain

With bacon

With bacon, scallions, and extra black pepper

IDEAS FOR TOPPING A BOWL OF SOUP

Chopped fresh herbs • a squeeze of fresh lemon, lime, or orange juice • flavored olive oil • hoisin sauce • hot sauces of all kinds • chile sauce with garlic • horseradish sauce • a bloop of sour cream or crème fraîche • a little spoonful of tahini • grated cheeses of all kinds • chutneys • chopped pickled jalapeños • minced olives • leftover chopped cooked bacon or ham

And from the spice drawer: a sprinkle of cayenne, paprika, smoked paprika, sesame seeds, nutmeg, mace, or cardamom; be judicious with your sprinkling.

Lentil, Tomato, and Rice Soup

Serves 6 to 8

This is part soup, part stew.

Sometimes we all fall into the trap of making knee-jerk assumptions about what our kids will and won't eat, and we avoid serving something new because we anticipate that it won't be met with open arms. Beans and lentils often fall into this category. I will say for the record that while my oldest, now twelve, is slightly amenable to beans in certain soups and dishes, my younger one, currently nine, will eat half a can of garbanzos in a single sitting. He really adores bean soups and stews, which makes it very easy to get some good protein and fiber into him without making meat the centerpiece of every dinner.

Just to reiterate a favorite "just try it" tip: Sometimes when I'm offering up a new thing in my house, I'll put a few tablespoons in a small bowl or ramekin and give it to my kids to taste—much less overwhelming than being presented with a full bowl of something they're feeling skeptical about.

This lentil soup is quite simple, with straightforward ingredients and seasonings. It's pleasingly thick and hearty. The rice adds to the substantial texture. If you're enthusiastic, as we are, about tossing crisp bacon pieces on top of the soup before you dig in, taste when you are adding any salt to the soup at the end; you'll want to see how salty, or not, the bacon and broth are.

Cooking Tip: Just to confirm: The alcohol in the wine cooks off in the soup, and all that's left is a nice flavor boost.

Make Ahead: The lentil soup can be made up to five days ahead of time and refrigerated or it can be frozen for up to six months. You will probably want to add some water or broth when you reheat the soup, as it thickens considerably when it is chilled. Sprinkle the additional bacon and cheese, if using, on top of each portion just before serving.

What the Kids Can Do: Crumble the cooled, cooked bacon and sprinkle it and the cheese over the servings of soup.

4 to 6 slices bacon, sliced crosswise into ½-inch pieces

2 teaspoons olive oil

I cup chopped onion

¾ cup peeled chopped carrots

½ cup rice, preferably Arborio (see Risotto Rices, page 240)

1½ teaspoons minced garlic

I teaspoon dried thyme

Splash of red or white wine (optional)

I can (28 ounces) crushed tomatoes

5 cups low-sodium chicken broth, or more as needed

¾ cup dried lentils (see Note), rinsed and picked through

Kosher or coarse salt and freshly ground black pepper

Freshly grated Parmesan or cheddar or crumbled feta cheese (optional), for serving

1. Heat a large pot over medium-high heat. Add the bacon and cook, stirring occasionally, until crisp, 4 to 5 minutes. Using a slotted spoon, transfer the bacon to paper towels to drain. Pour off all but 2 teaspoons of the bacon fat from the pot, add the olive oil, onion, and carrots and cook over medium-high heat, stirring, until the vegetables soften, about 5 minutes.

2. Add the rice, garlic, and thyme and cook, stirring, until well combined, about 3 minutes. Add the wine, if using, and stir until it's almost evaporated, about 1 minute.

3. Add the tomatoes, chicken broth, lentils, and half of the bacon and stir to combine. Season with salt and pepper to taste.

4. Let the lentil mixture simmer, uncovered, over medium-low heat, stirring occasionally, until the lentils and the rice are tender, 20 to 30 minutes. Feel free to add more liquid if you like a thinner soup. Serve the soup in bowls with the rest of the bacon and a sprinkling of Parmesan, cheddar, or feta cheese on top, if desired.

Note: Look for the tiny Le Puy variety of lentils; they have a wonderful flavor. You can buy Le Puy lentils at specialty food stores, some supermarkets, and online (see page 343). (While you don't have to use Le Puy lentils or Arborio rice, those ingredients do take the soup to a different level.)

A WORD ABOUT BOUILLON CUBES

I would like to say that I never use bouillon cubes, that I use stock I made myself from the tender meat of organic chickens that were given spa treatments up until the moment they lost their lives for my soup. Barring that, I would like to say that I use only organic store-bought chicken broth, which is certainly a bit more truthful than the previous sentence. The whole truth is, I use homemade chicken stock rarely, store-bought chicken broth almost all of the time—sometimes organic, sometimes not—and sometimes (she glances nervously to one side and whispers), a bouillon cube. Look, different days call for different realities, and if most of us held out for the pot of homemade organic liquid gold, we would get many fewer meals on the table. And wouldn't that be a shame?

Vegetarian Note: For a strictly vegetarian soup, skip the bacon and use a couple of teaspoons of olive oil instead of the bacon fat. And substitute vegetable broth for the chicken broth.

Halfway Homemade Chicken Noodle Matzoh Ball Soup

Serves 4 to 6

Every time I ask my kids what they want for dinner, this is the dish they call out first. It's a bit of a sham that the words *matzoh balls* are listed in the title of the recipe, since I don't make them from scratch and am not going to be hypocritical and suggest that you do. When I first met my husband's (then boyfriend's) extended family one Passover I went out of my way to lavishly praise his matriarchal Aunt Lois for her fluffy and delicious matzoh balls. I flattered her, and I begged for the recipe, which I supposed was a family one passed down for generations. Anyway, she imperially led me into the kitchen where I thought she would dictate the secret ingredients, but instead she shoved a box of matzoh ball mix in my hands. And who am I to question Aunt Lois? You do not even have to make the matzoh balls, of course; a bowl of chicken noodle soup is lovely on its own.

4 to 6 pounds skin-on, bone-in chicken thighs (preferred), or breasts, or a combination of the two

I onion, coarsely chopped

4 large carrots, 2 peeled and coarsely chopped and 2 peeled and thinly sliced

10 cups low-sodium chicken broth

I envelope matzoh ball mix (optional), including the other ingredients called for on the box (usually oil and eggs)

2 tablespoons minced fresh dill, or I tablespoon dried dill (see Green Flecks: Pro or Con?, opposite page)

Kosher or coarse salt and freshly ground black pepper

½ pound dried egg noodles, your choice of width, cooked according to package directions until just tender

You can make matzoh balls from scratch . . . but I don't.

Make Ahead: You can make this soup up to four days ahead of time. If you're planning in advance, you may want to make the soup, and cook the noodles and the matzoh balls, but keep them in separate containers. When you are ready to serve, add the noodles and matzoh balls to the soup and simmer until everything is heated through. This prevents you from having overcooked soggy noodles and matzoh balls.

What the Kids Can Do: Kids can shred the cooled, cooked chicken and help stir together the matzoh ball mix and form the matzoh balls.

1. Place the chicken in a large soup pot or Dutch oven, add the onion and the chopped carrots, and pour the chicken broth and 2 cups of water over all. Place the pot over high heat and let the liquid come to a full simmer. Reduce the heat to medium-low and let simmer, partially covered, until the chicken is fully cooked, about 1 hour. If the level of liquid seems like it's reducing too quickly, you can add 1 or 2 more cups of water.

2. Meanwhile, if you are making the matzoh balls, make them according to the package directions. I form mine into 1½-inch balls before poaching them for the soup.

3. Carefully strain the soup into a large bowl and set aside the chicken to cool slightly (you can toss out the cooked carrots and onion). Return the soup to the pot. When the chicken is cool enough to handle, shred the meat into nice bite-size pieces, discarding the skin, bones, and any gristle.

4. Bring the soup to a simmer over medium heat and add the sliced carrots and the dill. Let simmer until the carrots are tender, 8 to 10 minutes. Season the soup with salt and pepper to taste. Return the chicken to the pot (adding as much as you like and setting the rest aside for another use). Add the cooked noodles and the matzoh balls, if using. Let the soup simmer until everything has heated through, then ladle the soup into bowls and serve.

GREEN FLECKS: PRO OR CON?

Dill is what makes chicken soup taste like chicken soup to my family. My kids are cool with seeing green flecks in their soup. If yours aren't, but you agree that dill makes the soup, then you should feel free to add it to the broth when you are simmering the chicken (if you're using fresh dill, just throw in a couple of nice sprigs), and then you can strain it out with the cooked chicken and veggies, leaving behind a delicate dill flavor but no icky flecky things. If you'd rather not add dill while you're cooking the soup, another option is to snip a bit of fresh dill into the individual portions of soup for those who like it.

Cooking Tip: Now, sometimes I'm in a make-my-own-broth-entirely-from-scratch phase, but more often than not I'm in a we-want-soup-now phase. This soup is a compromise between using only broth from a can or box and making your own. Here's the scoop: When you cook chicken in water to create broth, pretty much all of the flavor of the chicken goes into the water to create the broth, leaving the chicken itself pretty tasteless. So then you have to go and roast a whole other batch of chicken to shred and add to the soup. That's a lot of chicken, and a lot of time.

In this soup, you're basically poaching chicken in premade chicken broth, which simultaneously enriches the broth (soup) and the chicken itself. A win-win kind of a thing.

If you go for the larger amount of chicken, you will have a richer soup and probably some leftover cooked chicken, which can be used to make Cheesy Chicken Enchiladas (page 164) or anything else that calls for simply cooked chicken, and I often use the larger amount just for that very reason. Whew, that sounds more complicated than it is.

Corn Chowder

Serves about 6

Does the word *chowder* conjure up appealing, summery images for you? It's crazy good made with fresh corn, but you can make this in the non-fresh-corn months with frozen or canned corn and still revel in the pale creamy sweetness of this soup.

If you're interested in a seafood chowder, see the variation on the facing page. I often make some version of this after a summer dinner party that featured corn and seafood, since it is a very lenient recipe, and facts being facts, any time you combine cream, corn, and just about anything else in a pot you're heading in a good direction.

- 4 slices bacon, sliced crosswise into ½-inch pieces
- I teaspoon unsalted butter
- I tablespoon all-purpose flour
- I cup chopped onion, or ½ cup chopped shallots
- ½ cup chopped peeled carrots
- ⅓ cup chopped red bell pepper (about ½-inch pieces)
- ¾ teaspoon minced fresh thyme, or ½ teaspoon dried thyme
- Kosher or coarse salt and freshly ground black pepper
- 2 cups diced potatoes (about ½-inch dice), preferably Yukon Gold
- 2 cups low-sodium chicken or vegetable broth
- I bay leaf
- 3 cups fresh corn kernels (from about 5 ears), or 3 cups frozen corn kernels
- 2 cups milk (I percent, 2 percent, or whole)
- ½ cup heavy (whipping) cream
- 2 tablespoons thinly sliced scallions, both white and light green parts, or minced fresh chives (optional), for serving
- Extra cooked crumbled bacon (optional), for serving

Cooking Tip: Yukon Gold potatoes are the potatoes of choice here for their buttery flavor and their great texture. They're firm enough to hold their shape and have some bite to them when cooked, but they're also able to be crushed up a bit, adding to the texture and body of the soup. The crushing-up step really turns the soup from a broth with things floating in it to a chowder.

Make Ahead: If you are planning to make the chowder in advance, prepare the recipe through Step 3 and refrigerate the soup. It will keep, covered, for up to two days. Reheat the soup, adding the milk and cream just before serving. If you want to reheat leftovers that already have the dairy added, make sure to heat the soup over medium-low heat until just warmed through so it won't separate.

1. Heat a large pot over medium-high heat. Add the bacon and cook, stirring occasionally, until crisp, 4 to 5 minutes. Using a slotted spoon, remove the bacon and set it aside on paper towels to drain. Pour off all but 2 teaspoons of fat from the pot.

2. Add the butter to the pot and melt over medium heat. Add the flour and stir until it starts to turn golden, about 2 minutes. Add the onion or shallots and carrots and cook, stirring occasionally, until tender, about 4 minutes. Add the bell pepper and thyme, season with salt and pepper to taste, and cook, stirring, until everything is well combined, about 1 minute. Add the potatoes, broth, bay leaf, and the reserved bacon. Reduce the heat to medium-low, let come to a simmer, and simmer until the potatoes are tender, 10 to 12 minutes.

3. Add the corn and let simmer until the corn is tender, 4 to 6 minutes. Using a potato masher or a wooden spoon, press against the side of the pot to smush up some of the potatoes and veggies so that they break up a bit and thicken the chowder.

4. Add the milk and heavy cream, increase the heat to medium, and cook, stirring frequently, until tiny bubbles form along the edge of the pot, about 7 minutes. Don't let the soup come to a boil or it might separate. Taste for seasoning, adding more salt and/or pepper as necessary. Fish out the bay leaf, then ladle the soup into bowls and top with the chives and/or bacon, if using.

Variation

Corn and Shrimp (or Lobster or Crab) Chowder

Add one cup 1/2-inch diced uncooked shrimp or lobster or crab just after you smush up some of the potatoes and corn at the end of Step 3. You can also use cooked seafood; add it at the end, right when the little bubbles form after you've stirred in the milk and cream, and let it heat through, about 2 minutes, but don't let the soup boil.

Let everyone customize their own bowl of chowder.

What the Kids Can Do: Ask the kids to crumble the cooled crisped bacon and, if they are old enough to be wary of a hot pot, smush up the potatoes and vegetables after they have been cooked in Step 3 (take the pot off the stove first). Kids can also sprinkle individual portions with scallions or chives, and/or bacon, if desired.

Vegetarian Note: If you want a vegetarian soup, skip the bacon and add a couple of teaspoons of olive oil when you melt the butter.

Cheddar and Cauliflower Soup

Serves 6

Getting your kids to eat vegetables *and* soup—who made you queen of the block? The great thing about this soup is that it uses the whole head of cauliflower, not just the florets, since everything gets pureed. Using white cheddar keeps the soup a pretty pale color, while yellow cheddar will . . . well, you know what yellow cheddar will do. And for those of us who see heavy cream and think "hold on, just a sec," let's all hold hands and remember that a little heavy cream goes a long way for texture, flavor, and just pure satisfaction. Let's save our raised eyebrow, food-related hackles for something else.

If you have some fresh herbs on hand, and your kids won't make gagging noises when they see them floating around, skip the dried thyme and add a teaspoon or so of minced fresh herbs (try thyme, marjoram, oregano, whatever you have, whatever you like), but add them during the final simmer. Or go for the nutmeg, a different flavor, and a strong one, so just add a pinch. You can also pass hot sauce at the table for those who are interested.

Let it simmer, but watch that it doesn't boil.

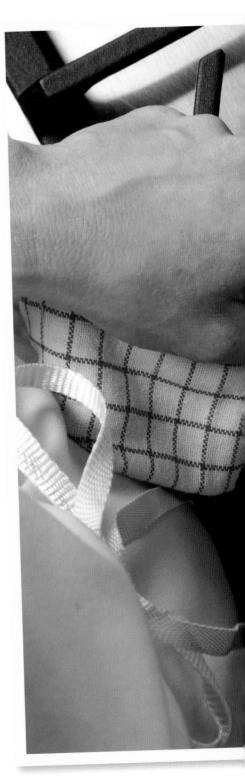

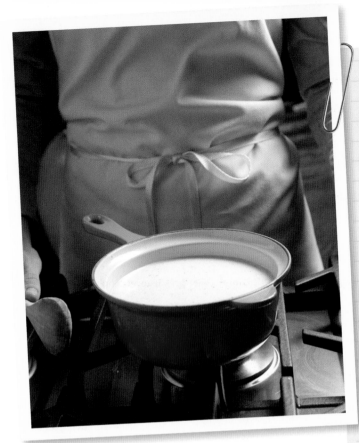

I tablespoon kosher or coarse salt, plus more to taste

I large head cauliflower (about 2 pounds),
   cored and cut into I-inch pieces

2 tablespoons (¼ stick) unsalted butter

I onion, chopped

½ teaspoon minced garlic

2 tablespoons all-purpose flour

½ teaspoon dried thyme, or I big pinch ground nutmeg

4 cups low-sodium chicken or vegetable broth
   (see Vegetarian Note)

2 teaspoons Dijon mustard

⅛ teaspoon cayenne, or a few shakes Tabasco sauce,
   or I squirt Sriracha sauce (all optional)

I cup heavy (whipping) cream or whole milk,
   or a combination of the two

I½ cups (6 ounces) grated sharp or extra-sharp cheddar cheese

Freshly ground black pepper

AN APPLIANCE WORTH THE STORAGE SPACE

Buying lots of kitchen appliances or tools that do one job or another is fun, but as you attempt to find storage for your egg poaching trays, heart-shaped pancake molds, individual asparagus tongs, and madeleine pans, you probably wonder, what was I thinking? Or, more often, what were my kind-hearted houseguests thinking?

The immersion or stick blender is the opposite of the one-off tool. It's a blender on a stick that you can put right into a mixture, hot or cold, press a button, stir it around, and puree the whole shebang. It's brilliant, and for some of us (for example, me) the number of times I feel sure I would have burned (read: did burn) myself transferring hot soups to a blender to puree them pays for the immersion blender over and over again. Seriously, a good immersion blender costs like thirty bucks, and you may be aware that that is equal to a few tubes of Neosporin and some packages of gauze. All of this is to say, buy one if you use your food processor or blender regularly, and you'll find yourself reaching for it often.

1. Pour water to a depth of 1 inch into a large pot and bring to a boil over high heat. Add 1 tablespoon of salt and the cauliflower, cover the pot, reduce the heat to medium-high, and let simmer until the cauliflower is tender, 7 to 9 minutes. Drain the cauliflower and set it aside.

2. Melt the butter in the same pot over medium heat. Add the onion and cook, stirring frequently, until tender but not browned, about 4 minutes. Add the garlic and cook until the garlic starts to turn golden and becomes fragrant, 1 to 2 minutes. Whisk in the flour and thyme or nutmeg and cook, whisking, until the flour starts to color, about 3 minutes.

3. Gradually whisk in the broth, mustard, and whatever spicy ingredient you may be using, if you are using one at all. Let come to a simmer and cook until the liquid thickens slightly, about 5 minutes, then stir in the cooked cauliflower.

4. At this point you can transfer the soup to a blender or food processor (working in batches if necessary) and puree it or, better yet, use an immersion blender (see An Appliance Worth the Storage Space, opposite page) to puree it right in the pot until smooth. Make the soup as smooth or chunky as you like.

5. Return the soup to the pot if necessary and reheat it over medium-high heat. Add the cream or milk and cheddar cheese and stir until the cheese is melted and everything is hot, about 3 minutes. Don't let the soup come to a boil or it might separate. Taste for seasoning, adding more salt as necessary and black pepper to taste.

Make Ahead: Most soups freeze very well, but this soup (and most other soups with a dairy base) loses its texture when frozen and reheated. If you are planning to make the soup in advance, prepare the recipe through Step 4. The soup can be refrigerated, covered, for up to four days. Reheat the soup, adding the cream or milk and cheddar just before serving. You can refrigerate leftover soup for two or three days; just make sure to reheat it gently over low heat, not allowing it to boil, so it won't separate.

What the Kids Can Do: The kids can break the cauliflower into small pieces, help blend the soup (with serious supervision), and add the cream or milk and cheese to the soup, but take the pot off the heat first.

Vegetarian Note: If you use vegetable broth in the Cheddar and Cauliflower Soup, it's a vegetarian soup.

There's a bowl of soup hiding in
your refrigerator right now . . .

Vegetable Bin Stone Soup

Makes about 4 quarts

Remember the stone soup fable? It's is about a man who came to a village and asked for something to eat; all of the villagers felt too poor to share, so he then embarked on the elaborate public enterprise of creating soup from a mere stone. However, of course he needed a bit of potato to make it thicker, and some parsley for flavor, and a bit of carrot for color, and so on, and it turned out that all of the villagers were in fact willing to donate a bit of this and that, out of curiosity and with the promise of soup on the horizon. A few hours later the entire village had created a cauldron of the most aromatic, amazing soup, all by pooling their resources. So, to summarize, stone soup provides a way to: (1) engage kids in cooking; (2) clean out the vegetable bin; and (3) include a meaningful if slightly pious little lesson, all in one soup.

This is called Vegetable Bin Stone Soup because it makes use of pretty much everything that's hanging out in your vegetable drawer in the fridge (and some other pantry staples, too). You can also feel free to add some frozen vegetables in place of fresh; there are a lot of high-quality frozen vegetables available these days. Add them closer to the end of the cooking time. The whole thing will take from forty-five minutes to one hour from the time the liquid comes to a simmer—just keep tasting until it starts to taste like soup. You can also sprinkle cheese on each serving, if you like. And, the soup will taste even better the next day. It makes a lot, so you may want to invite over some villagers to help you make and eat it.

You will want somewhere between 8 and 10 cups of vegetables total, depending on how flavorful they are and how thick you want your soup to be.

ONION   +   CARROT   +   CELERY

+   SQUASH   +   BEANS   +   CABBAGE

+   TOMATO   +   CORN   +   PEAS

+   BROCCOLI   +   RED PEPPER   +   POTATO

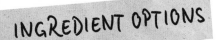

INGREDIENT OPTIONS

LONGER-COOKING INGREDIENTS TO ADD AT THE BEGINNING

Chicken, beef, or vegetable bouillon cubes (read the package to determine the amount in proportion to liquid)

Chopped onion • chopped shallots • broccoli, chopped or small florets • cauliflower, chopped or small florets • chopped cabbage • sliced or chopped carrots • sliced or chopped celery • chopped fennel • diced winter squash or pumpkin • diced potatoes • canned chopped or crushed tomatoes • dried herbs, such as thyme, basil, oregano, rosemary, or an Italian mix, about 1 to 2 teaspoons total

SHORTER-COOKING INGREDIENTS TO ADD DURING THE LAST 15 TO 20 MINUTES OR SO OF COOKING

Corn kernels • peas • sliced or chopped zucchini or summer squash • chopped fresh tomatoes • any leftover cooked vegetables, chopped • rinsed and drained canned beans • cooked rice, barley, or orzo • shredded or cubed cooked beef, pork, turkey, or chicken • chopped fresh herbs, such as thyme, basil, oregano, rosemary, and/or parsley, 1 to 2 tablespoons total • kosher or coarse salt and freshly ground black pepper • grated or crumbled cheese, such as cheddar, Parmesan, Provolone, Romano, feta, and so on (optional), for sprinkling on at the end

1. Bring 3 quarts of water to a simmer in a large soup pot over high heat. Add the bouillon cubes. Reduce the heat to keep the liquid at a simmer and add your choice of the longer-cooking ingredients. Let them simmer away until everything becomes fairly tender, about 30 minutes.

2. Add your choice of the shorter-cooking ingredients, season with salt and pepper to taste, and let the soup simmer for another 15 to 20 minutes or so. Start tasting the soup toward the end, and when the flavors seem to be blended and the consistency of the ingredients is as you like it, serve it up—it's soup! Sprinkle some cheese on top, if you like.

Make Ahead: Depending on what you've put in the stone soup, it will last covered in the fridge for about four days. Sprinkle the cheese on top, if desired, just before serving.

What the Kids Can Do: This is tailor-made for kids to take the reins. Let them hunt through the refrigerator and the pantry. Depending on your kids' ages and how hard or soft the vegetables are, kids may be able to help with some of the prep work (leftover cooked veggies are usually soft enough for beginner chefs to cut up with a table knife). Be sure to supervise kids while they add the various ingredients to the simmering pot. It's so much fun for them to see how a bunch of very separate ingredients comes together into one special dish.

You might encourage your kids to take photos of the process, the different ingredients, and then the homemade soup. It's great for kids to document the action, and they will feel even prouder of what they have made when they have something to remember it with and to show to friends and family.

Vegetarian Note: If you stick to vegetarian ingredients and broth, you've got a vegetarian soup!

STONE SOUP

Chapter 6

4 Salads and a Couple of Vinaigrettes

"I don't like salad." Whenever that sentence comes out of a kid's mouth it's a real conversational dead end. Where do you go with that? "You don't like all salads, Sam?" "What in particular don't you like about salads, Zoe?" "Have you actually ever even taken a bite of salad, Penelope?"

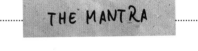

THE MANTRA

Be brave—serve salad.

Sigh. Look, there's not much to do here except to keep trying, and in this chapter there are four salads that may turn the situation around for you and yours. Three come with their own very different dressings (with various modifications). The fourth salad calls for a vinaigrette, and because an endless number of salads in your future will, too, the chapter ends with a recipe for a classic vinaigrette that has plenty of variations, as well as a lemon-based dressing.

How to crack open the door? Let your kids dip a cucumber or a carrot into some dressing and take a bite. Let them help pick out vegetables at the supermarket or farmers' market and concoct their own beautiful, colorful salads. As far as lettuce goes, kids lean toward crunchy, and you can slide from iceberg to romaine to Bibb lettuce in short time, then broaden your leafy options.

Salad dressings are one of the very best kid projects in the kitchen; no cooking, just pouring, stirring, shaking, tasting, and adjusting seasonings, with ample opportunity for inventiveness.

Bibb Lettuce with Ranch Dressing

Serves 4; Makes about 1¾ cups of dressing
Vegetarian

Two of my nieces will essentially only eat a vegetable if there is ranch dressing to dip it in, so in preparation for a visit from them, it was time to start getting a dressing recipe together. Let's not pretend that this is a low-fat dressing; *however,* the buttermilk, which (contrary to its name) contains very little fat, does offset the other ingredients, and you can also make the lower-fat variation, which uses thick Greek yogurt in place of the sour cream. The dressing is creamy and refreshing and delicious. It may get some reluctant vegetable eaters to embrace salad, so that's a good thing. The recipe makes more dressing than you'll need for one salad, but leftovers keep for a week in the refrigerator.

If you want to make an even thicker version, which serves well as a more substantial dunk for crudités, try the Ranch Dip variation (you'll find it on the next page).

This is a good beginner salad.

FOR THE RANCH DRESSING

⅔ cup buttermilk

½ cup mayonnaise, preferably Hellmann's

½ cup sour cream

I tablespoon white wine vinegar

I tablespoon chopped fresh Italian (flat-leaf) parsley

I teaspoon Dijon mustard

¾ teaspoon finely minced garlic or garlic powder

½ teaspoon dried dill, or I teaspoon chopped fresh dill

½ teaspoon dried thyme, or I teaspoon chopped fresh thyme

⅛ teaspoon sweet paprika

Kosher or coarse salt and freshly ground black pepper

FOR THE SALAD

6 cups torn Bibb or butter lettuce, rinsed and dried

I cup peeled and thinly sliced seedless or English cucumber (optional)

I cup cherry or grape tomatoes (optional)

1. Make the ranch dressing: Place the buttermilk, mayonnaise, sour cream, vinegar, parsley, mustard, garlic, dill, thyme, and paprika in a small bowl and whisk to combine. Season with salt and pepper to taste.

2. Make the salad: Place the lettuce, cucumber and tomatoes, if using, in a large serving bowl and drizzle about ½ cup of the dressing on top, or more if desired. Toss the salad and serve.

Variations

#1: Lower-Fat Ranch Dressing

Substitute ½ cup 1 percent fat Greek yogurt for the sour cream, or you can also use low fat mayo if you wish.

#2: Ranch Dip for Veggies

Reduce the buttermilk to ½ cup and increase both the mayonnaise and the sour cream to ⅔ cup each.

Make Ahead: The ranch dressing will keep for one week in a covered container in the fridge.

What the Kids Can Do: Kids will enjoy measuring and whisking and tasting and tossing the dressing and salad.

MY LESS FAT GREEK YOGURT DRESSING

Greek yogurt is thicker, creamier, and has less of a tart-tangy taste than regular yogurt. It gets its thick texture from being strained, so that the whey is removed from the yogurt. It has become increasingly available in the U.S. over the past several years and can in many cases be used as a substitute for sour cream, cutting down on the fat and calories in a recipe. Greek yogurt is full of protein and available in fat free, I percent, 2 percent, and whole versions. As with milk, the more fat, the creamier the texture and the richer the flavor. Most Greek yogurt available here in the States is made with cow's milk.

Japanese Restaurant Salad

Serves 4 to 6; with about 2 cups of dressing, there's enough for a few more salads
Vegetarian

This salad happens to be my older son's favorite part of dinner at any Japanese restaurant. It's a great change of pace from the usual vinaigrette and a perfect companion to any of the Asian dishes in this book such as Broiled Miso Cod Fingers (page 146), Teriyaki Chicken and Beef Skewers (page 230), Asian Salmon (page 144), Soy-Ginger Flank Steak (page 120), Shrimp Stir-Fried Rice (page 150), or any other Asian dish, for that matter.

The thick dressing also makes a great topping for steamed or roasted veggies like broccoli, asparagus, sugar snap peas, green beans, or cauliflower and is a nice dunk for raw veggies, too. You might sauté some tofu or chicken, mound it on hot rice, and spoon the dressing on top—that to me is comfort food.

MIRIN

A rice wine used in Japanese cooking, mirin is a bit like sake, but sweeter and with less alcohol. In fact, one kind—*shin mirin*—has only a trace amount of alcohol; so if you're buying a fresh bottle for family cooking, that's the one to choose. You can also leave it out completely, and no one will miss it.

This sweet and tangy dressing has carrots built right in.

FOR THE JAPANESE CARROT-GINGER DRESSING

3 medium-size carrots, peeled and cut into about 1-inch chunks

1 piece (2-inches) fresh ginger, peeled and cut into disks

1 shallot, minced, or ¼ cup minced onion

3 tablespoons unseasoned rice vinegar, or 1½ tablespoons white wine vinegar

¼ cup canola, peanut, or vegetable oil

1 tablespoon Asian (dark) sesame oil (see Note)

1 teaspoon granulated sugar

4 teaspoons miso paste (optional, but recommended; see Miso Paste, page 146)

2 teaspoons mirin (optional; see Mirin, opposite page)

FOR THE SALAD

6 to 7 cups thinly sliced romaine lettuce (about 1½ heads lettuce or 2 hearts of romaine)

½ cup shredded peeled carrots

½ cucumber (preferably seedless or English), peeled, cut in half lengthwise, and thinly sliced crosswise

Handful of cherry or grape tomatoes

1 cup steamed tiny broccoli florets (optional)

1. Make the Japanese carrot-ginger dressing: Place the carrot chunks, ginger, shallot or onion, rice vinegar, canola oil, sesame oil, and sugar in a food processor fitted with the metal blade. Pulse until well combined. Add the miso and mirin, if using, and ¼ cup of water and puree until nicely blended and fairly smooth. If you want your dressing a little thinner, you can add another tablespoon or two of water and puree again.

2. Make the salad: Place the lettuce, shredded carrots, cucumber, tomatoes, and broccoli, if using, in a large serving bowl and drizzle about ½ cup of the dressing on top, or more if desired. Toss the salad and serve.

Note: Asian (or dark or roasted) sesame oil is made from toasted sesame seeds and has a deep, nutty, very appealing flavor.

Make Ahead: The Japanese carrot-ginger dressing lasts in the fridge for at least a week, so that's why this is a recipe for a big batch, more than double what you would use for a salad for a family of four or so. Might as well make it worthwhile to rev up the food processor, right? The salad part is just a suggestion—use whatever lettuce and veggies your family is into.

What the Kids Can Do: Did you know you can peel ginger with a teaspoon? It's true—the skin is very thin, and if you take a teaspoon and turn the bowl part in toward the ginger and scrape away with the edge of the spoon, it will take the skin right off quickly. A spoon can get into those creases and crevices of the ginger better than a regular vegetable peeler. This task can safely keep a young sous chef busy for a while. Kids can also measure and dump things for the dressing into the food processor. And they can assemble the salad.

Croutons and anchovies both
optional (but recommended).

Caesar Salad with Garlicky Croutons

Serves 4 to 6

This is how much my older son Jack loves salad: When he was in nursery school they took a poll in his class to see what everyone's favorite food was and charted the results. Among all the ballots cast for pizza, chicken nuggets, ice cream, and so on, there was little Jack's lone vote: salad. Kind of dorky, but adorable. And while he can put away platefuls of salad with a simple vinaigrette, a Caesar salad is what really gets his blood pumping.

It's hard to talk about Caesar salad without embarking upon a conversation about anchovies. Some people hate them, but what's more relevant is that many people *think* they hate them. Sure, sucking down a tiny and slightly hairy fish fillet is an acquired taste for most, but when an anchovy is very finely chopped and becomes part of a sauce or a dressing all it's doing at that point is adding a slightly salty, slightly briny note, a richness of sorts, a depth. And no one would know it was there until you leaned over and said, "Hey, how about those anchovies? Delicious, right?" at which point your guest may decide he no longer liked what he was eating . . . or you, for that matter. Having said that, if you are at all worried that the mere presence of an anchovy in your kitchen might ruin everything, just leave it out.

The other hot button in a Caesar salad dressing is raw eggs. These are not an issue in this recipe, which takes its lead from an ingenious Caesar dressing created by New York restaurateur Frank Falcinelli that relies on mayonnaise for emulsification. Brilliant.

FOR THE CROUTONS, OPTIONAL

2 cups day-old firm white bread cubes (about ¾-inch)

¼ cup extra-virgin olive oil

I clove garlic, pressed through a garlic press
   or very, very finely minced into a paste (see Note)

½ teaspoon kosher or coarse salt

FOR THE CAESAR SALAD DRESSING

¼ cup mayonnaise, preferably Hellmann's

2 tablespoons extra-virgin olive oil

I to 2 tablespoons fresh lemon juice,
   depending on how lemony you like it

½ teaspoon Worcestershire sauce

I anchovy rinsed and very finely minced,
   or ½ teaspoon anchovy paste (optional)

I clove garlic, pressed through a garlic press
   or very, very finely minced into a paste (see Note)

¼ teaspoon kosher or coarse salt, or more to taste

Freshly ground black pepper

You can top this salad with some sliced chicken, or a piece of salmon or tuna, or some poached or grilled shrimp for a restaurant-ey entrée.

FOR THE CAESAR SALAD

4 hearts of romaine lettuce, or 2 heads of romaine lettuce, rinsed and dried

½ cup freshly grated Parmesan cheese

1. Make the croutons, if using: Preheat the oven to 350°F.

2. Spread the bread cubes on a rimmed baking sheet. Mix together the olive oil, garlic, and salt in a small bowl. Drizzle the garlic oil over the bread cubes and toss to coat. Bake the bread cubes until golden and toasted, 12 to 14 minutes. Set the croutons aside.

3. Make the Caesar salad dressing: Place the mayonnaise, olive oil, lemon juice, Worcestershire sauce, anchovy, if using, garlic, salt, and 1 tablespoon of water in a blender or food processor and process until blended (or just shake everything up in a tightly sealed jar). Taste for seasoning, adding more salt as necessary, and pepper to taste.

4. Make the Caesar salad: Tear or thinly slice the romaine lettuce and place it in a large serving bowl (you should have about 8 cups). Drizzle about two thirds of the Caesar salad dressing on top and toss to combine. Sprinkle the Parmesan over the salad and toss it again until everything is evenly mixed. Add more dressing as needed but don't drown the salad. Leftover dressing may be stored in the refrigerator, covered, for up to 5 days. Top the Caesar salad with the croutons, if using, before serving.

Note: To achieve a pureelike texture while mincing garlic by hand, here are a couple of tips. One, mince the garlic on a cutting board along with the coarse salt called for in the recipe; the salt will act as an abrasive, roughing up the little pieces of garlic. Also, periodically scrape together the garlic-salt mixture and slide the blade of the knife sideways across it, crushing and smearing it into the cutting board, until the whole thing looks more like a paste than a mince.

What the Kids Can Do: If you're making the croutons, kids can toss the bread with the garlicky olive oil. They can add all of the ingredients for the dressing to the blender or jar, and they can shake it if you're mixing this by hand. They can tear the lettuce for the salad, or even cut it, depending on their knife skills. They can toss.

Vegetarian Note: For a vegetarian-friendly version, leave out the Worcestershire sauce (it is made with anchovies) and skip the optional anchovy.

Kitchen Sink Chopped Salad

Serves 4 to 6
Vegetarian

Years ago, when my kids were very young, an oversize, green, gently serrated plastic knife appeared in our kitchen, probably having migrated there from an old Play-Doh set or some kiddie kitchen kit that was given to them. Anyway, it became Charlie's knife. "Where's my knife?" he'd demand, with a certain amount of Gordon Ramsay-ish inflection. It is a great knife, sharp enough to actually cut things like cheese and tomatoes, not sharp enough to cut things like Charlie. It has been used by Charlie to make many a salad in our house. If you can find a knife like this it's a great thing to have on hand, especially if your child feels a sense of ownership about it, which leads naturally to participation in the kitchen. Curiouschef.com has kid-friendly knives, for your young *chef garde manger* (French for "the cold food sous chef guy").

This is a kitchen sink salad. As in, Step 1: Open vegetable bins and peer inside. Step 2: Save any slightly depressing looking vegetables for soup (see Vegetable Bin Stone Soup on page 79) and pull out the rest for this big-bowl salad. The veggies listed are merely suggestions. You might also try slices of pear or apple. Moreover, this immediately becomes a main dish (though possibly non-vegetarian) salad if you add chopped cooked chicken, steak, tuna fish, shrimp, tofu, hard-boiled eggs . . . let your leftovers be your guide.

2 hearts of romaine lettuce, sliced crosswise into ½-inch ribbons

I red bell pepper (or orange, yellow, or green), stemmed, seeded, and diced

2 large carrots, peeled and sliced or shredded

What the Kids Can Do:
Look in the vegetable bins and the pantry for things they would be happy to see in their salads. And of course kids can help toss together the salad, whether it's one big salad or their own individual creations.

- 1 can (14 ounces) artichoke bottoms, cut into ¼-inch dice, or 1 jar (6 ounces) marinated artichoke hearts, drained and coarsely chopped

- 1 cup thinly sliced seedless or English cucumber

- 1 cup cherry or grape tomatoes, cut in half

- ½ cup chopped or slivered red onion

- ¼ cup sliced pitted black olives (any kind)

- ¼ to ½ cup shredded or grated cheese, such as Parmesan, cheddar, Swiss, mozzarella, or whatever cheese your family likes (optional)

- ¼ to ⅓ cup Classic Vinaigrette (page 94), to taste, or a salad dressing of your choice

Mix together the lettuce, bell pepper, carrots, artichokes, cucumber, tomatoes, onion, and olives in a large serving bowl (alternately you can line up the ingredients on a bed of the lettuce). Toss in the cheese, if using. Add the vinaigrette and toss again. Serve.

If you're presenting the salad in a "ta-da" fashion, you can line up the ingredients in neat rows before tossing it up.

Classic Vinaigrette (aka Salad Dressing)

Makes about 1 cup
A Fork in the Road Recipe
Vegetarian

Salad dressing is somewhat of a hot button for many of us. We either have a little fear of it and keep hitting the bottle (bottled dressing, of course), which is often pretty gross, or we get stuck in a one-dressing rut.

First of all, vinaigrette is just French for oil and vinegar. Okay, no, that's not quite true, but it certainly is partly true and this is helpful in making things much less scary. This basic recipe lets you make a vinaigrette in two minutes.

My family likes their dressing pretty vinegary. If you don't, use less vinegar. And try adding the minced shallot at least once; I really think (along with the Dijon mustard) it's what makes a vinaigrette a vinaigrette.

Finally, vinaigrette is so forgiving. Too oily? Add more vinegar. Too tart? Add more oil. Too bland? Add more salt, or maybe a bit of mustard. Too salty? Add more oil, and maybe some vinegar. When you get your perfect balance you'll just have a bigger stash of vinaigrette to tuck in the fridge.

- ½ cup extra-virgin olive oil
- ½ cup vinegar(s) of your choice, such as red wine, white wine, balsamic, unseasoned rice, and cider
- I tablespoon finely minced shallot (optional)
- I teaspoon Dijon mustard, or more to taste
- ½ teaspoon kosher or coarse salt, or more to taste
- Freshly ground black pepper

1. Put the olive oil, vinegar(s), shallot, if using, mustard, and salt in a container with a lid, cover it. You can continue with Step 2 or go directly to Step 3.

Cooking Tip: Here's my favorite very basic vinaigrette tip: Use two different vinegars in your dressing. This creates a very nice kind of layering of flavors and just takes it to a slightly higher level, all for the extra 20 seconds it takes to open a second bottle of vinegar. Some favorite combos: red wine and sherry vinegars; balsamic and red wine vinegars; white wine and unseasoned rice vinegars.

What the Kids Can Do: Vinaigrettes are a really nice way to have some fun in the kitchen with your kids that doesn't involved baking. Mine are endlessly experimenting in the vinaigrette department— it's like a chemistry project that you can eat.

Make Ahead: You can store it in the refrigerator, covered, for up to a week. Let the vinaigrette sit out for 10 to 15 minutes to come to room temperature and give it a good shake to mix it again before using.

2. ![fork] See the Fork in the Road suggestions for seasoning the dressing on this page.

3. Shake the vinaigrette to mix. Taste for seasoning, adding more mustard and/or salt if necessary and pepper to taste. Use about 1 teaspoon of dressing per cup of salad.

BONUS SOLUTION

Lemon Vinaigrette

Makes about 1¼ cups
Vegetarian

Now, for those of you who need a moment away from the classic vinegar-based dressing, this one is a favorite in my house. A friend was quite sick for a while, and a simple salad with this dressing was one of the few foods she craved. It's very fresh and clean, and apparently restorative. Nice with Bibb or butter lettuce, romaine, slivered fennel, and spring veggie salads. The rice vinegar softens the acidity of the lemon juice.

¼ cup chopped shallots

¼ cup strained fresh lemon juice (from about I big juicy lemon)

¼ cup unseasoned rice vinegar

2 to 3 teaspoons Dijon mustard

½ cup extra-virgin olive oil

Kosher or coarse salt and freshly ground black pepper

Put the shallots, lemon juice, rice vinegar, mustard, and olive oil in a container with a lid, cover it, and shake away. Season the dressing with salt and pepper to taste and shake once more.

![fork] Fork in the Road

Put half of the basic vinaigrette in a separate container and add any of the following to the rest of the vinaigrette, alone, or in combination.

1½ teaspoons to 1 tablespoon finely chopped onion, or ¼ teaspoon finely minced garlic, with, or instead of, the optional shallot • ¼ to ½ teaspoon dried herbs, or ½ to 1 teaspoon minced fresh herbs—either a single herb or a combination; basil, oregano, thyme, and parsley are some good choices • ½ to 1 teaspoon minced sun-dried tomatoes • 1½ teaspoons to 1 tablespoon minced black olives • 1 to 1½ tablespoons crumbled or grated cheese, such as goat cheese, feta, blue cheese, or Parmesan

Bring a pretty jar of vinaigrette next time you visit a friend.

Lemon Chicken (page 104)

Chapter 7

4 Chickens and a Turkey (Sort of)

You've probably had a lot of chicken pass through your kitchen. You've also probably stood there staring listlessly at that package of chicken breasts, waiting for inspiration to strike. And you've probably all heard your family whine, "Chicken, again?"

Well, yes, chicken again because, grousing aside, it's simply one of the most well-liked and the most versatile proteins out there. And there's life beyond chicken nuggets, although you'll find a very simple recipe right here for making your own chicken fingers, a much more satisfactory alternative to anything found in your grocer's freezer.

Having a handful of great chicken (and some turkey) recipes at the ready gives you a money-in-the-bank kind of feeling, because chicken is undeniably one of the best common denominator dinners in terms of pleasing the most people at one time. While we've all been stuck in our chicken ruts, these recipes should break the "Chicken, again?" spell, at least for a while.

You'll find quite a few more chicken and turkey recipes in this book, in other chapters like Souped Up (Halfway Homemade Chicken Noodle Matzoh Ball Soup, page 70), Hearty Comfort Foods (Cheesy Chicken Enchiladas, page 164, and Moist Make-Ahead Parmesan Turkey Meat Loaf, page 157), Potluck (Turkey or Chicken Chili, page 215), and Mixed Company Dinners (Chicken, Piccata-ed (or Plain), page 233); see page 339 for a complete list of all recipes involving poultry.

THE DILEMMA

Enough with the frozen chicken nuggets.

Roast Chicken, Several Ways

Serves 4
A Fork in the Road Recipe

While a whole roast chicken is a wonderful thing, it does involve the post-cooking job of cutting it up, which takes time and can be a little daunting. Since buying chicken already cut into parts allows you to pick the pieces or assortment of pieces your family likes, takes less cooking time, and cuts out that pesky carving step, roasting chicken pieces is a great way to go. You still get the wonderful qualities of roasting: the juiciness, the moistness, the tenderness, the flavor. This recipe may call for a higher heat than you usually use, but that's how to get that amazing crispy skin (which you can pull off, if you wish, you model of self-restraint you, but do it after the chicken is cooked). You will need to buy skin-on, bone-in chicken; that's the key. Other than that, thighs, breasts, drumsticks, even whole legs or chicken halves are fair game (ha! I didn't even see that one coming).

Make Ahead: You can rub the chicken with any of the rubs a day ahead; this allows the seasonings to permeate the meat more.

What the Kids Can Do: They can help measure the ingredients for any of the rubs, and if your kids aren't grossed out by the prospect, they can rub the rubs onto the chicken. Follow this by a lengthy hand washing in warm, soapy water (and a reminder not to stick their hands in their mouths until after the soapy water bit).

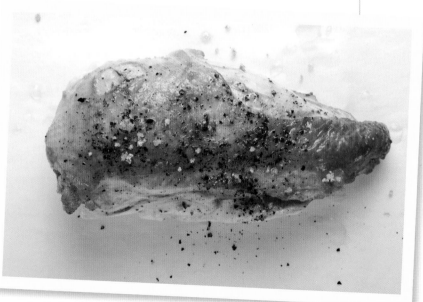

One perfectly plain roasted chicken breast.

Nonstick cooking spray (optional)

2 tablespoons olive oil, plus more olive oil for oiling the baking sheet (optional)

1 chicken (about 4 pounds), cut into 8 pieces, or about 4 pounds skin-on, bone-in chicken parts

2 teaspoons kosher or coarse salt (optional)

Freshly ground black pepper (optional)

1. Preheat the oven to 425°F. Place a rack in the lower third of the oven. Spray a large rimmed baking sheet with nonstick cooking spray or lightly oil it with olive oil.

2. Using your hands, rub the chicken pieces with the olive oil. You can continue with Step 3 or go directly to Step 4.

3. ⟜⟜⟜ See the Fork in the Road suggestions for rubs on page 102.

4. Arrange the chicken pieces on the prepared baking sheet in a single layer skin side up with at least 1/2 inch between each piece. Sprinkle the chicken on both sides with the salt and some pepper if you didn't use one of the rubs.

5. Bake the chicken until fully cooked and the juices run clear when you cut into a piece (see Note), 35 to 50 minutes, depending on the size and thickness of the pieces (dark meat also takes longer). If the skin needs a bit more crisping, place the chicken under the broiler for a few minutes. And you should let the chicken sit for at least 5 minutes before serving so the juices can regroup back into the meat. Serve the chicken hot or warm or cold.

Note: If you want to test the chicken for doneness using an instant-read thermometer, the FDA recommends an internal temperature of 165°F for both chicken breasts and dark meat. Remember, though, that the chicken will continue to cook slightly more after it is removed from the oven, particularly if it sits on the baking sheet.

TO RINSE CHICKEN OR NOT TO RINSE?

There has been a fair amount written about this, and much of what is written also includes subopinions on what to do depending on where your chicken hails from. You should make up your own mind, but if you do rinse the chicken, pat it dry so that you can rub it lightly with olive oil and the oil will stick.

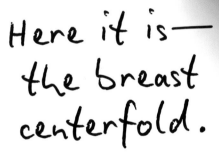

Here it is—
the breast
centerfold.

GREEK

GARLIC, LEMON

+ ROSEMARY

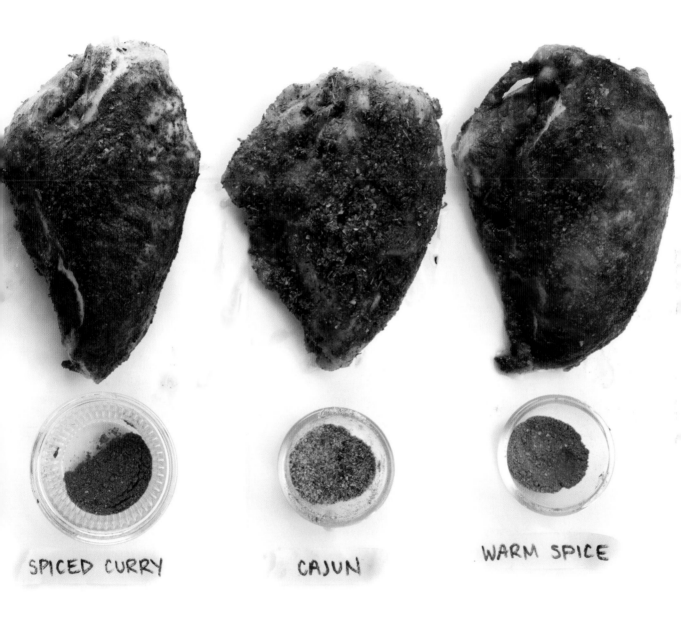

SPICED CURRY

CAJUN

WARM SPICE

Spiced Curry Rub

Makes about ¼ cup; good for 3½ to 4 pounds of chicken parts

- 4 teaspoons curry powder
- 4 teaspoons chili powder
- I teaspoon ground cumin
- I teaspoon ground allspice
- I teaspoon ground cinnamon
- ½ teaspoon kosher or coarse salt

Combine the curry powder, chili powder, cumin, allspice, cinnamon, and salt in a small bowl.

Warm Spice Rub

Makes about ¼ cup; good for 3½ to 4 pounds of chicken parts

This has a nice slightly Caribbean flavor.

- 2 tablespoons sweet paprika
- 2 teaspoons ground ginger
- 2 teaspoons ground cinnamon
- I teaspoon kosher or coarse salt
- ¼ teaspoon cayenne pepper

Combine the paprika, ginger, cinnamon, salt, and cayenne in a small bowl.

Greek Rub

Makes about ¼ cup; good for 3½ to 4 pounds of chicken parts

This Greek-seasoned rub is also great with lamb and fish. For fish, use about one teaspoon per pound.

- 2 tablespoons dried oregano
- I teaspoon dried dill
- I teaspoon finely minced garlic, or I teaspoon garlic powder
- 1½ teaspoons kosher or coarse salt
- ¼ teaspoon freshly ground black pepper
- Juice of I lemon (optional), strained, for serving

Combine the oregano, dill, garlic, salt, and pepper in a small bowl. After the chicken is cooked, sprinkle with lemon juice, if desired.

Fork in the Road

Looking for something with a little more pizzazz? Check out the five fast rubs for chicken here and pick your flavors. You can also rub half of the chicken pieces with a rub and leave half plain, making everyone happy with one chicken. Feel free to double or even triple the rub recipes, depending on how much chicken you're making. If you need to use more than one baking sheet to keep the pieces from crowding, do. Switch the baking sheets on the racks midway through the cooking time.

In general, you want to use one tablespoon of rub for every pound of meat, although if you're introducing young palates to certain spices for the first time, perhaps go a bit lighter. If you are using the rub on chicken with skin and plan to take the skin off before eating the chicken, work a bit of the rub up under the skin so that it penetrates the meat itself.

Each of these recipes make enough for 3½ to 4 pounds of chicken cut into pieces, about the size of one average chicken. I heartily recommend making double or triple batches of the rubs once you find the ones you like; keep them around for future dinners. Dry rubs will keep in a sealed plastic or glass container for up to three months in a cool dark place. If the rub contains fresh ingredients, such as garlic or lemon juice, that rub can be kept in the fridge for up to ten days.

Garlic, Lemon, and Rosemary Rub

Makes about ¼ cup; good for 3½ to 4 pounds of chicken parts

The Garlic, Lemon, and Rosemary Rub can be kept in the refrigerator for up to ten days. It's a bit different from the dry rubs in that it contains fresh ingredients. When you use it you'll want to coat the chicken parts a bit more generously with olive oil first, then massage in the rub, making sure you work it all over the pieces and under the skin a bit.

- 1 tablespoon finely minced garlic, or 1 tablespoon garlic powder
- 1 tablespoon grated fresh lemon zest
- 1 tablespoon minced fresh rosemary, or 1½ teaspoons dried rosemary, crumbled
- 2 teaspoons kosher or coarse salt
- ¼ teaspoon freshly ground black pepper
- Juice of 1 lemon (optional), strained, for serving

Combine the garlic, lemon zest, rosemary, salt, and pepper in a small bowl. After the chicken is cooked with this rub, sprinkle the lemon juice over it, if desired.

Cajun Rub

Makes about ¼ cup; good for 3½ to 4 pounds of chicken parts

I really love this Cajun Rub; it has just the perfect amount of heat and lots of flavor.

- 1 teaspoon garlic powder
- 2 teaspoons onion powder
- 2 teaspoons dried thyme
- 2 teaspoons dried oregano
- 2 teaspoons sweet paprika
- ¼ teaspoon cayenne pepper
- 1 teaspoon kosher or coarse salt
- ¼ teaspoon freshly ground black pepper

Combine the garlic powder, onion powder, thyme, oregano, paprika, cayenne, salt, and black pepper in a small bowl.

COOKING CHICKEN; BEST PRACTICES 101

Hopefully you've gotten a little hungry at this point, but now it's time for the boring but important safety tips from our friends at the FDA. Some people get nervous about knowing when chicken is cooked through. If you stick a fork into a piece, especially when it's dark meat, and press gently and the juices that come out are clear, then your chicken is properly cooked through. And for those of us who can find our instant-read meat thermometers, here's what the FDA has to say about chicken temperatures.

- Cook whole poultry to 165°F. Insert the food thermometer into the thigh for an accurate temperature; don't let it touch the bone.
- Cook chicken breasts to 165°F.

The FDA also has this to say:
- Wash hands thoroughly with warm water and soap before and after handling raw poultry, meat, and seafood.
- Wash cutting boards, dishes, utensils (including knives), and countertops with soap and hot water after they come in contact with raw poultry, meat, or seafood.

These basic pieces of information are important, especially when you are encouraging your young helpers to get involved with preparing raw poultry. But, internalize this info, tuck it away, and get to the more interesting topics: Lemon Chicken or turkey tacos tonight?

Lemon Chicken

Serves 8 to 10

In New York City's East Harlem there is an Italian restaurant called Rao's. It's known for its Neapolitan cuisine, but it is notorious for the fact that it is completely impossible to get a reservation there. The tables are "owned" by regulars (there has been a lot of speculation about what it takes to be a regular—think *The Sopranos*), and unless one of them lends his table to you for a night, you will probably not be eating there in this lifetime. You may also recognize the name Rao's from the label of some pretty pricey pasta sauces available in many supermarkets and wherever pretty pricey pasta sauces are sold.

I actually did get behind the velvet ropes one time, with friends who knew someone. The two things I remember the most are that (1) I announced that I was pregnant with my first child (although the combination of adult acne and the fact that I was drinking a Shirley Temple had probably tipped everyone off) and (2) the Lemon Chicken, one of Rao's most famous dishes, was amazing.

Over the years I've worked up a modified version of this lemon chicken, and it's a great take on simple broiled chicken. The lemon sauce is wonderful, and there is lots of it. Serve this with rice, crusty bread, and/or Mashed Potatoes (page 253).

Cooking Tip: Don't be nervous about broiling. You will certainly want to keep an eye on the chicken to make sure it doesn't burn. But once you've cooked whole pieces under a broiler and see how juicy they come out, and how quickly the cooking goes, you'll become attached to this form of high heat cooking (think grilling). Feel free to use a different mixture of chicken pieces.

Make Ahead: You can broil the chicken and make the sauce a day ahead. Refrigerate the sauce and chicken separately, or toss the chicken with the sauce and refrigerate them together for an even deeper lemony flavor. Let the chicken come to room temperature about twenty minutes before broiling it with the sauce. This last five minute broil won't heat the chicken all the way through, just warm it up on the outside. Leftovers are also fantastic cold or at room temperature.

What the Kids Can Do: Let the kids juice the lemons, combine the ingredients for the sauce, shake it up, and pour over the chicken.

I cup fresh lemon juice (from 4 to 6 lemons)

⅔ cup olive oil

I tablespoon red wine vinegar

2 teaspoons finely minced garlic

I teaspoon dried oregano or thyme

Kosher or coarse salt

¼ teaspoon freshly ground black pepper

4 bone-in chicken breast halves with skin
   (2 to 2½ pounds total)

6 bone-in chicken thighs with skin (2½ to 3 pounds total)

¼ cup Italian (flat-leaf) parsley (optional, see Note)

1. Preheat the broiler with the rack placed about 8 inches away from the heat source.

2. Put the lemon juice, olive oil, red wine vinegar, garlic, oregano or thyme, ½ teaspoon of salt, and ¼ teaspoon of pepper in a container with a lid and shake well to blend.

3. Place the chicken pieces skin side down on a rimmed baking sheet and salt them lightly. Broil for 15 minutes. Turn the pieces, lightly salt them, and broil them until the skin is crisp and golden brown and the juices run clear when the pieces are pierced with a fork, 15 to 20 minutes longer.

4. Remove the chicken from the broiler, leaving the broiler on. Cut the breasts and thighs in half (you can use a clean dish towel to hold the chicken steady so you don't burn yourself; cut across the bone if you have a very strong sharp knife or cut just alongside the bone if a crosswise cut is too difficult). Pour off all but 1 tablespoon of fat, and return the chicken to the baking sheet.

5. Shake the lemon sauce again and pour it over the chicken. Turn the pieces over so they are evenly coated with the sauce, making sure all of the pieces end up skin side down.

6. Broil the chicken until it has browned a bit more, another 2 minutes, then turn the pieces skin side up and broil them until the skin is browned a bit more, about 3 minutes longer. Remove the chicken from the baking sheet and, if you are using the parsley, stir it into the sauce still in the baking sheet. Pour the sauce over the chicken and serve.

Make sure to serve with something starchy to soak up all that sauce.

Note: The parsley is optional only because if you happen to have one of those kids who runs screaming from the table if anything has a fleck of green in it, you will not want to inflict the horrors of parsley upon your little prince or princess.

Barbecued Chicken

Serves 6; makes about 6 cups of barbecue sauce; you'll have sauce left over

Why should you make your own barbecue sauce? Good question. There are a number of quite good barbecue sauces on the market, including some supermarket varieties (KC Masterpiece is a brand favored by many barbecue aficionados), and you can find lots more gourmet offerings in specialty food stores and other fancy outlets.

But if you're reading this, then you are at least partially sold on the idea of making your own sauce. First, you won't be adding any artificial sweeteners or miscellaneous ingredients with chemical names. Also, it's ridiculously easy. And finally, the sauce keeps in the fridge for weeks, so it's one of those great big batch things to make. And how much fun is it to have your very own house barbecue sauce? I'll tell you, fewer things make your friends and family look at you with glowing admiration than when you pass around a bowl of homemade barbecue sauce, about which you nonchalantly say, "Oh, you like it? I'm so glad."

This is an easy recipe to play around with. Use all honey, or all brown sugar, spice it up, spice it down, use chili sauce and less ketchup, add some cumin or lemon juice. This makes a hefty quantity but is also a great recipe to double batch: Split the batches between two containers and punch up the level of heat and spice in one so you have a version with kick for those who like sauce with kick. Label the two containers so you know which is which. Bring a jar to someone's house as a thank-you-for-having-us gift.

Basting with sauce at the end lets the chicken caramelize, but not burn.

FOR THE BARBECUE SAUCE

2 tablespoons vegetable or canola oil

1½ cups chopped onion

2 tablespoons finely chopped garlic

4 cups ketchup, preferably Heinz (see Notes)

½ cup cider vinegar

¼ cup firmly packed light or dark brown sugar

¼ cup honey

¼ cup tomato paste (see Cooking Tip #1, page 157)

3 tablespoons Worcestershire sauce

2 tablespoons Dijon mustard

I tablespoon chili powder

Kosher or coarse salt and freshly ground black pepper

5 pounds skin-on, bone-in chicken pieces, your choice of breasts, thighs, and drumsticks

Save the fancy serving platter for another dish.

1. Make the barbecue sauce: Heat the oil in a large saucepan over medium heat. Add the onion and garlic and cook, stirring occasionally, until slightly softened, about 3 minutes (don't let the onion and garlic get more than light golden in color). Add the ketchup, cider vinegar, brown sugar, honey, tomato paste, Worcestershire sauce, mustard, and chili powder. Season the sauce with salt and pepper to taste, stir well, and let simmer over medium low heat until the flavors meld, about 15 minutes.

2. If you like your sauce a bit chunky with the chopped onions, it's ready to go. If you like it nice and smooth, let it cool a bit and then puree it in a blender or food processor, or use an immersion blender.

3. Preheat a grill to medium or preheat the broiler with the rack placed about 8 inches away from the heat source.

4. Cook the chicken, naked at first, on the grill with the grill covered or under the broiler until it is, to your best estimation, two thirds of the way cooked through, about 10 minutes on each side. Watch carefully for smoke and flare-ups. Baste the chicken with some of the barbecue sauce, turn the chicken, and baste the second side. Grill the chicken another 5 minutes or so on each side, basting as necessary and checking to see that it's caramelizing nicely but not burning. Adjust the heat as necessary. When the outside looks the way you like it and the chicken is cooked through (see Notes), let it sit for a few minutes off the heat. Serve the chicken hot, warm, or at room temperature.

Notes: You can substitute 1 cup of Heinz chili sauce for 1 cup of the ketchup if you want a zestier sauce.

To check for doneness you can stick a fork in a piece of chicken and see if the juices run clear. Or, use an instant-read thermometer to determine whether the chicken has reached a temperature of 165°F; insert the thermometer in the thickest part of the meat but do not let it touch a bone. That temperature is from the FDA, but note that the chicken will continue to cook and the temperature will continue to rise after you've taken the chicken off the grill.

Cooking Tip: This recipe calls for skin-on, bone-in chicken pieces, but of course you can use skinless, boneless breasts or thighs, or even pull the skin off bone-in chicken before cooking it. It's all good. And other than chicken, you can slather barbecue sauce on anything you like.

Make Ahead: The barbecue sauce can be made up to three weeks ahead and stored in the fridge. (I've given it a boil and used it after a couple of months but I think I probably shouldn't admit that.) The chicken can be made a couple of days ahead and reheated or eaten cold.

What the Kids Can Do: After the onion and garlic are cooked, kids can carefully add the rest of the ingredients for the barbecue sauce to the pot and if they are old enough, stir the simmering sauce, watching for bloopy splatters. If you take the chicken off the grill to baste it with the barbecue sauce, they can help with that, too.

SIMPLE

CRISPY

CRISPIER

PARMESAN

Homemade Chicken Tenders (or Nuggets or Fingers, or Whatever You Call Them)

Serves 4 to 6

I once was asked to write an article where I had to test and evaluate as many types of nationally branded frozen or refrigerated chicken nuggets as I could find. At first my children could not believe their luck and were giddily high-fiving each other all over the house (as you might imagine, frozen chicken nuggets do not normally make many appearances on our dinner table). "This is awesome!" they cried, beaming at me as though I had invented video games.

Well, sixty-three nuggets, tenders, fingers, popcorn bites, and sticks later they (and a group of their stalwart friends) were a little green around the gills. Often there were six or seven varieties of nuggets at a tasting, with the kids having to taste only one bite of each kind. In the end they didn't find all that many that were worth a second nugget. There is an awful lot of ground up, dry "chickenesque" filling in some of these nuggets, and in many cases not a whole lot that actually tasted like chicken. One brand had somewhere near thirty-five ingredients, a few of which were sodium diacetate, silicon dioxide, sodium tripolyphosphate, and artificial flavoring. Gosh, I must have run out of sodium tripolyphosphate and not even realized it. How embarrassing.

Although Charlie and Jack still often go for the nuggets on the kids' menu when we're at a restaurant with a kids' menu, they are happy to dig into these very fast, very simple chicken nuggets at home. And you can rest assured that these are nothing more than simple floured chunks of real chicken, served up on a stick, if you like, just for fun.

There are four versions: One is super simple. The next

You're going to need a nugget recipe, and these are ones you can be proud of.

is a bit crunchier (and only involves adding a couple of measly eggs). The third even crunchier version has some bread crumbs as a final coating. And the fourth is the "Mom, that's so cool!" showstopper—Chicken Parmesan on a Stick, which we have yet to encounter on a kiddie menu.

FOR THE CHICKEN

I pound chicken tenders, or I pound skinless, boneless chicken breasts or thighs

¾ cup all-purpose flour

I teaspoon kosher or coarse salt

¼ teaspoon freshly ground black pepper

About 3 tablespoons olive oil

FOR SERVING (OPTIONAL)

Ketchup

Yellow, brown, or honey mustard

Barbecue sauce, homemade (see page 108) or store-bought

YOU'LL ALSO NEED

10 to 15 wooden skewers (optional)

1. If you are using pieces of chicken, not tenders, cut them lengthwise into 1 inch–thick strips. There should be between 10 and 15 pieces in all.

2. Place the flour, salt, and pepper in a shallow bowl and, using a fork, mix them together. Coat the chicken strips in the flour mixture.

3. Heat about 1½ tablespoons of olive oil in a large skillet over medium heat. Cook half of the chicken until lightly browned and cooked through, about 3 minutes per side. Transfer the browned chicken to a plate. Add about 1½ tablespoons of olive oil and cook the remaining chicken strips the same way.

4. Insert a skewer lengthwise into each of the chicken strips, if desired. Serve the chicken with ketchup, mustard, barbecue sauce, or whatever other dipping sauces your kids are into.

What the Kids Can Do:
They can do any of the dipping and dredging of the chicken and, if your children are of the right age, even skewer the chicken strips. A good scrubbing with soap and warm water follows all contact with raw meat, of course.

Crispy Chicken Version

Lightly beat 2 eggs in a shallow bowl. After coating the chicken pieces with the flour mixture, dip them in the eggs, let the excess drain off, then dip the chicken back into the flour mixture to coat. Proceed with Step 2 of the recipe; you may need a bit more olive oil in the skillet and you will need to cook the chicken strips for 30 seconds to 1 minute longer on each side, 3½ to 4 minutes per side.

Crispier Chicken Version

Place ¾ cup of *panko* (Japanese bread crumbs) in a shallow bowl. Then follow the instructions for the Crispy Chicken Version, but instead of the second dip in the flour mixture after the egg dip, make the final dip in the *panko* crumbs. You may need a bit more olive oil in the skillet to achieve the crispiest crust for this version, and you will likely need to cook the chicken strips for 4 minutes per side for them to be done through.

Chicken Parmesan on a Stick

You'll need ½ cup of marinara or spaghetti sauce (or the sauce from Good Old Spaghetti and Tomato Sauce on page 174), ½ cup of shredded mozzarella cheese, preferably fresh mozzarella, 2 tablespoons of freshly grated Parmesan cheese, and 10 to 15 wooden skewers. Preheat the oven to 350°F.

Make the Crispy Chicken or the Crispier Chicken, cooking it for only 2 minutes per side for Crispy Chicken, 3 minutes per side for Crispier. Insert a skewer lengthwise into each strip of chicken, making sure it's secure. Place the skewered chicken on a baking sheet with a rim. Spoon a little bit of marinara or spaghetti sauce down the center of each strip of chicken. Line up a few pieces of the shredded mozzarella down the center of each strip, on top of the sauce. Evenly sprinkle the Parmesan over the mozzarella. Bake the skewered chicken until the cheese is melted, 4 to 5 minutes. Ta-da.

EVERYTHING TASTES BETTER ON A STICK

If you were at a state fair and someone handed you a cornbread-encrusted hot dog on a plate with a fork and a knife, it wouldn't be all that appealing, right? But put it on a stick and now it's a corn dog and maybe the best thing you've eaten all week.

Of course none of us wants to see anyone get poked with a skewer. (I have horrible memories of the time Jack, then two years old, ran into the wall face first while playing a plastic flute—a narrowly averted disaster.) You have to use your judgment about when your kids are old enough to handle a pointed stick. It's definitely a good idea to have the kids seated at a table when they do. You can also try using chopsticks, which are less pointy.

Taco Night

Serves 8

Taco night is a big deal in our house. Everyone in the family loves them, and there is something inherently festive and fun about a hands-on, interactive meal. If you're looking for a dinner to counterbalance a cranky day, this is the one. I usually go with ground turkey or chicken, instead of beef. You choose, and if you choose beef, drain it well. And if you choose turkey, don't go for the extra lean, get the 93 percent lean/7 percent fat or the 85 percent lean/15 percent fat ratio—they're juicier.

I have certainly been known to reach for a package of store-bought taco seasoning at times, but with an extra few minutes you can make a homemade seasoning blend that tastes amazing, and the sodium level won't be through the roof. Then throw together a big salad, or some steamed broccoli or cauliflower, and you've got dinner.

Cooking Tip: This makes enough taco seasoning for two pounds of meat, but because doubling or tripling the recipe takes no extra time, wouldn't you want to make a big batch and throw the extra in a small plastic container or zipper-top bag, and be happy with the knowledge that your next taco night is halfway complete? Or, if you have a smaller group, make the seasoning, put half in a container, and use just one pound of meat.

FOR THE TACO FILLING

1 tablespoon chili powder

2 teaspoons ground cumin

2 teaspoons onion powder

1 teaspoon kosher or coarse salt

1 teaspoon cornstarch

1 teaspoon garlic powder

½ teaspoon dried oregano

½ teaspoon sweet paprika

½ teaspoon freshly ground black pepper

Pinch of cayenne or red pepper flakes (optional)

Nonstick cooking spray

2 pounds ground turkey or beef

FOR SERVING

Shredded lettuce

Salsa or taco sauce

Shredded cheddar, Monterey Jack, or a Mexican cheese blend

Low-fat or regular sour cream

Diced tomatoes

Diced avocados

About 12 taco shells

1. Preheat the oven to 350°F.

2. Place the chili powder, cumin, onion powder, salt, cornstarch, garlic powder, oregano, paprika, black pepper, and cayenne or red pepper flakes, if using, in a small bowl or plastic container. Blend well.

3. Spray a large skillet with nonstick cooking spray and place it over medium-high heat. Add the turkey or beef and cook, stirring and making sure to really break it up into small crumbles, until it is browned throughout, about 5 minutes. Drain off any liquid. Add the spice mixture and cook stirring, until you can smell all of the spices, about 1 minute. Add ¾ cup of water and stir until the water is mostly evaporated, the meat is evenly coated with the spices, and there is still a little bit of liquid in the pan, about 4 minutes.

Charlie wants credit for assembling this perfect taco.

4. To serve, place your choice of toppings in small individual bowls. Heat the taco shells on a baking sheet (or right on the oven rack, whichever you prefer) in the oven until warm and toasty, about 5 minutes. Transfer the meat to a serving bowl. Place the taco shells on a plate and cover them with a napkin or clean dish towel to keep them warm, setting them out with the bowls of toppings. Let everyone serve him or herself.

What the Kids Can Do:

The kids can measure away, and this is a really good recipe to use as a teaching tool to discuss how many teaspoons go into a tablespoon (three, of course), and if you double or triple this recipe it's an awesome math moment in the kitchen. Kids can also put the different toppings in small bowls.

Soy-Ginger
Flank Steak
(page 120)

Chapter 8

Main Dish Meat

lthough there are some meat recipes in other sections of the book, this chapter is where five of my family's be-still-my-heart favorites lie. The flank steak is my kids' hands-down favorite steak. Leftover meatballs (if there are any) are requested for the next day's breakfast. The brisket is a no-frills, fork-tender cut of meat that makes everyone feel all is right with the world. The ribs are a summertime staple, although the oven version makes them a year-round option. And the pork chops are a newer house darling, with appley sweet flavors that appeal to milder taste buds.

You will also want to check out the Teriyaki Chicken and Beef Skewers (page 230), Lamb Chops with Lemony White Beans and Spinach (page 227), Big Batch Turkey Meat Sauce with Ziti (page 178), and lasagna (page 160, made with beef instead of turkey), Simplest Beef Stew (page 210), and One-Skillet Cheesy Beef and Macaroni (page 155). And never forget Pigs in a Blanket (page 56).

THE DILEMMA

The kids can't get beyond hamburgers and hot dogs.

Soy-Ginger Flank Steak

Serves 6 to 8

The combination of garlic and soy and ginger with a bit of brown sugar are just a complete home run, and this glaze sure has enough going on to make the grown-ups happy. There's a simplified teriyaki quality to the whole thing.

Serve this with generous scoops of rice and Roasted Asparagus (page 262) or broccoli (see page 264) or a big green salad with Classic Vinaigrette (page 94)—or maybe the Japanese Restaurant Salad (page 86).

I tablespoon vegetable or canola oil

1½ tablespoons finely grated peeled fresh ginger

I tablespoon minced garlic

⅔ cup low-sodium soy sauce, or ½ cup regular soy sauce and 3 tablespoons water

½ cup lightly packed light or dark brown sugar

½ teaspoon red pepper flakes (optional)

I flank steak (2½ to 3 pounds)

Freshly ground black pepper

Thinly sliced scallions, both white and light green parts (optional), for serving

Lime wedges, for serving

Hot cooked rice, for serving

1. Preheat the broiler and if you have an adjustable rack make sure it is as close to the heat source as it can get.

2. Heat the oil in a small saucepan over medium heat. Add the ginger and garlic and cook, stirring, until you can really smell everything and the garlic turns golden, about 3 minutes. Add the soy sauce, brown sugar, and red pepper flakes, if using. Increase the heat to medium-high and let the soy glaze simmer until slightly reduced and syrupy,

HOW DONE IS DONE?

If you have an instant-read meat thermometer you can be pretty accurate in your assessment of how well cooked your steak is: 125°F for rare, 155°F for medium, and 185°F for well-done, but you can also use your hand as a guide to determine the doneness of the meat by pressing on the meat with your finger and comparing its texture to the firmness of different parts of your palm. Rare meat should feel fairly soft, similar to pressing the fleshy pad at the base of your thumb. Medium should feel like the center of your palm, firmer than rare, obviously, but not too firm. For well-done compare the meat to the area of your palm directly below your pinky finger; it should offer little resistance.

Remember, no matter what the degree of doneness, the meat will continue to cook for a few minutes after you take it off the heat, so err on the side of softness! You can't uncook meat, as we've all learned the hard way.

stirring occasionally, about 5 minutes. Set the glaze aside to cool for about 5 minutes.

3. Season the flank steak lightly with black pepper. Brush the top side of the flank steak with some of the soy glaze, then broil it for 4 minutes. Using tongs, turn the steak, then brush the second side with the glaze. Broil the flank steak until it is done to your liking, about 4 minutes longer for medium-rare. Transfer the steak to a cutting board and let it sit for 5 minutes. Meanwhile, bring the remaining soy glaze to a simmer over low heat.

4. Thinly slice the flank steak across the grain and brush the slices with some of the reheated soy glaze. Transfer the sliced steak to a platter and scatter the scallions, if using, on top. Arrange the lime wedges on the edge of the platter for people to squeeze over their steak if they like. Put the rest of the soy glaze in a small pitcher or bowl to serve at the table for drizzling over the rice.

Thin slices make this steak very approachable.

Cooking Tip #1: Flank steak is a thin and somewhat chewy cut of meat, so you'll want to broil or sear it quickly, and don't forget about Carryover Cooking (see page 136). If you want to use skirt steak, or even London broil, that will work, too. You can also prepare this steak on a grill or use a grill pan and sear it on top of the stove.

Cooking Tip #2: Slicing steak on the bias (diagonally) is not really any harder to do than just slicing it straight up and down, but it just looks so much nicer on the plate. I'm not suggesting that the smaller members of your household will notice this, but you and other adults might appreciate the slightly sexier looking slices with their greater surface area.

What the Kids Can Do: Let the kids add the ingredients for the glaze, being careful with the hot pot. They can brush the sliced steak with extra glaze.

Pasta with Meatballs and Sauce

Makes about 20 meatballs; serves 6

Cloudy with a chance of delicious. My friend Leigh Galione is no slouch in the kitchen and, as you've correctly guessed, is Italian American. And not just Italian American, Brooklyn Italian American. When Leigh asked me for my meatball recipe, that was validation.

You have three options for cooking the meatballs. The main recipe calls for baking them, but you can also sauté the meatballs in a little oil before you finish cooking them in the sauce, or you can also cook them right in the sauce. Baking and simmering the meatballs is easier and frees you up for other pursuits, like mah-jongg. Or laundry. Or Irish folk dancing. Seriously, has any mom ever been able to identify extra time?

A classic meat combo for meatballs (and traditional meat loaf, for that matter) is about one third each of veal, beef, and pork. You can often find this in the meat area of the supermarket labeled "meat loaf mixture," and if so, your work is done. If not, you can ask the butcher (who may well sell this mixture already), or buy the three meats and mix them together in any proportion you like (do *not* make yourself in any way crazy about the one third, one third, one third thing), or buy two meats, or even just one. You can also use ground turkey—see the variation for more info.

You can bake, sauté, or simmer the meatballs, whatever works best.

I slice plain bread

¼ cup milk

1¼ pounds ground meat, preferably a combination of beef, pork, and veal

I large egg, lightly beaten

¼ cup finely freshly grated Parmesan cheese, plus more for serving (optional)

2 tablespoons finely minced fresh Italian (flat-leaf) parsley (optional)

½ teaspoon finely minced garlic

½ teaspoon kosher or coarse salt, plus more for cooking the pasta

¼ teaspoon freshly ground black pepper

Nonstick cooking spray, if you are baking the meatballs

4 cups sauce from Good Old Spaghetti and Tomato Sauce (page 174), or 4 cups store-bought tomato sauce

2 tablespoons olive oil, if you are sautéing the meatballs

I package (16 ounces) dried pasta, anything from spaghetti to ziti to rigatoni

1. Tear the bread into pieces and place them in a small bowl. Pour the milk over the bread, stir to combine, and let sit until the bread has absorbed most of the milk, about 5 minutes. Squeeze out the excess milk and shred the bread into little pieces.

2. Place the meat in a large bowl. Add the soaked bread, egg, Parmesan, parsley, if using, garlic, salt, and pepper. Using your hands, blend the meat mixture well but try not to squeeze it too much. Form the meat mixture into nice round meatballs about 1½ inches in size.

3. Preheat the oven to 350°F. Spray a rimmed baking sheet with nonstick cooking spray.

4. Arrange the meatballs on the baking sheet so that they are not touching. Bake the meatballs until almost cooked through, about 15 minutes. Meanwhile, bring the tomato sauce to a simmer in a medium-size pot over medium-low heat. Add the partially cooked meatballs to the sauce and let them simmer until fully cooked, about 10 minutes.

THE FEAR OF RAW MEAT

When I was a kid, my mother used to give me pinches of raw ground meat to nibble on while she cooked, which now makes my stomach curl to think about, though the thought of raw salmon sashimi makes my heart sing. Now we all have it drilled into our heads that if you do let your little one help you roll the meatballs (and you should, it's much fun), we need to make sure they immediately wash their hands well with soap and warm water before they touch anything, especially their mouths. Because who wants to mess with salmonella? With all that said, people are still scarfing down steak tartare in fine restaurants that clearly vetted their raw meat in a serious way.

5. While the meatballs are cooking, bring a large pot of water to a boil over high heat. Add salt and let the water return to a boil. Add the pasta and cook according to the package directions. Drain the pasta and serve it with the sauce and meatballs. Serve extra Parmesan on the side to sprinkle over the meatballs, if you like.

Variations

Other Meatballs

You can use all beef, all pork, or all veal, or any combo of the three. You can also use turkey (in this case the mixture will be a bit softer and so a little trickier to handle and keep in perfectly round balls). You can even use a mixture of turkey and one of the other meats, if you just want to lighten the meatballs up a bit.

Other Cooking Methods

To sauté the meatballs: Heat a large skillet over medium-high heat and add 1 tablespoon of olive oil. When the oil is hot, add half of the meatballs and brown them on all sides, about 5 minutes in total. Remove the browned meatballs. Repeat with the remaining 1 tablespoon of olive oil and the rest of the meatballs. Set the meatballs aside and pour off all but 2 teaspoons of fat. Heat the tomato sauce in the skillet over medium heat (if you are making the tomato sauce from scratch, you can do this right in this skillet). Scrape the bottom of the skillet to incorporate all of the nice little crusty bits into the sauce. When the sauce is simmering, slide the browned meatballs into the skillet and gently stir so they are all coated with the sauce. Reduce the heat to medium-low and cook the meatballs, stirring occasionally, until they are cooked through and tender, 15 to 20 minutes.

To cook the meatballs right in the sauce: Bring the tomato sauce to a simmer in a medium-size pot over medium-low heat. Add the raw meatballs to the sauce, increase the heat to medium, partially cover the pot, and let simmer, without stirring, for about 5 minutes. Very carefully shake the pot to prevent breaking up the meatballs and let them cook in the sauce, partially covered and stirring gently and occasionally so that the sauce doesn't stick to the bottom of the pot, until the meatballs are fully cooked, about 25 minutes in all. If some of the fat from the meat rises to the top of the sauce, you can spoon it off if you like.

What the Kids Can Do:
Kids can tear the bread into pieces, soak it in the milk, and squeeze it out. They can combine the raw meat with the other ingredients (wash hands!), and form it into meatballs (wash hands again!). Older kids can also carefully grate the Parmesan.

Make it Sunday. Eat it hot on Monday.
In sandwiches on Tuesday. As soup on Wednesday.
Go vegetarian on Thursday.

Monday Night Brisket

Serves 8 to 10

Brisket is interesting because two different groups can claim it as "their" dish; the Jews and the Texans. And I guess if you're a Jewish Texan you get double helpings. Down South brisket is usually slow cooked over indirect heat, with basting and smoking often involved. The brisket here is from the Jewish camp, with the meat being braised in the oven for a long time. It's a pot roast, essentially. Other cultures have their versions, too, and we could discuss them for a while, but this is not that kind of cookbook.

Many of us think of brisket during the Jewish holidays, and rarely otherwise, but like Potato Pancakes (page 255) my family is so crazy about brisket that it makes no sense not to make it all throughout the colder months. First, it's a pretty inexpensive cut of meat. Second, aside from acknowledging that it needs to cook for a few hours, it really takes little work. Don't you just love a main course that you can ignore? Some recipes call for browning the brisket first, which is a nice step if you have extra time on your hands (pause for laughter). But it's just not necessary for a nice tender brisket, and not only do you save the extra time, you also save having to clean up the splatters all over the stove (at least that's what Gary tells me). The reason this is called Monday Night Brisket is because it's the kind of dish you want to start early in the day, when you have a stretch of time, for example on a Sunday afternoon, and refrigerate overnight for the next night's dinner.

First-cut brisket means brisket with much of the fat cut off (but not all, you don't want that). If you get a bigger piece of meat and want to cut it into two pieces, you can overlap them in the pot. On the whole, brisket is fairly resilient.

Brisket is great served with Roasted Potatoes (page 250), Mashed Potatoes (page 253), or some simple buttered noodles.

DO NOT READ THIS IF YOU KEEP KOSHER

This is a lovely condiment to serve with the brisket, if you feel like providing a creamy yet piquant counter note to the unctuous meat.

- ¼ cup heavy (whipping) cream
- ½ cup regular or low-fat sour cream
- 3 tablespoons prepared horseradish, drained
- I tablespoon Dijon mustard
- I tablespoon minced onion
- Juice of ½ lemon
- Kosher or coarse salt and freshly ground pepper to taste

Place all the ingredients through the lemon juice in a small bowl and stir to blend. Taste and add salt and pepper as needed.

1 teaspoon olive oil

2 teaspoons minced garlic

1 teaspoon dried thyme

1 teaspoon kosher or coarse salt

¼ teaspoon freshly ground black pepper

1 first-cut beef brisket (4 to 5 pounds)

2 cups chopped onions

4 large carrots, peeled and thickly sliced

3 bay leaves

3 tablespoons tomato paste (optional; see the Cooking Tip)

1 cup low-sodium beef or chicken broth

1 can (28 ounces) crushed tomatoes in juice or puréed

1 cup red wine (any kind is fine), or an additional cup crushed tomatoes or broth

2 tablespoons finely chopped Italian (flat-leaf) parsley (optional), for garnish

1. Preheat the oven to 325°F.

2. Place the olive oil, garlic, thyme, salt, and pepper in a small bowl and stir to mix. Rub the mixture all over.

3. Place the brisket, fat side up, in a large casserole or Dutch oven with a tight-fitting lid. Toss in the onions, carrots, and bay leaves. If you are using the tomato paste, blend it into the broth then pour over the meat and vegetables. Then pour the crushed tomatoes and red wine, if using, on top. The liquid should cover the meat and most of the vegetables. Cover the casserole and bake the brisket until the meat is very tender, 3 to 3½ hours.

4. *If you are serving the brisket the next day,* let it cool then put the entire casserole in the refrigerator. About an hour before serving, skim off any hardened fat, then take out the meat and cut off any excess fat from the top of the meat. Slice the brisket across the grain, as thin or thick as you like, then neatly return the sliced meat to the cooking liquid. Reheat the brisket on the stovetop over medium-low heat, or in a preheated 325°F oven, until everything is warmed through and the cooking liquid has reduced and thickened up a bit, about 30 minutes in the oven, maybe less on the stovetop. Adjust seasonings as needed.

Cooking Tip: You'll see that the brisket recipe calls for three liquids: broth, tomatoes, and wine. If you use only one or two of these, and just make the quantity equal to about 6 cups of liquid, the results will be fine. The tomato paste adds richness to the cooking liquid and is great, but if you don't have any, add some squirts of ketchup or skip it altogether. The reason brisket tastes so good is mostly because of its long slow cooking in liquid, and it's fairly magnanimous about what kind of liquid it is braised in.

Make Ahead: There are a few reasons to make the brisket a day or two ahead of time. (1) It tastes better; the flavors really meld and blend and all of that stuff, and the meat is at its most tender. (2) Your life will be easier the next day because dinner is basically made. (3) You can skim off the fat from the cooking liquid, which will create a more concentrated cooking liquid with no greasiness. (4) It's much easier to slice the brisket when it's cold.

What the Kids Can Do: The kids can peel carrots, if they can handle the peeler. They can also measure ingredients and add them to the pot with the brisket.

If you are serving the brisket right away, remove the meat from the casserole and let it rest on a platter, loosely tented with aluminum foil. Let the cooking liquid and vegetables sit for about 15 minutes, then spoon off any fat that has accumulated. Place the casserole over medium-high heat and simmer, stirring occasionally, until the liquid reduces a bit, about 10 minutes. Adjust seasonings as necessary. Slice the meat neatly across the grain, return it to the pot, and remove and discard the bay leaves.

5. You can serve the brisket in the casserole or transfer it to a large shallow bowl. Remove and discard the bay leaves and sprinkle the parsley on top of the brisket, if desired.

THE DUTCH OVEN

What in the world is a Dutch oven? Doesn't it sound like some sort of archaic potbelly stove that needs to have its wood stoked at regular intervals? Or possibly a cauldron of some sort that hangs in a fireplace? This is kind of what it was, once upon a time. What a Dutch oven is today is just this: a big pot, preferably made of enameled cast iron, that has a tight-fitting lid.

BONUS SOLUTION

Beef Barley Soup

Serves 4 to 6

If you have any doubt that you'll have enough leftovers to make this soup, be prudent and remove some of the meat and liquid before serving the brisket. It stretches what is essentially a couple of portions of brisket into another meal.

I tablespoon olive oil

½ cup chopped onion

½ cup chopped peeled carrots

½ cup pearl barley

2 cups low-sodium beef or chicken broth

2 cups liquid from cooking the brisket, or I cup of the liquid and an additional I cup beef broth

2 cups chopped leftover brisket, plus cooked carrots from the brisket

Chopped fresh Italian (flat-leaf) parsley (optional)

1. Heat the olive oil in a large saucepan over medium-high heat. Add the chopped onion and carrots and cook until slightly softened, about 3 minutes. Add the barley and cook, stirring, until the barley is nicely coated with the oil, about 2 minutes. Add the 2 cups of beef broth, the brisket liquid with the beef broth, if using, and 2 cups of water. Partially cover the pan and let the liquid come to a simmer. Reduce the heat to medium-low and let the soup simmer until the barley is pretty tender, 30 to 35 minutes.

2. Increase the heat to high, add the chopped brisket and any stray cooked carrots, and let come to a simmer, uncovered. Reduce the heat to medium-low and let the soup simmer, about 10 minutes. Now you have soup.

These ribs are glazed with sauce
(though with just the rub they're pretty fine, too).

Ribs with a Rub
(and Maybe a Glaze)

Serves 4 to 6

When my friend Pam's daughter Maya was very young she used to call spareribs "steak on the cob," which killed me. Still, I was always intimidated by cooking spareribs. They seemed likely to turn out tough and chewy, instead of tender and juicy. And once I started reading about different theories and methods of cooking spareribs, it was easy to become even more unsettled. Barbecue has such hard-core followers that any friendly question can turn into hours of heated debate. I swear it's safer to walk into a La Leche League meeting and say "I think formula is as good as breast milk" than to walk into a room full of pit masters and say "I think boiling ribs makes them more tender."

Barbecue genius Steven Raichlen opened my eyes to the magic of rubs, and since then I've been massaging all kinds of foods with flavorful herb and spice blends. This one is the result of many racks of happy experimentation and calibration, cooked low and slow, either in the oven or on the grill. Sometimes I go with just a rub, no sauce, which makes a less sticky rib but one that still has lots of flavor. Then I pass a heated pitcher of homemade (see page 108) or store-bought barbecue sauce on the side. Or for a shiny glaze and an even deeper flavor I brush the ribs with the sauce for the last twenty minutes or so of grilling or baking. Even when I am grilling, I find it less chancy to start the ribs in the oven where the temperature is more even and controlled.

As for all of the other rib-related topics, sometimes I like a healthy culinary debate on technique . . . but what I really like is making something delicious and not having to take a graduate course in the subject to get there.

KOSHER SALT

BROWN SUGAR

PAPRIKA

BLACK PEPPER

GARLIC POWDER

OREGANO

RED PEPPER FLAKES

ADOBO

You might want to rethink that white T-shirt.

FOR THE SPICE RUB

2 tablespoons kosher or coarse salt

2 tablespoons light or dark brown sugar

2 tablespoons sweet paprika

1½ teaspoons freshly ground black pepper

1½ teaspoons garlic powder or minced garlic

1½ teaspoons dried oregano

½ teaspoon adobo seasoning (optional; see Notes)

¼ teaspoon red pepper flakes

1 rack pork spareribs (6 to 7 pounds)

Barbecue sauce, homemade (page 108) or store-bought, for serving or basting or both

TO GRILL THE SPARERIBS START TO FINISH

If you'd like to grill the ribs from beginning to end, preheat to medium-low a gas or charcoal grill set up for indirect grilling. Arrange the ribs on the hot grill, but not directly over the fire, with the meatier side up and cook them for 2¼ hours with the grill lid closed.

Then, increase the heat to medium (if you are using charcoal, add fresh coals), baste the meaty side with the barbecue sauce, if desired, and turn the ribs meaty side down. Close the lid and grill the ribs for 15 minutes. Baste the underside, turn the ribs, and grill with the lid closed until nicely browned, 15 minutes longer. Be sure to watch for flare-ups.

1. Make the spice rub: Mix together the salt, brown sugar, paprika, black pepper, garlic, oregano, adobo seasoning, if using, and red pepper flakes in a small bowl. Set the spice rub aside.

2. Rinse the spareribs and pat them dry. Rub them with about 1/4 cup of the spice blend and place them meaty side up on a wire rack set on a rimmed baking sheet. If the rack of ribs is too big for the wire rack, cut the rack in half and arrange the 2 pieces so they overlap slightly but do not overlap the meatier parts. Let the ribs sit, uncovered, in the refrigerator for a few hours (if you have to skip this step don't worry; the ribs will still be great, the flavors just won't permeate the meat as deeply).

3. To bake the ribs and finish cooking them on the grill, preheat the oven to 250°F.

4. Place the baking sheet with the ribs in the oven and bake until tender, 2½ hours (see Notes).

5. When ready to grill, preheat the grill to medium.

6. Arrange the ribs on the grill meatier side down. If you want more glazed ribs baste them with the barbecue sauce. Grill the ribs for 15 minutes with the grill lid closed. Turn the ribs over, baste the meaty side with the barbecue sauce, and grill until the ribs have good grill marks, 15 minutes longer with the lid closed. Check the grill frequently; once the barbecue sauce is added, it can cause a flare-up.

7. Remove the ribs from the grill and let them sit for 5 to 10 minutes or so. Warm the remaining barbecue sauce in a small saucepan over medium heat. Slice the ribs and serve them passing a pitcher of the warm barbecue sauce on the side.

Notes: Adobo seasoning is a dried spice blend popular in Mexican cooking, available in most supermarkets. The spices vary, but blends traditionally include garlic, onion, oregano, and pepper. A hit of adobo in the rib rub ups the flavor nicely.

After 2½ hours, if you'd prefer to finish cooking the ribs in the oven, increase the oven temperature to 400°F and continue baking them for another 30 minutes, until nicely browned, basting them with barbecue sauce, if desired.

Cooking Tip: You can use this spice rub on really anything: chicken, steaks, pretty much any meat you like. This recipe makes twice as much as you'll need for the ribs here because you'll be very happy to have the rest on hand for another round, but you can make it with half measures of the ingredients if you prefer. Conversely, you can multiply the recipe to make as much rub as you like. Keep in mind the rule of approximately 1 tablespoon rub to 1 pound of meat (and you might use less if your crowd prefers a less intensely seasoned rack of ribs).

Make Ahead: If you use fresh garlic the spice rub will keep in the fridge for a couple of weeks, but if you use powdered garlic it will keep for months in a tightly sealed container in your spice drawer.

Especially handy when guests are coming, you can bake (or grill) the ribs for two and a half hours and leave them at room temperature for an hour or so, then finish them at the higher heat—grilled or in the oven—for the last thirty minutes just prior to serving.

What the Kids Can Do: Kids can measure the ingredients for the rub and massage the rub into the meat if that appeals to them (wash hands!).

Apple Glazed Pork Chops

Serves 6

Buy nice thick pork chops for this dish. The lightly sweet glaze browns up beautifully under the broiler, but you'll need the thickness so the chops don't over-cook and dry out before the outside caramelizes (see Cooking Pork Properly, below).

This recipe makes a bit more sauce than you'll need for marinating and glazing the chops, but that is no accident. If you make a pot of rice or maybe mashed potatoes to go with the chops, the reserved glaze is fabulous drizzled over either. You can also trickle it over plain old steamed carrots, broccoli, or cauliflower, or some plain roasted squash.

The sautéed apple topping is simple to prepare and turns the dish into something almost restaurant-ey. There is no reason a kid shouldn't like sliced apples sautéed with some butter and maple syrup or sugar, but you can run that up the old flagpole and see if anyone salutes it, as the old saying goes.

COOKING PORK PROPERLY

There's no meat that causes more consternation in the timing department than pork. Cooked too long, it's dry and tough. Cooked too little, it's scary. But really, there's not much to worry about. First of all, better farming practices have reduced the possible health hazards of undercooked pork. In fact, because the risks are so much less prevalent, the USDA has changed their guidelines from a 185°F internal temperature to 160°F. This means you don't have to cook pork until it becomes completely grayish-white and shoe-leathery throughout. Instead, you can take it off the heat when the pork is tender and juicy, and the interior still has a nice pink blush. It's quite liberating.

FOR THE PORK CHOPS

⅓ cup firmly packed light or dark brown sugar

½ cup apple cider or apple juice

3 tablespoons canola or vegetable oil, plus more for brushing the pan

2 tablespoons regular or low-sodium soy sauce

2 tablespoons cider vinegar

I teaspoon grated peeled fresh ginger

Kosher or coarse salt and freshly ground black pepper

2 teaspoons cornstarch

6 pork chops (each about 6 ounces and I-inch thick), either boneless or bone-in is fine

FOR THE SAUTÉED APPLES (OPTIONAL)

I tablespoon unsalted butter

2 Granny Smith apples, peeled, cored, and sliced

I tablespoon maple syrup or light or dark brown sugar

Pinch of kosher or coarse salt

¼ cup heavy (whipping) cream (optional)

CARRYOVER COOKING

Carryover cooking is just a term that means that food continues to cook after it's removed from the heat, so you want to take foods off the stove or out of the oven just before they are done to your liking. This is true for meat, vegetables, even brownies!

So, a simple but good tidbit of kitchen know-how: Whenever you finish cooking a piece of meat (steak, chicken, lamb chops, whatever), you will want to let it sit for at least 5 minutes or so before you cut into it. For a roast, even longer, I5 to 20 minutes.

Why wait? During the cooking process, the fibers of the meat contract, forcing out the liquid into the spaces between them. As the meat sits, the cells relax, reabsorbing the juices, which then stay in your steak, instead of running out onto the cutting board, leaving you with a hunk of dry tough meat. Also, when it comes to a bigger piece of meat, like a roast, the outside is much hotter than the inside when it comes out of the oven. Letting the meat rest evens out the temperature; the inside of the meat will continue to cook, with the internal temperature rising up to ten degrees—which is why you want to take it out before it's cooked to the level of doneness you are looking for.

You can cut your kid's chop into inviting slices.

1. Prepare the chops: Combine the brown sugar, apple cider, 2 tablespoons of the oil, soy sauce, cider vinegar, and ginger in a small saucepan. Season with salt and pepper to taste. Bring to a boil over medium-high heat, then reduce the heat to medium and keep the brown sugar mix at a simmer. Combine 1/3 cup of water and the cornstarch in a small bowl and whisk this into the brown sugar mixture. Let simmer, stirring occasionally, until thick, about 3 minutes. Let the marinade cool to room temperature.

2. Meanwhile, place the pork chops in a nonreactive dish large enough to hold them in a single layer and season them lightly with salt and pepper. When the marinade is cool, pour it over the pork chops, turning them to coat both sides. Cover the dish with plastic wrap and refrigerate the chops for at least 1 hour, and up to 8 hours.

3. Remove the chops from the marinade, scraping off any extra back into the dish. Transfer the marinade to a small saucepan and heat it over medium heat until simmering. Let the marinade simmer for 3 minutes to eliminate any risk from its having been in contact with the raw meat (this will become your sauce).

4. Heat a large skillet over medium-high heat and add the remaining 1 tablespoon of oil. When it is hot, arrange the pork chops in the skillet, without crowding them (you may need to cook the chops in two batches or in two skillets). Let the chops cook without moving them around until the undersides are nicely browned, about 4 minutes. Turn the chops over and let them sear, largely undisturbed, until the second sides are browned and the inner temperature of the meat is at or near 160°F, 4 to 5 minutes. (When cut into, they should still have a blush of pink, see the note on Carryover Cooking on the facing page.) Remove the chops from the heat and let them sit for 2 minutes before serving them with the reheated marinade on the side.

5. Meanwhile, while the chops are cooking, make the sautéed apples, if using: Melt the butter in a skillet over medium heat. Add the apples and cook until tender, but not too soft, 4 to 5 minutes. Add the 1 tablespoon of maple syrup or brown sugar and the salt and cook, stirring, until the apples become glazed, about 1 minute longer. Add the cream, if using, and cook until heated through, about 2 minutes. Serve the apples with the pork chops.

Cooking Tip: You may also grill or broil these chops, although broiling them may not make them as caramelized on the outside. Either way you cook them let the chops sit for 2 minutes before serving them with the simmered marinade on the side (see the note on Carryover Cooking on the facing page).

To broil the chops, preheat the broiler. Lightly oil a rimmed baking sheet or a broiler-proof baking pan. Broil the pork chops until browned, 4 to 5 minutes per side, brushing them with the reserved marinade if desired. Remove the chops when they are cooked through but still have a hint of pink inside, 160°F on an internal thermometer.

To grill the chops, brush the grate of an outdoor grill lightly with oil and preheat the grill to high. Grill the chops until nicely browned and juicy but still a bit pink inside, about 4 minutes on each side, basting them with the reserved marinade, if desired.

What the Kids Can Do: Let the kids measure and dump the ingredients for the marinade into the saucepan, season the chops with salt and pepper, and possibly peel the optional apples.

Broiled Miso Cod Fingers
(page 146)

Chapter 9

Fish and Seafood

So you're rolling up your sleeves to take a stab at serving fish to your family. Good for you. Such drama. My friend recently told me that when she mentioned she was making fish for dinner her kids reacted the same as when she announced that they were going to the doctor for flu shots.

I know I should be cheerfully extolling the virtues of fish and the myriad ways I have found to get my kids not only to eat fish but to applaud when they see it on the table. I can't do that. This chapter was like giving birth to a third child. A ten-pound child with a big head who was breech.

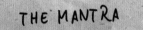

THE MANTRA

Just eat the damn fish.

When Charlie was young, he liked fish. Jack didn't. I figured I just had to keep trying and wait it out. Now Jack likes fish. Most of the time. And Charlie doesn't much. Unless you count smoked salmon, which he loves. And recently he ate a bowl of seafood gumbo with gusto at a party. When I responded with pleasant surprise he said, "But, mom, I like soup, remember?" Right.

Kids and fish have long been at a standoff. Well, I guess it's not a standoff, in that fish don't have anything against kids, but by and large getting your kids to try, never mind like, fish is something of an ongoing struggle for many parents. You are not alone.

Here's the current status in our house: Everyone's good with shrimp— sometimes even enthusiastic. Jack is quite fond of the Asian Salmon and really likes the Flaky Fish with Balsamic Glaze. Both kids have found the miso cod fingers to be to their liking. I'm stunned at how much they love mussels and clams, but I know that those may be a hard sell to many other kids. In short, I won't tell you how may recipes hit the cutting-room floor during the making of this chapter. For example, I thought Charlie and Jack would like scallops way more than they did. Charlie recently asked me if I would make scallops only when he was out at a sleepover.

A few things I've learned along the way:

1. Buy very fresh fish. The fresher it is, the cleaner and "unfishier" the flavor. If you can buy it from a good fish shop, do. Cook it within 1 or 2 days.

2. Avoid "fishy" fish. If you attempt to get your kids started on a fish habit with mackerel or bluefish you will have only yourself to blame. Good beginner fish: cod, halibut, sole, tilapia, salmon (although wild salmon tends to have a much stronger flavor).

3. Use seasonings that your kids already like and ones that will cut through any lurking "fishiness." Try the teriyaki marinade on page 232 as well as soy sauce, balsamic vinegar, butter, garlic, lemon, or tomato sauce.

4. Urge your kids to try things at a buffet or from your plate, instead of making fish the main course.

5. Serve small portions. These make the fish seem less overwhelming and more accessible, resulting in less waste. They might also result in a request for seconds (but let's not get ahead of ourselves here).

6. Be patient and unruffled. Kids can smell your neediness the way dogs can smell fear. Be cool, be casual.

7. If you're in the mood, bribe them. I don't usually take this tack, but apparently there's nothing like a plate of brownies sitting on the kitchen counter to give a reticent eater a little more incentive to take just one bite of fish for God's sake.

A tangle of shrimp
scampi and spaghetti.

Flaky Fish with Balsamic Glaze

Serves 4

Balsamic vinegar is a perfect flavoring for seafood because it has a built-in sweetness that more than compensates for any of the "fishiness" that makes kids scrunch up their noses in that *adorable* way. And in this dish there's a pinch of brown sugar added for good measure. This recipe was born on a rushed evening when I had some fish that was demanding to be cooked and a container of leftover balsamic vinaigrette in the fridge. Necessity is the mother of invention, but some nights motherhood is the necessity of invention, and any mom can prove that.

Jack was fish averse for so long that the fact that he loved this came as a pleasant shock. The fact that he asked for his brother's leftovers was stunning. The fact that he asked for this the very next night was weird.

As for a side dish, the beans that go along with the lamb chops on page 227 would be lovely as would any of the vegetables in the vegetable side chapter (see pages 259 to 271) and any of the recipes in the carb chapter (see pages 245 to 257). And you can't go wrong with plain cooked rice.

The balsamic and a touch of brown sugar create a sweet sauce.

Nonstick cooking spray (optional)

2 tablespoons extra-virgin olive oil, plus extra for greasing the
   baking sheet (optional)

2 tablespoons balsamic vinegar

1 tablespoon Dijon mustard

2 cloves garlic, finely minced

1 tablespoon light or dark brown sugar

Kosher or coarse salt and freshly ground black pepper

4 cod, halibut, or sea bass filets (each about 6 ounces and
   ¾ inch thick)

1. Spray a rimmed baking sheet with nonstick cooking spray,
   brush it lightly with olive oil, or line it with parchment
   paper.

2. Place the olive oil, balsamic vinegar, mustard, garlic, and
   brown sugar in a shallow bowl and whisk to mix. Season
   with salt and pepper to taste. Dip the fish fillets in the
   balsamic vinegar mixture, turning to coat them well, and
   place the fillets on the prepared baking sheet. Let the fish
   sit at room temperature for 15 to 20 minutes (see Cooking
   Tip).

3. Meanwhile, preheat the oven to 450°F.

4. Bake the fish fillets until just opaque throughout, about
   8 minutes (the rule is about 10 minutes per inch of
   thickness, so eyeball your fish and take it from there).
   The fillets should be nicely glazed on the outside and they
   should flake when you insert a fork into them. Transfer
   the fish to serving plates or a serving platter and serve.

Variation

Balsamic Glazed Scallops

Try this with large sea scallops instead of the fish fillets. Marinate
1 pound of sea scallops in the balsamic vinegar mixture for 20 minutes,
then pat them dry. Heat a large skillet over medium-high heat, add
a tablespoon of olive oil, and when hot, add the scallops without
crowding them. Sear the scallops, without fiddling with them, until
the bottoms are nicely browned, about 3 minutes. Turn the scallops
and sear them until they are browned on the second side and the
insides are almost opaque, about 3 minutes longer. Remove the
scallops from the heat and let them sit for a minute before serving.

Cooking Tip: The fish
fillets marinate at room
temperature because they
need to sit for only 15 to
20 minutes. But use your
judgment; if it's very warm out,
put the fish in the refrigerator
instead and let it marinate a
little longer, maybe half an
hour.

What the Kids Can Do:
Whisk up the balsamic vinegar
glaze and dip the fish fillets
in it. And they can try not to
make obnoxious comments
about fish.

Asian Salmon

Serves 4

Salmon is one of the most popular fish eaten in the United States, and from anecdotal observation, also one of the most popular (okay, make that tolerated) fish with kids, too. Again, the use of a few well-chosen ingredients cuts through any offputting oiliness—in this case the popular Asian flavors of soy and garlic coupled with a subtle lift from the mustard. A little bit of brown sugar adds a touch of sweetness. This recipe turned Jack from a non-salmon eater into a salmon eater.

Serve this with plain rice, mashed potatoes (page 253) and roasted asparagus (page 262), or with the Sautéed Corn, Spinach, Bacon, and Scallions (page 268).

Cooking Tip: If the salmon fillets have skin on them, this will actually keep the fillets moister as they cook. After the salmon has cooked, you can slide a spatula cleanly between the fish and the skin, leaving the skin behind on the baking sheet.

What the Kids Can Do: Let the kids measure and whisk together the ingredients for the soy sauce marinade and pour some of it over the salmon. Once the salmon has finished cooking, they can drizzle the reserved marinade on top.

The extra reserved marinade makes a good drizzle.

Nonstick cooking spray

4 salmon fillets (each 6 to 7 ounces), with or without skin
(see the Cooking Tip)

3 tablespoons low-sodium soy sauce, or 2 tablespoons regular
soy sauce and 1 tablespoon water

2 tablespoons extra-virgin olive oil

1 tablespoon Dijon mustard

1 tablespoon light or dark brown sugar

½ teaspoon finely minced garlic

Hot cooked rice, for serving

Lime wedges, for serving (optional)

1. Spray a rimmed baking sheet or broiler pan with nonstick cooking spray.

2. Place the soy sauce, olive oil, mustard, brown sugar, and garlic in a small bowl and whisk to mix. Arrange the salmon fillets about 1 inch apart on the prepared baking sheet, skin side down (even if the skin has been removed). Evenly pour about three quarters of the soy sauce marinade onto the salmon, using your fingers to make sure it coats the fillets thoroughly, including the sides. Let the salmon sit at room temperature for about 20 minutes (see Note). Set the remaining soy sauce marinade aside for a sauce.

3. Meanwhile preheat the broiler.

4. Broil the fish on the baking sheet for 10 minutes, watching so that it doesn't burn. If the salmon starts to get too brown on top, turn off the broiler, set the oven temperature to 400°F, and let the fish continue cooking (still about 10 minutes in total). Take the salmon out when it is slightly less cooked in the middle than you like it; it will continue to cook as it sits (see Carryover Cooking on page 136). Drizzle the reserved soy sauce marinade over the salmon fillets, or drizzle it over the rice. Serve the salmon with lime wedges, if desired.

Note: The salmon marinates at room temperature because it needs to sit for only 20 minutes. But use your judgment; if it's very warm out, tuck the salmon in the fridge instead and let it marinate a bit longer, maybe half an hour.

SMALL STROKES OF MANIPULATIVE PARENTAL GENIUS

While I usually advocate being straight up with kids about what they are eating and, without being a pedant, explaining why different foods are more healthful or not, I have to tip my hat to my brother-in-law, Jeff, whose little girls were eating salmon with gusto at a very, very young age. He dubbed the pink fish "Barbie Chicken," and the rest was history. It took years for the truth to come out.

My other favorite manipulative parent story belongs to my college roommate's father. There were four little girls in the family and a backseat big enough for only three, so all car trips began with him saying, "Who wants to sit in the pretty girl seat?" (otherwise known as the "way-back"), and they couldn't scramble fast enough to sit among the suitcases and spare tires. (I add the disclaimer that of course all small children should absolutely ride in car seats, and it's lucky so many of us survived after spending our childhoods driving cross-country sliding across backseats with nary a safety belt in sight).

One last piece of admiration for that family: Early in the child-rearing process, the mom somehow managed to negotiate an agreement that for any long trips she would fly and meet everyone at their destination, not travel in the station wagon with her husband and four little girls. I don't know what she had to trade for this perk, but it was probably worth it.

Broiled Miso Cod Fingers

Serves 4

This may sound ridiculously sophisticated in terms of kid-friendly meals, but it's a total winner. Maybe you've never cooked with miso, usually encountered in soup form at Japanese restaurants—I didn't attempt it until just a few years ago, but now it's a happy staple in our fridge, with a fantastically long shelf life. It's hard to get a definitive answer on how long it will keep, but a year in an airtight container seems to be a conservative estimate. Miso's distinctive flavor works beautifully with the subtle, slightly sweet taste of the cod. (For more about miso, see Miso Paste below.)

One thing that sometimes helps kids get over their distrust of fish is presenting it in strips, which may feel a bit less intimidating than staring down at a big slab. Cod is a nice firm "unfishy" fish that holds its shape when you slice it.

Serve the cod fingers with rice, with the steamed vegetable of your choice, and maybe the Japanese Restaurant Salad on page 86.

¼ cup white or yellow miso (see Miso Paste, this page)

¼ cup mirin (sweet rice wine; see Mirin, page 86)

2 tablespoons granulated sugar

2 teaspoons minced peeled fresh ginger

1 teaspoon Asian (dark) sesame oil

4 skinless cod fillets (each 5 to 6 ounces), cut into 1 inch–thick strips

Vegetable oil or nonstick cooking spray

Thinly sliced scallions (optional), for garnish

No, of course cod don't have fingers.

MISO PASTE

Miso is usually made from fermented soybeans (a fact you may not want to mention). It has a rich but soft smoky flavor and is a bit salty, very savory, and kind of earthy. You can find miso in lots of supermarkets and, of course, at Asian and specialty food stores as well. There are hundreds of kinds of miso, but you needn't make yourself crazy trying to figure out the nuances of each type, unless you decide to be a miso master. Just buy either the mildly flavored white miso or the yellow, which is a little more pungent, and use those for all your miso-flavored dishes, including these savory cod fingers.

1. Place the miso, mirin, sugar, ginger, and sesame oil in a 13 by 9-inch baking pan. Add the cod strips and turn them so they are well coated with the marinade. Cover the baking pan with plastic wrap and refrigerate the cod for at least 2 hours; if you can marinate the cod overnight, all the better.

2. Preheat the broiler. Generously oil a rimmed baking sheet or spray it with nonstick cooking spray.

3. Remove the cod from the marinade, using your fingers to scrape off any excess (it's a rich marinade; too much will be overpowering to the fish, not to mention to your children). Discard the marinade.

4. Arrange the cod strips on the prepared baking sheet at least 1/2 inch apart. Broil the cod until cooked through and golden brown, 6 to 10 minutes. Sprinkle the cod with the scallions before serving, if desired.

What the Kids Can Do:
Kids can mix up the marinade and coat the fish with it, as well as remove the excess marinade before the fish goes in the oven.

Garlic Shrimp (or Shrimp Scampi . . . or, Literally, Shrimp Shrimp)

Serves 4 to 6

Did you know that *scampi* is actually the Italian word for prawn or shrimp? So the name shrimp scampi is actually a redundancy. But who cares? Sometimes the shrimp are broiled whole, and sometimes they are butter-flied, but in the houses of busy people with children shrimp is usually made somewhat like what you see here.

You may think that's a lot of garlic for little palates, but when garlic is gently cooked it becomes mellower and sweeter. A pinch of hot pepper flakes boosts the flavor, but of course if you have heat-sensitive offspring, skip it. As for the scal-lions and parsley, they contribute a nice color and a bit of freshness, but there's no point in adding them to the whole batch if it means you'll be scraping untouched portions into a Tupperware container.

Cooking Tip: If you're planning to serve the shrimp over a tangle of pasta or mound of rice you will want it to be more saucy, so add the optional cup of chicken broth. If you're just serving the shrimp as is, there's enough sauce. Have hunks of crusty bread on hand to soak it all up.

What the Kids Can Do: Peel the shrimp (sorry—you still have to do the deveining) and juice the lemons. Make sure the kids wash their hands well after peeling the shrimp.

- 2 tablespoons (¼ stick) unsalted butter
- 1 tablespoon olive oil
- 4 teaspoons finely minced garlic
- 2 pounds extra-large (21 to 25 count per pound) shrimp, peeled and deveined (see Frozen vs. "Fresh" Shrimp, page 62)
- 4 scallions, both white and light green parts, sliced (optional)
- Big pinch of red pepper flakes (optional)
- ¼ cup dry white wine
- 1 cup low-sodium chicken broth (optional; see the Cooking Tip)
- 3 tablespoons fresh lemon juice (from about 2 lemons)
- 2 tablespoons minced fresh Italian (flat-leaf) parsley (optional)
- Kosher or coarse salt and freshly ground black pepper

1. Heat the butter and olive oil in a large skillet over medium heat. Add the garlic and cook until softened (do not let it brown), about 2 minutes.

2. Increase the heat to medium-high, add the shrimp, scallions and red pepper flakes, if using, and cook, stirring frequently, until the shrimp just turn pink, about 4 minutes.

3. Add the white wine and cook until the wine is almost evaporated, 1 to 2 minutes. Add the chicken broth, if using, and let come to a simmer. Add the lemon juice and parsley, if using, and season the shrimp with salt and pepper to taste. Toss well and you're done; serve it up!

Parsley and pepper flakes can also be sprinkled on individual portions.

Shrimp Stir-Fried Rice

Serves 4 to 6

This fried rice dish is lighter than many and has an appealing simplicity to it. We don't really want to know how much oil is in the stir-fried rice we've all indulged in at Chinese restaurants. Let's just say that the rice is glistening for a reason, and that this version tastes terrific without so much fat.

You can substitute chicken or pork cut into half-inch dice. You can add a couple of tablespoons of hoisin or oyster sauce or a couple of teaspoons of sesame oil along with the soy sauce for a more flavorful stir-fried rice dish (see Sauce It Up on the next page for more about these Chinese ingredients). You can also add some other veggies along with the carrots or even make this into a purely vegetarian fried rice (see the Vegetarian Note).

I pound large (31 to 40 per pound) peeled and deveined shrimp, cut in half crosswise

Kosher or coarse salt and freshly ground black pepper

3 tablespoons vegetable oil

3 large eggs, beaten

3 cups cold cooked white or brown rice (see Cooking Tip)

½ cup chopped carrots

I tablespoon minced peeled fresh ginger

2 teaspoons finely minced garlic

¼ cup low-sodium soy sauce, or 3 tablespoons regular soy sauce and I tablespoon water

I cup frozen shelled edamame or peas, thawed

½ cup thinly sliced scallions, both white and light green parts

2 tablespoons chopped fresh Italian (flat-leaf) parsley, or I additional thinly sliced scallion, for garnish

Cooking Tip: Day-old cooked rice is best for stir-fries. If you are cooking rice specifically for this dish use a bit less water than usual and let it cook until it is quite dry, so that the grains stay separated. If you have both time and forethought (understood, it's unlikely that a busy mom might have both time *and* forethought at the same moment), you'll make a pot of rice a day or two ahead. You can also spread out freshly cooked rice on a dish towel or baking sheet and leave it uncovered for an hour or two so that it dries out nicely.

What the Kids Can Do: Kids can peel the shrimp (wash hands well afterward!) and garnish the finished dish with parsley or the scallion, if desired.

Vegetarian Note: Skip the shrimp and sauté about 4 cups of chopped veggies, such as chopped broccoli florets or more chopped carrots, slivered cabbage or sugar snap peas, sliced asparagus, and/or more edamame or peas.

Leftover rice never tasted so good.

1. Season the shrimp lightly with salt and pepper. Heat a wok or a large saucepan over high heat until very hot. Add 1 tablespoon of the oil and, when it is hot, add the shrimp and quickly stir-fry them until they are pink, about 2 minutes. Transfer the shrimp to a plate and set them aside.

2. Heat 1 more tablespoon of oil in the same wok or saucepan over high heat. Add the eggs and scramble them quickly with a whisk or fork. Slide the eggs onto the plate with the shrimp when they are just cooked through, about 1 minute.

3. Return the wok or saucepan to the burner over high heat, add the remaining 1 tablespoon of oil, then add the cooked rice and cook, stirring occasionally, until it is lightly browned in spots, about 5 minutes. Add the carrots, ginger, and garlic and cook, stirring, until they become fragrant, 1 to 2 minutes. Add the soy sauce, edamame or peas, and scallions and cook, stirring often, until everything is hot and the carrots are tender, 3 to 4 minutes. Return the cooked shrimp and scrambled eggs to the wok or saucepan and stir until everything is well mixed and heated through, about 1 minute.

4. Garnish the stir-fry with the parsley or scallion and serve.

SAUCE IT UP

Hoisin is a rich, vegetarian Chinese sauce made from sugar, soybeans, white vinegar, garlic, chile peppers, and some starch. It is used in cooking, as a dipping sauce, and as a glaze, and its flavor is a bit sweet, a bit spicy, and a bit salty. Hoisin's very strong in large amounts.

Oyster sauce is another thick, savory Chinese sauce that usually does have oysters involved, although vegetarian versions are available. It has a piquant, rich flavor, often contains sugar, salt, and cornstarch, and can also be used as an ingredient, a glaze, or a dipping sauce.

Sesame oil, with its concentrated smoky, toasty sesame flavor, should be used in small doses. The Sesame Edamame (page 35), Japanese Restaurant Salad (page 86), and Tofu-Veggie Stir-Fry (page 194) are all flavored with sesame oil.

You're not going to get a mac and cheese like this from a box.

Chapter 10

Hearty Comfort Foods

The words *comfort foods* should make you extremely cheerful. This and the Potluck chapter have much in common, because both kinds of dishes are often a meal in a dish, perhaps needing a simple salad or vegetable to round it out, sometimes not even needing that. Most of these dishes can be put together ahead of time and cooked or reheated just before serving, so if you make one the day before, or in the morning, then as the dinner hour rolls around you will be mentally high-fiving yourself. (Don't actually ask your kids to high-five you; take it

THE QUEST

I need a "food is love" recipe.

from me, they won't share your self-congratulatory enthusiasm, and their confused or condescending looks may dampen your pleasure.)

The One-Skillet Cheesy Beef and Macaroni makes my husband giddy, the Lasagna with Turkey Meat Sauce is just what you want when you close your eyes and think "lasagna," and the Moist Make-Ahead Parmesan Turkey Meat Loaf is just that. Cheesy Chicken Enchiladas are inherently festive, and the mac and cheese has become one of my most-requested dishes from people of all ages.

Other comforting dishes are sprinkled throughout the book: Look for the Mexican Tortilla Casserole on page 203, the One-Pot Arroz con Pollo on page 219, and for brunch, Lazy Oven French Toast on page 274.

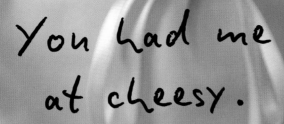

You had me
at cheesy.

One-Skillet Cheesy Beef and Macaroni

Serves 8 with a lot of leftovers, which you will be grateful for
(so I guess it really serves 10 to 12)

Very possibly the least sophisticated recipe in the book, this may be the one dish that my husband in particular eats as though he will be fasting for the following week. The kids love it, but Gary's eyes get kind of teary whenever I make it. He'll show up for dinner early. It's nothing new under the sun, but once you try it, you will understand the deepest meaning of the word *crowd-pleaser.* And, it all cooks in one skillet. Even the pasta, which cooks right in the sauce! I know, I know! It's the little things.

Get a huge pan, a twelve or thirteen incher (best pan in the world if you cook for a group regularly), make a vat of this, and keep it in the fridge. If you don't have a huge honking pan, cut the recipe in half. If you have bigger kids who are constantly running in and out of the house with their friends, all of them starving and in need of fuel before or after soccer practice, then you, my friend, may never again be without a pot of this awaiting reheating and inhalation. My sister-in-law Lisa, with her three large boys and revolving cast of visiting teenagers, swears by it. It is reminiscent of something that rhymes with Flamberger Felper, but it's better and it's yours.

YOU SAY TOMATO . . .

Crushed tomatoes have become my go-to canned tomato for most dishes. They have a more interesting consistency than a puree, more body than a sauce, and involve less work than chopping up whole canned tomatoes. But not all brands of crushed tomatoes are created equal—some are thinner, some thicker, and of course the acidity and saltiness come into play in the flavor. You should taste several brands and see if one jumps out at you. Of course, there's always the I-like-the-one-that's-on-sale method of choosing, which also works.

2 pounds lean ground beef

I tablespoon olive or vegetable oil

I cup chopped red, yellow, orange, or green bell pepper
(about ¼-inch pieces)

I cup peeled chopped carrots

I cup chopped onion

I tablespoon minced garlic

I teaspoon dried basil

2 teaspoons dried oregano

2 cans (28 ounces each) crushed tomatoes in juice
(see You Say Tomato . . . , page 155)

I tablespoon Worcestershire sauce

2 to 3 teaspoons chili powder (optional but recommended)

Kosher or coarse salt and freshly ground black pepper

¾ pound dried elbow macaroni

2 cups (8 ounces) grated cheddar cheese

1. Heat a very large skillet over medium-high heat (for this full recipe, it should be a deep 12-inch skillet). Add the beef and cook it until browned, stirring until no pink remains, about 5 minutes. Place the browned beef in a strainer and let the fat drain off, then set the beef aside.

2. Wipe out the skillet, add the oil, and heat it over medium heat. Add the bell pepper, carrots, onion, and garlic and cook until almost tender, about 5 minutes.

3. Return the beef to the skillet and add the basil, oregano, tomatoes with their juice, Worcestershire sauce, chili powder, if using, and 2 cups of water. Season with salt and black pepper to taste. Increase the heat to high and let come to a simmer. Add the elbow macaroni, stir, and cover the skillet. Reduce the heat to medium and let simmer, stirring occasionally, until the macaroni is tender and most of the liquid has been absorbed, 8 to 10 minutes. Taste for seasoning, adding more salt and/or black pepper as necessary.

4. Sprinkle the cheddar on top, then cover the skillet and cook until the cheese is melty, about 1 minute. Serve this right out of the skillet.

PICK A COLOR, ANY COLOR

Green bell pepper is often called for in dishes like this, and it's fine. But red (or orange or yellow) bell peppers are sweeter and usually more kid-friendly, so give them a try if the green variety isn't your family's cup of tea.

Cooking Tip: Leftovers can be reheated on the stovetop over medium-low heat, or in a preheated 350°F oven, for 10 to 15 minutes (you may want to add a bit of water if it seems like the macaroni is drying out). If possible, don't add the cheese until the very end, otherwise it has a way of dissolving right into the casserole and not staying on top in that appealing melty way. If you are serving half of the dish on one day and saving the other half for another, sprinkle one cup of the cheese over half of the skillet, leaving the other half naked for later.

What the Kids Can Do: Kids can add ingredients to the skillet, with supervision, and letting them sprinkle on the cheese during the final step often locks in their appetite for the dish, because it smells great.

Moist Make-Ahead Parmesan Turkey Meat Loaf

Serves 8 (which you may not think you need, but make it and you'll be so happy you did)

Is it me, or do some of you feel like meat loaf has gotten somewhat of a bad rap? I certainly won't argue that it's the sexiest main course on the block, but it just has that Rodney Dangerfield "I don't get no respect" quality to it.

Give it another chance. My kids pronounced this meat loaf just plain delicious, which is saying a lot after the number of turkey meat loaves that were plunked down on our dining table. It's also lighter than you'd expect yet still solidly in the category of comfort food. It's quite large so you will certainly have leftovers if you're feeding a family of four or five. And leftover meat loaf in the fridge is one of the most soul-soothing, happy-making thoughts I know. You may hear it calling to you, late at night . . . "Hi . . . it's me . . . your fabulous meat loaf . . ." Or maybe that's really just me. Meat loaf sandwiches make some people exceptionally cheerful.

Meat loaf is in the category of highly forgiving dishes—don't get anxious about exact quantities. And if your gang is game you can really have fun by looking around in your fridge and pantry for add-ins: some slivered sun-dried tomatoes, sliced black olives, a bit more garlic, chopped roasted peppers, fresh herbs. You can also sauté other finely chopped veggies along with the shallots; think carrots, broccoli, bell peppers, celery, or fennel. Use barbecue sauce instead of the ketchup to top the meat loaf off if you like, or chili sauce if you're feeling frisky. Or you can make the meat loaf exactly the way it is here and be very happy.

Cooking Tip #1: If you don't have tomato paste, or don't feel like opening a whole can just for 2 tablespoons, use ketchup instead. Most of us always have an open bottle of ketchup in the fridge. And also see the Cooking Tip on page 196 about storing extra tomato paste.

Cooking Tip #2: Make sure there are a few inches of space all around the meat loaf—this is so the hot air can get to the sides and brown the meat loaf nicely without steaming it.

GROUND TURKEY INFO

When you buy ground turkey, don't go for ultralean. Buy packages marked at least 93 percent lean/7 percent fat, preferably 85 percent lean/15 percent fat. Some brands of ground turkey come in 1.3 pound packages; use two of them. And make sure to buy the unseasoned turkey; some have Italian seasoning added in, which you don't need here.

A just-the-right-size meat loaf is
a little heartbreaking.

Nonstick cooking spray

2 tablespoons olive oil

⅔ cup minced shallots (about 3 large shallots)

½ cup thinly sliced scallions, both white and light green parts

1 teaspoon finely minced garlic

1 teaspoon kosher or coarse salt

½ teaspoon freshly ground black pepper

½ teaspoon dried oregano, rosemary, or thyme

2 tablespoons Worcestershire sauce

2 tablespoons tomato paste (see Cooking Tip #1, page 157)

1 tablespoon Dijon mustard

2 large eggs

½ cup milk, preferably whole milk

2½ pounds ground turkey (see Ground Turkey Info, page 157)

¾ cup panko (Japanese bread crumbs; see Note, page 171)

½ cup finely freshly grated Parmesan cheese

½ cup minced fresh Italian (flat-leaf) parsley

½ cup ketchup

1. Preheat the oven to 350°F. Spray a rimmed baking sheet with nonstick cooking spray.

2. Heat the olive oil in a medium-size skillet over medium heat and add the shallots. Cook, stirring frequently, until tender, about 5 minutes; try not to let them get too brown.

3. Add the scallions and garlic and cook until you can smell the garlic, about 2 minutes. Add the salt, pepper, oregano, Worcestershire sauce, tomato paste, and mustard and mix well. Let the mixture cool slightly.

4. Place the eggs and milk in a large bowl and beat to mix. Add the turkey, *panko,* cooled shallot mixture, Parmesan, and parsley. Mix well (use your hands!) and shape into a rectangular loaf on the prepared baking sheet, making sure there is space on all sides of the meat loaf (see Cooking Tip #2). Spread the ketchup over the meat loaf.

5. Bake the meat loaf until cooked through, 60 to 65 minutes. Let it sit for at least 10 minutes, then slice and serve.

Make Ahead: The "make ahead" in the title is kind of superfluous because really all meat loaves can be made ahead of time. You just mix it all up, mold it into its loaf shape, put it in a large baking pan, cover it with plastic wrap or aluminum foil, and tuck it in the fridge. Then about an hour before dinner you unwrap it and stick it in the preheated oven, adding an extra five to ten minutes if it's going from fridge to oven. Leftovers keep for up to four days. Reheat slices in the microwave.

What the Kids Can Do: Crack eggs, measure seasonings, and with clean hands mix everything up in one bowl (encourage the kids to handle things gently—not too much squeezing and squishing) and form the meat loaf into its shape on the baking sheet. They can also spread the ketchup over the top—slimy but fun. And of course wash their hands well again with soap and warm water when they're done. (Best to remind them not to put their hands in their mouths till after giving them a good wash post–meat loaf mixing.)

Lasagna with Turkey Meat Sauce

Serves 6 to 8

My husband says that when he eats a really good lasagna it tickles the back of his throat—do with that thought what you will. But let's hold hands and face the reality of lasagna together: It *always* takes much more time than you thought it would. Yet it's quite similar to childbirth: The result is so delicious and charming that you forget all about the pain involved in bringing it into the world. You might even make another lasagna. Maybe even two.

And here's the thing: It's worth it. Every layered, savory, flavor-melded bite is so good you forget that you were up late the night before muttering to yourself. And there are some good shortcuts. The next time you're making a meat sauce (see page 180) or the tomato sauce from the spaghetti recipe on page 174, think about setting aside half for making lasagna later in the week. Or, freeze some of the sauce and pull it out when you're in a lasagna state of mind. Or just say screw it, and grab a couple of jars of your favorite store-bought sauce, add some browned meat—beef, turkey, sausages, your choice—and mix that into the sauce, along with some extra basil, oregano, and sautéed minced garlic, if you like.

This is a very unsnobby lasagna that allows you to make it at the fanciness level of your choosing. If you shop for ingredients at an authentic Italian market you will create something company-worthy elegant. If you are rummaging through your pantry or making a last minute trip to a run-of-the-mill supermarket, you will end up with a damn fine lasagna.

CHEESE CHOICES

I use part-skim ricotta in my lasagna, because my family thinks it tastes just great and it takes some of the edge off that pesky indulgent feeling of lasagna. If you have the opportunity to find fresh ricotta—skim, whole milk, or otherwise—absolutely buy it and think about fat and calories another time. The fresh flavor is so light and delicate, as is the texture, it's really another quality level of ricotta altogether.

Speaking of quality of cheese, you've probably heard all about how fresh mozzarella is head and shoulders better than the stuff in the supermarket dairy case, which the food world regularly snubs as "rubbery bricks," "bouncy cubes of plastic cheese," and other condemning metaphors. Well, it's true that very fresh mozzarella has an entirely different flavor and texture, and it's miles apart from those factory-sealed cheeses. There's fresh fresh mozzarella, made in the place where you buy it. Then there are prepackaged sorta "fresh" mozzarella balls often found in the fancier cheese sections of the supermarket, sometimes near the deli area, which are pretty good. But, life being what it is, sometimes fresh mozzarella is not in the picture for any number of reasons, and you can make a perfectly good, family-friendly lasagna with blocks of supermarket mozzarella. One of the basic mantras of getting a real dinner on the table for your family is this: A pretty good lasagna is a whole lot better than no lasagna. Repeat three times, and dig in.

what is it about lasagna?

3 large eggs

I container (32 ounces) ricotta cheese
(see Cheese Choices, page 160)

I teaspoon dried basil

2 teaspoons dried oregano

I cup freshly grated Parmesan cheese

Kosher or coarse salt and freshly ground black pepper

5 cups Turkey Meat Sauce (page 180), or 5 cups store-bought
meat or pasta sauce

12 no-cook lasagna noodles (see the Cooking Tip)

I pound (4 cups) very thinly slivered or shredded mozzarella,
preferably fresh mozzarella

Nonstick cooking spray (optional)

1. If you are planning to bake the lasagna right away, preheat the oven to 375°F.

2. Place the eggs in a medium-size bowl and lightly beat them. Add the ricotta, basil, oregano, and ¾ cup of the Parmesan and stir to blend. Season with salt and pepper to taste.

3. Ladle a little of the sauce onto the bottom of a 13 by 9–inch baking dish. Arrange all 12 of the lasagna noodles on a work surface and spread them evenly with the ricotta mixture. Place 4 ricotta-covered noodles in the baking dish, covering the bottom. Spoon about 1½ cups of the sauce on top, covering the ricotta mixture entirely. Evenly sprinkle one third of the mozzarella over the sauce. Repeat until you have 3 layers of noodles, sauce, and mozzarella. Sprinkle the top of the lasagna with the remaining ¼ cup of Parmesan.

4. Cover the lasagna with aluminum foil. (Hint: Spray one side of the foil with nonstick cooking spray and place that side down on top of the lasagna; when you remove the foil, the cheese won't stick to it! Amazing, right?) Tuck the lasagna in the refrigerator for a day or two if you like and cook it later; don't preheat the oven yet if this is your plan.

5. Bake the covered lasagna for 1 hour, removing the foil after 30 minutes so that the top gets bubbly and browned. You may wish to put a rimmed baking sheet on an oven rack placed below the lasagna pan to catch any drips. Let the lasagna sit for 10 to 15 minutes before cutting it, so that the pieces hold together better.

Cooking Tip: If you haven't discovered the no-boil lasagna noodles in the pasta aisle of the supermarket you will fall in love with this gift of a convenience product. Purists may turn up their noses at them, but you don't have to invite those people to dinner. You can certainly cook your lasagna noodles; they'll have a more toothsome and authentic texture. Toss the noodles in a little olive oil after cooking to keep them separated, or leave them in a pot of cool water and pat them dry before layering them in the baking dish. However, one of the things that deters me from making lasagna more often is that step of boiling a huge pot of water, cooking the noodles, taking them out, and keeping them from sticking. The creator of no-boil lasagna noodles is right up there with the inventor of Post-it notes as worthy of sainthood in my book.

Make Ahead: Like most soups and stews, baked lasagnas that sit for a day before serving develop even more depth of flavor. They can be baked up to three or four days ahead of time and reheated. Or assemble the lasagna and store it unbaked in the fridge for up to two days. Then, bake the lasagna the day you plan to eat it—that way works, too.

No-boil lasagna noodles are a mom's best friend.

Lasagna is busy, messy work, and perfect fodder for getting kids elbow deep in the kitchen. They can help with smearing the noodles with the ricotta mixture, layering all the elements, spooning on the sauce, and sprinkling on the cheese.

NO-BOIL LASAGNA NOODLES SANCTIONED (WHEW)

Through my friend, crazy-talented food writer Eugenia Bone, I have been lucky enough to hang out with her father, Edward Giobbi, who wrote some of the groundbreaking Italian cookbooks published in the 1970s and eighties. Anyway, a very long story short (not my forte), I have been fortunate to make regular trips to Arthur Avenue, the mecca of Italian food in the Bronx, with Gena and her dad, and I have never come back with less than a truckload of ingredients that make me want to weep with pleasure. I could go on—I'd like to go on—but with this recipe on my mind, during a recent trip I sheepishly mumbled something about liking the convenience of no-boil noodles and Ed firmly led me over to the Delverde brand and said he thought these were the best. I loved that an old-school authority was embracing no-boil noodles, and as always, his recommendation was just right. If Ed Giobbi recommended I put a piece of ricotta under my pillow for sweet dreams, I would do it.

Cheesy Chicken Enchiladas

Serves 4 to 6
A Fork in the Road Recipe

This is a dish that makes people happy. Feel free to buy a large store-roasted chicken and use the meat from that. Dark meat or white meat, all fine. And since in this dish the chicken is tucked away inside a tortilla you may not hear as many observations about it from your white meat–loving peanut gallery. Or you can use meat from any leftover semi-plainly cooked chicken (poached, roasted, fried) that you have in the fridge, or you can make the simple roasted chicken on page 98 and use the meat from that, or add extra meat from the chicken noodle matzoh ball soup on page 70. And if you want to knock two meals out with one thought, roast a double batch of chicken for dinner and reserve half of the pieces for these enchiladas. In short, any chicken will do, unless it is heavily seasoned with non-Mexican flavors, so don't go peering into leftover Chinese food containers; that won't work.

FOR THE ENCHILADAS

About 2 tablespoons canola or peanut oil, plus oil for the baking dish (optional)

Nonstick cooking spray (optional)

14 small (6-inch) corn tortillas

1 medium-size onion, chopped

1 clove garlic, minced

1 tablespoon chili powder

1 teaspoon ground cumin

½ teaspoon dried oregano

1 can (28 ounces) enchilada sauce, or Quick Homemade Enchilada Sauce (recipe follows)

4 cups shredded cooked chicken

2 cups (8 ounces) shredded cheddar cheese or a Mexican cheese blend

FOR SERVING, PICK AND CHOOSE

Chopped fresh cilantro

½ cup thinly sliced scallions

Thinly sliced avocado

Sour cream

Salsa

You can't eat enchiladas and be in a bad mood at the same time.

1. Make the enchiladas: Preheat the oven to 350°F. Lightly oil a 13 by 9-inch baking dish or spray it with nonstick cooking spray.

2. Line a plate with paper towels. Heat a large skillet over medium-high heat, add 1 teaspoon of the oil, and swirl it around. Add a tortilla and cook until it is just beginning to become very pliable, literally 2 to 3 seconds. Using tongs, a fork, or a spatula, flip the tortilla and cook it until it is floppy but not mushy, 2 to 3 seconds longer. Quickly transfer the tortilla to the paper towel-lined plate. Repeat with the remaining tortillas, stacking them up as they are cooked and adding more oil in tiny amounts as needed.

3. ►══════ You can continue with Step 4 or see the Fork in the Road suggestions for adapting the enchiladas to suit your family on the facing page.

4. Add another teaspoon of oil to the skillet and heat it over medium heat. Add the onion and garlic and cook until they begin to soften, about 3 minutes. Add the chili powder, cumin, and oregano and stir until fragrant, about 1 minute, then add the enchilada sauce and stir well. Increase the heat to medium-high and let the sauce come to a simmer. Turn off the heat. Place the shredded chicken and half of the sauce in a medium-size bowl and stir to mix. Set the remaining sauce aside.

5. Place a tortilla on a work surface, spoon a generous ¼ cup of the chicken filling along one edge, and gently roll up the tortilla, making sure the filling doesn't pop out the ends (don't worry about a tiny tear here or there). Carefully place the enchilada seam side down in the prepared baking dish. Repeat with the remaining tortillas and filling, lining up the rolls tightly and neatly against each other.

6. Pour the reserved sauce evenly over the enchiladas, making sure they are all covered, and sprinkle the shredded cheese on top. Bake until everything is hot and the cheese is melted, about 20 minutes.

7. Serve the enchiladas with cilantro, scallions, avocado, sour cream, and/or salsa, if desired (the sour cream is usually highly desired).

Cooking Tip: Warming the tortillas in a bit of oil is an added step but really makes the dish. After a brief moment in the skillet the corn flavor becomes more developed and the tortillas also become more pliable and easier to wrap around the filling with less cracking. It takes about 3 minutes from start to finish to warm all of the tortillas, *and* you can use that same skillet when you make the very fast doctored-up enchilada sauce so you are not dirtying one more pot. However, you can also just wrap the stack of corn tortillas in a double layer of paper towels, put them on a microwave-safe plate, and microwave them until they are hot, about 45 seconds or so, if that's what will get the enchiladas on the table.

Make Ahead: You can assemble the enchiladas up to a day ahead of time, but don't sprinkle the cheese on top. Cover the baking dish with aluminum foil or plastic wrap and refrigerate it. Uncover the dish and if possible let the enchiladas sit at room temperature for twenty to thirty minutes before baking. Sprinkle on the cheese right before the enchiladas go in the oven. Know that you will need to allow several extra minutes of cooking time for the enchiladas to become heated through. Leftovers can be reheated in the oven or in the microwave.

Quick Homemade Enchilada Sauce

Makes about 3 cups

If you're game, make your own enchilada sauce from scratch. It takes about fourteen extra minutes, and it's basically starting with regular tomato paste and adding a little more of the enchilada seasonings. Use all of this sauce instead of the twenty-eight-ounce can of enchilada sauce called for in the chicken enchilada recipe.

- 3 tablespoons canola or peanut oil
- 1 tablespoon all-purpose flour
- 2 tablespoons chili powder
- 1 teaspoon garlic powder
- 1 teaspoon ground cumin
- 2½ cups low-sodium chicken broth
- 1 can (8 ounces) tomato paste (½ cup)
- 1 teaspoon dried oregano
- Kosher or coarse salt

Heat the oil in a saucepan over medium heat, add the flour, and whisk until well incorporated and lightly browned, about 2 minutes. Whisk in the chili powder, garlic powder, and cumin, followed by the chicken broth, tomato paste, and oregano. Season the sauce with salt to taste. Increase the heat to medium-high, let the sauce come to a simmer, and cook, whisking occasionally, until slightly thickened and smooth, about 10 minutes.

What the Kids Can Do: Shred cooked chicken, measure spices, combine the chicken and sauce, and if your kids are older and/or especially dexterous, roll the enchiladas up. You may want to have a few extra tortillas on hand if you plan on letting the kids help because tortillas do have a tendency to tear when not handled carefully. Kids can pour the rest of the sauce over the enchiladas and sprinkle them with cheese. They can choose their favorite condiments and put them in small bowls to serve.

Make Ahead: The enchilada sauce can be held at room temperature for a few hours or covered and refrigerated for up to four days.

Fork in the Road

First of all, the amount of spices called for in this recipe is not insignificant, so if your kids have more delicate palates, cut down a bit on the chili powder and garlic. Then, to cut back further on the heat, if you think your kids might not like the enchiladas swathed in a layer of the piquant sauce, you can divide the enchiladas between two smaller baking dishes and only pour the reserved sauce over one batch (use half of the remaining sauce, or as much as seems reasonable), leaving the other naked except for the sprinkled cheese.

Macaroni and Cheese

Serves 8 to 10 as a main dish
A Fork in the Road Recipe
Vegetarian

My kids like Kraft macaroni and cheese. There, I said it. I haven't made it in a long time although, like most of us, I have succumbed to the call of the blue box at times. But even now when they eat it at a friend's house I definitely get to hear about it later: "Kiefer gets to have the macaroni and cheese in the box every night. Why can't we ever have that?"

Still, they seem to be willing to shovel in this homemade version at a pretty fast clip, and we can pronounce all of the ingredients. Laced with a blend of cheeses and enriched with milk and cream, even grown-up guests tend to sigh with pleasure while looking at the browned *panko* crust sitting atop a bubbling casserole of cavatelli nestled in a sauce fragrant with a mixture of Gruyère and cheddar. (Although we call it macaroni and cheese, the actual pasta shape is up for grabs.) It's hard to think of a single dish with more universal kid appeal.

The Dijon mustard and red pepper flakes give the macaroni and cheese a little kick, a little edge, and save the dish from being too intensively rich and creamy (not that there's anything wrong with that). And, no, this isn't low fat. Thanks for asking.

WHO MOVED MY CHEESE TO THE BACK OF THE FRIDGE?

I keep changing up the cheese in this dish, depending on what I have on hand, and so my mac and cheese never tastes the same twice, which I find part of the thrill. My lovely dish-washing husband, however, has been known to look sadly at the last few globs on the plates and say wistfully, "Well, we'll never eat that again," already mourning the delicious, undocumented combination of cheeses that has come and gone.

Some good basic cheeses to start with are sharp or extrasharp cheddar, Gruyère, Swiss, Manchego, and fontina, or any combination of these. You can also use bits of softer cheeses, like Brie or fresh, mild goat cheese if you have some small pieces lingering about. Remove all rinds you wouldn't want to see floating around in your mac and cheese and unless you really know your audience, stay away from very potent cheeses like blue cheese or smoked cheese or anything particularly stinky.

FOR THE PANKO TOPPING

3 tablespoons unsalted butter

3 cups panko (Japanese bread crumbs, see Note)

½ cup freshly grated Parmesan cheese

FOR THE PASTA AND CHEESE SAUCE

4 tablespoons (½ stick) unsalted butter, plus butter for greasing the baking dish(es)

4 tablespoons all-purpose flour

½ teaspoon red pepper flakes (optional)

4½ cups 2 percent or whole milk (however indulgent you're feeling)

1 cup heavy (whipping) cream

5 cups coarsely grated flavorful cheese, such as sharp cheddar or Gruyère, or a mix (see Who Moved My Cheese to the Back of the Fridge? page 169)

½ cup freshly grated Parmesan cheese

4 teaspoons Dijon mustard

1½ teaspoons kosher or coarse salt, or more to taste

½ teaspoon freshly ground black pepper, or more to taste

1½ packages (24 ounces) dried cavatelli, ziti, penne, or any short pasta

1. Preheat the oven to 400°F. Butter a shallow 4-quart baking dish (or use 2 smaller baking dishes, or one smaller baking dish and some individual ramekins; see the Fork in the Road, opposite page).

2. Bring a large pot of water to a boil, salt it generously, and let the water return to a boil.

3. Meanwhile, make the *panko* topping: Melt the butter in a small saucepan over low heat or place it in a medium-size microwave-safe dish and heat it in a microwave oven until melted, 15 seconds. Add the *panko* and the Parmesan and stir until well combined. Set the *panko* topping aside.

4. Make the pasta and sauce: Melt the butter in a large heavy saucepan over medium heat. Whisk in the flour and red pepper flakes, if using. Cook, stirring, until the flour is blond in color, about 4 minutes. Gradually whisk in the milk. Increase the heat to medium-high and let come to a

Make Ahead: You can prepare the macaroni and cheese up to the point of baking and let it sit at room temperature for up to two hours. If you want it to keep longer, you can refrigerate it for up to one day. Either let the macaroni and cheese come to room temperature before baking or, if you're taking it straight from the refrigerator, add about fifteen minutes to the baking time.

Also, you can wrap the macaroni and cheese very well with aluminum foil and freeze it for up to three months. Either defrost it in the fridge (this takes about twenty-four hours), or add about thirty minutes to the baking time—leave the foil on the casserole for the first thirty minutes of baking so the top doesn't get too brown.

No matter what, if you're going to refrigerate or freeze the dish before baking, hold off on the *panko* topping. It's best if you add it just before baking.

What the Kids Can Do: Kids can grate cheeses, if they are old enough to handle a grater. They can measure all of the ingredients and mix together the *panko* topping. If they can be safely near a hot stove they can help stir together the sauce. And they can sprinkle the crumb topping over the casserole.

simmer, whisking frequently. Reduce the heat to medium-low and let the sauce simmer until it starts to thicken, about 5 minutes. Add the cream, grated cheese, Parmesan, mustard, salt, and black pepper, stirring until everything is smooth. Taste for seasoning, adding more salt and/or black pepper as necessary.

5. Add the pasta to the boiling water and cook it until barely al dente (follow the package directions but stop a minute or two before the pasta is completely tender). Set aside 1 cup of the pasta cooking water, then drain the pasta.

6. Whisk the reserved pasta cooking water into the cheese sauce, combining it thoroughly. Add the pasta to the cheese sauce and stir to combine. Spoon the pasta mixture into the prepared baking dish. There will appear to be a lot of sauce. Some of it will be absorbed into the pasta as it cooks, and in my book saucy is better than dry.

7. ➤—⪦ You can continue with Step 8 or see the Fork in the Road suggestion on preparing the mac and cheese for kids below.

8. Sprinkle the *panko* topping evenly over the pasta and bake it until golden and bubbling, 30 to 40 minutes. Let the pasta sit for a few minutes before serving.

Note: *Panko* are light Japanese dried bread crumbs. Although they are available at most supermarkets and at any Asian market, you can substitute 3 cups of fresh bread crumbs or 2 cups of regular unseasoned dry bread crumbs.

➤—⪦ Fork in the Road

If you happen to have a bunch of ramekins or gratin dishes lying around, make individual portions. Kids just love having their own little dish of something.

Also, young kids often would rather pass on the crunchy topping, alas, preferring their creamy pasta unpunctuated by contrasting textures. With individual portions, you can skip the topping on theirs and keep it all for the grown-ups. Make sure to put the hot dishes on cool plates and remind the kids not to touch the dishes. You can share your *panko*-covered version later, once the kids realize what they are missing.

FERTILITY MAC AND CHEESE

Among a small group of my friends this dish is referred to as "fertility mac and cheese." I made it for one friend at her request because it was the comfort food dish she was craving the night of her in vitro fertilization. When I received the news that she was pregnant . . . with *twins,* I happened to be visiting another friend who was about to embark on fertility shots. She insisted I make the mac and cheese that night and put another in the freezer for the night she began her fertility regime, which I did. One month later, she was pregnant. With twins.

Yes, yes, we all know that the fertility medications were probably more responsible for the pregnancies than the mac and cheese, but who's to know for sure if there might not have been a little correlation? If you are in baby-making mode, it can't hurt to toss this dish into the mix, though if you are trying for a baby but not going to be excited about twins, *caveat emptor.*

There are only 3 or 4 ingredients in this shortcut dish (see page 176).

Chapter 11

Pasta and Pizza—the Magic Words

Pasta is probably the biggest mainstay in most of our kid-friendly weeknight repertoires. Some kids are just plain-with-butter kids, some maybe a-sprinkle-of-cheese-too kids. But turning kids on to different kinds of dishes is important, and pasta is just the vehicle for the job.

THE QUEST

I'm looking for some new surefire hits.

We have all opened many jars of store-bought sauce and found some just fine, and some not as fine, but being able to whip up your own red sauce and meat sauce is an awfully good tool to have in your culinary tool belt. Plus, big batches provide imminently freezable leftovers that will serve you very well in the days and weeks to come.

A simple pasta casserole is a quick and easy weeknight dinner, and Sesame Noodles move away from the more traditional Italian offerings into something Asian and different. This chapter also contains a recipe for Grilled Pizza, a fantastic Fork in the Road dish that makes it possible for people to choose their own toppings (or lack thereof). And you do not have to make the crust from scratch to achieve this kind of pizza nirvana.

Other pasta recipes in this book include Lasagna with Turkey Meat Sauce (page 160), Macaroni and Cheese (page 169), and One-Skillet Cheesy Beef and Macaroni (page 155).

Good Old Spaghetti and Tomato Sauce

Serves 6; makes a little less than 7 cups of sauce, more than you need for 1 pound of pasta, but the sauce keeps well
Vegetarian

I have used tomato sauce from a jar so many times I couldn't even tell you. There are plenty of decent ones out there . . . and plenty of crappy ones as well. But once you make this sauce you will see how ridiculously easy it is and you'll have the pride of ownership that comes with homemade sauce with enough left for another pound of pasta later in the week. Or you can freeze that half for another time. Also, you can use the leftover sauce in Simple Fresh Mozzarella Pasta Casserole (page 176), as a pizza sauce (find the pizza recipe on page 187), or on Chicken Parmesan on a Stick (page 113). And it will get you halfway to Pasta with Meatballs and Sauce recipe on page 122.

FOR THE TOMATO SAUCE

3 tablespoons olive oil

I large onion, finely chopped (about I cup)

I teaspoon finely minced garlic

2 cans (28 ounces each) crushed tomatoes, preferably in puree (see Juice vs. Puree, opposite page)

3 tablespoons tomato paste (see Cooking Tip #1, page 157)

I teaspoon dried oregano (see the Cooking Tip, this page)

½ teaspoon dried basil (see the Cooking Tip, this page)

Pinch of red pepper flakes, or more to taste (optional)

Kosher or coarse salt and freshly ground black pepper

FOR THE PASTA

I package (16 ounces) dried spaghetti or any pasta you like

Freshly grated Parmesan cheese (optional), for serving

2 tablespoons slivered fresh basil or a handful of whole leaves (optional), for serving

Cooking Tip: If you have fresh oregano and basil you'll be able to make a lovely fresher tasting sauce. Instead of adding the dried oregano and basil at the beginning of the long simmer, finely chop about I tablespoon of each of the fresh herbs (not worrying about precision; the herb thing is really to taste). Add the fresh herbs for the last 5 or so minutes that the sauce simmers. And, as noted in the recipe, you can also sliver up some fresh basil and sprinkle it on top of the plates of whoever wants it, along with or instead of the optional Parmesan.

JUICE VS. PUREE

Crushed tomatoes in puree are thicker in consistency than crushed tomatoes in juice and therefore will yield a thicker sauce or finished dish. If you can't find canned crushed tomatoes in puree, you can certainly use crushed tomatoes in juice; if you cook them longer, the tomatoes will reduce and thicken up a bit more.

1. Make the tomato sauce: Heat the olive oil in a large saucepan over medium heat. Add the onion and cook until softened, about 5 minutes. Add the garlic and cook until it starts to turn golden, about 2 minutes. Add the tomatoes, tomato paste, oregano, basil, and red pepper flakes, if using (you can also wait and add the red pepper flakes to portions of the sauce at the end for those who like it hot). Season the sauce with salt and black pepper to taste and let come to a simmer. Reduce the heat to medium-low and let the sauce simmer gently until it thickens slightly and the flavors taste nicely melded, about 20 minutes (the sauce can simmer for much longer, if you want; it will get even richer and more concentrated). Taste for seasoning, adding more salt and/or black pepper or red pepper flakes as necessary.

2. Prepare the pasta: Bring a large pot of water to a boil over high heat. Add salt and let the water return to a boil. Add the pasta and cook it according to the package directions.

3. Drain the pasta, return it to the pot, and pour about half of the tomato sauce over the pasta, stirring to combine. Transfer the pasta to a serving bowl or serve it in individual bowls, topping it with Parmesan, fresh basil, and red pepper flakes, as desired, or pass the toppings in small bowls at the table.

Make Ahead: The tomato sauce can be refrigerated for five days and can be frozen for up to nine months. Let it cool and put it in well-sealed pint or quart plastic containers.

What the Kids Can Do: The kids can add the sauce ingredients to the pot and stir if they are old enough to stand near the stove—always with supervision. At some point they'll be interested in tossing the pasta with the sauce, although you'll need to decide when, factoring in the inevitability of tiny pink speckles of tomato sauce flying off over everything.

Simple Fresh Mozzarella Pasta Casserole

This is probably the easiest dinner in the book.

Serves 6
Vegetarian

This is one of those slightly magical dishes that comes together in a snap for a highly satisfying weeknight meal and yet can serve as an ooh-and-aah main course for company. I don't think I've ever seen anyone not take seconds, even the pickiest eater. There are quite a few very nice vodka sauces on the market, and it's actually one of the only sauces I buy more often than make.

There is something more than pleasing about the way the chunks of melted mozzarella stretch out as you lift your fork from plate to mouth. All this needs is a salad with a simple vinaigrette (see page 94) to be a perfect, easy, any night dinner.

> 1 package (16 ounces) dried pasta, such as ziti, penne, cavatelli, bow ties, or any chunky fun shape
>
> 1 jar (24 to 26 ounces) vodka sauce (see Is There Really Vodka in Vodka Sauce?, facing page), or 3 cups tomato sauce (page 174), or any other pasta sauce you may have
>
> 1 pound fresh mozzarella, cut into small cubes
>
> ½ cup freshly grated Parmesan cheese (optional)

1. Preheat the oven to 400°F.

2. Bring a large pot of water to a boil over high heat. Add salt and let the water return to a boil. Add the pasta and cook it until almost al dente (follow the package directions but stop a minute or two before the pasta is completely tender). Drain the pasta.

3. Return the pasta to the pot and add the vodka sauce. Mix it all up, stir in the mozzarella, then spoon the mixture into a 3-quart baking dish (see the Cooking Tip) and sprinkle the Parmesan on top, if desired. Bake the casserole until the top is a bit brown and everything is bubbly, 20 to 30 minutes.

Cooking Tip: If you are a family who likes the crusty part of a casserole, use a shallow baking dish so you have more surface area. Conversely, if you are a creamy family, use a deeper dish for a less crusty top and a more gooey inside.

Make Ahead: You can make the casserole ahead, cover it with aluminum foil or plastic wrap, and store it in the fridge for a day. While the oven preheats let the casserole sit at room temperature for half an hour, and know that it may need to bake for a bit longer than thirty minutes. If you forget to take it out of the fridge ahead of time, then just let the casserole cook for forty-five to fifty minutes, until it's hot and bubbly. Somehow, this thing is very hard to overbake!

What the Kids Can Do: Kids can cut the soft mozzarella with an age-appropriate knife and, if they are old enough, with supervision they can combine the sauce and any add-ins with the pasta. They can sprinkle the Parmesan on top, if you are using it.

Variations

Pasta Pluses

You can keep the casserole plain Jane or add slices of roasted pepper, sliced black olives, or sliced drained canned artichoke hearts. I also often add chunks of cooked chicken or shrimp, or slices of turkey kielbasa. Some crumbled cooked bacon is also an excellent addition.

IS THERE REALLY VODKA IN VODKA SAUCE?

Well, yes. But before you call the authorities, note that, as is the case with wine, almost all of the alcohol cooks off during cooking, and certainly there is not measurable alcohol in commercial sauce, which is intended for all ages. So, why use vodka at all? The alcohol cooks off, but while doing so it boosts the flavors of the other ingredients, especially the tomatoes. Vodka in particular does this without imposing another flavor onto the dish, as a splash or two of wine would, and that's why it became the key ingredient in this particular sauce, which has a lovely pinkish hue thanks to a bit of cream mingling with the red tomatoes.

Big Batch Turkey Meat Sauce with Ziti

Serves 6 to 8, with serious amounts of leftover sauce; makes about 20 cups of sauce

This makes *way* more sauce than you will need for a pound or two of pasta, but there's a reason to grab the big pot and make such a big batch. First, of course, you can cut the ingredient amounts in half. But ground turkey and turkey sausage are often sold in one pound packages, so if you buy one of each, this is the amount of sauce you will end up with. And that's about twenty cups of sauce. (Whoa!)

Here's another reason this recipe is so huge: Day one, you can boil one pound of pasta and serve it with several cups of sauce for dinner. The next day, make the Lasagna with Turkey Meat Sauce on page 160 and bake that for later in the week. Freeze the rest of the sauce in two or three containers, so that pasta with homemade meat sauce is an option any night you're in a pinch and you're halfway there to another lasagna.

The wine adds something to the sauce, and the alcohol burns off in cooking, so it won't affect the kids (and yeah, I know it's horribly politically incorrect even to have a fleeting wish that it might; shame on you for even thinking that). Almost any wine is good, adding another layer of flavor, unless it is sweet or has a very intense, unusual flavor.

If you want to use pork sausages and ground beef instead of the turkey, go ahead—it will be one hearty sauce.

THERE'S-NOTHING-IN-THE-HOUSE PASTA

You can make a quick and simple pasta sauce from lots of things already on hand in your refrigerator. Combining about a half cup of the water the pasta cooked in (which contains starch from the noodles and helps bind everything together into a sauce), with half to one cup of chicken broth and some cut-up steamed veggies, cooked chicken, pork, or shrimp, and other diced leftovers lingering around in the fridge can turn a pound of dried pasta into an impromptu dinner any night of the week. Just heat everything up together with the drained cooked pasta in the cooking pot. A sprinkle of grated cheese like Parmesan makes a flavorful finishing touch. It's another good opportunity for you to engage the kids in figuring out how to make something out of seemingly nothing (see Vegetable Bin Stone Soup on page 79 for another example).

This sauce is the very definition of rib sticking.

FOR THE TURKEY MEAT SAUCE

2 tablespoons olive oil

I pound ground turkey (don't buy the ultralean, use 93 percent lean/7 percent fat or 85 percent lean/I5 percent fat)

I pound fresh hot turkey sausage, removed from the casing (see Cooking Tip #2)

I pound fresh sweet turkey sausage, removed from the casing (see Cooking Tip #2)

I½ cups chopped onions

3 shallots, finely chopped

I tablespoon finely minced garlic

I tablespoon dried oregano

2 teaspoons dried basil

Big glug or two of red or white wine, if you have a bottle open

4 cans (28 ounces each) crushed tomatoes, preferably in puree (see Juice vs. Puree, page I75)

½ teaspoon red pepper flakes (optional)

Kosher or coarse salt and freshly ground black pepper

I package (I6 ounces) dried penne or ziti rigate (see Note)

Cooking Tip #1: You are more than welcome to use ground beef or pork and pork sausage and make this a full-on red meat sauce, if you like. The turkey version is a little lighter, and for us almost vegetarians (that is non-red-meat-eaters), it's a very satisfying meat sauce, which most kids seem to really go for.

Cooking Tip #2: Slitting the thin casing around the sausages makes it much easier to get the sausage out. There are two reasons for cooking the turkey sausages and the ground turkey together. One, it's easier and faster. Two, I have the impression that when they are cooked together the seasonings from the much more flavorful turkey sausages season the plain ground turkey and that these become one in a more delicious way than they would if they were cooked separately and simply met up later in the sauce. This is not based on scientific fact.

1. Make the turkey meat sauce: Heat 1 tablespoon of the olive oil in a large stockpot over medium-high heat. Add the ground turkey and the turkey sausage meat and cook, stirring frequently and breaking up the meat until it's very crumbly and browned throughout, 4 to 6 minutes. Place the browned meat in a strainer and let the fat drain off.

2. Heat the remaining 1 tablespoon of olive oil in the same pot over medium heat. Don't clean the pot! All those little browned bits of flavor from the meat will season the sauce. Add the onions and shallots and cook, stirring frequently, until softened, about 5 minutes. Add the garlic, oregano, and basil and cook, stirring, until you can smell the garlic and herbs, about 2 minutes. Add the wine, if using, and cook, scraping up any bits stuck to the bottom of the pot, until the wine pretty much evaporates, about 1 minute.

3. Add the tomatoes and red pepper flakes, if using, and stir to combine. Increase the heat to medium-high and let the tomato mixture come to a simmer, stirring it occasionally for about 10 minutes. Add the browned turkey and sausage mixture, reduce the heat to medium-low, and let simmer, stirring occasionally, until nicely thickened and the flavors have blended, about 20 minutes. Taste for seasoning, adding salt and black pepper as necessary. You won't need much; the sausages provide a whole lot of seasoning.

4. Bring a large pot of water to a boil over high heat. Add salt and let the water return to a boil. Add the pasta and cook it according to the package directions. Drain the pasta, return it to the pot, and toss it with as much of the meat sauce as desired.

Note: Rigate means ridged, and those ridges help catch the sauce in the pasta.

Make Ahead: The meat sauce can be kept for up to four days in the refrigerator, covered, and for at least six months well sealed in the freezer.

What the Kids Can Do: Some kids like squeezing the ground turkey sausage from the casing (you can slit the casing first, which makes this go faster, although it's less fun to remove the sausage); (wash hands!). Older children can help add ingredients to the pot and stir. And for this, and any other recipe, tasting to see if the sauce is seasoned properly and "done" is one of the most important jobs in the kitchen. It makes the kids feel important when you ask their opinion and may well be an opening for them to try something new.

This recipe should make enough sauce for three or four dinners for a family of four . . . not bad.

CILANTRO

PEPPERS

BROCCOLI

CHICKEN

CUCUMBER

CARROT

SCALLIONS

SESAME
SEEDS

Sesame Noodles

Serves 8 as a side dish, 4 to 6 as a main dish with add-ins
A Fork in the Road Recipe
Vegetarian

It took quite a few attempts to get the right balance of flavor and consistency for this perennially popular Asian noodle dish. Success had clearly been attained when Charlie took a first bite and said, "Put this in the book—I command you." After a gentle reminder about the best and most appropriate ways to ask people to do something, here it is.

FOR THE SESAME SAUCE

1 piece (2 inches) peeled fresh ginger

3 cloves garlic

2 tablespoons light or dark brown sugar

⅓ cup creamy peanut butter

2 tablespoons rice vinegar or sherry vinegar

2 tablespoons regular or low-sodium soy sauce

½ to 1 teaspoon chili pepper sauce, such as Sriracha or Tabasco

3 tablespoons vegetable, peanut, or canola oil

2 tablespoons Asian (dark) sesame oil

FOR THE NOODLES

Kosher or coarse salt (optional)

1 package (16 ounces) dried thin spaghetti, or any pasta that you like, such as rotini or linguine

FOR GARNISH, PICK AND CHOOSE

2 scallions, both white and light green parts, thinly sliced

1 tablespoon toasted sesame seeds (see Cooking Tip, page 184)

Fresh cilantro leaves (see Nobody's Neutral on Cilantro, page 185)

When kids can customize their dinner, they are more apt to give a new ingredient a shot.

1. Make the sesame sauce: Place the ginger and garlic in a food processor or a blender and run the machine until they are finely minced. Add the brown sugar, peanut butter, vinegar, soy sauce, chili pepper sauce, vegetable oil, and 1 tablespoon of the sesame oil. Process until smooth and reserve the sesame sauce in the food processor.

2. Prepare the noodles: Bring a large pot of water to a boil over high heat. Add salt and let the water return to a boil. Add the noodles and cook them according to the package directions until just tender. Set aside 1 cup of the noodle cooking water, then drain the noodles. Rinse them quickly with warm water and drain them again.

3. Add the reserved cup of cooking water to the sesame sauce and process to blend. Place the warm drained noodles in a large bowl and toss them with the remaining 1 tablespoon of sesame oil, then add the sesame sauce and mix everything until the noodles are well coated. Taste for seasoning, adding salt if necessary.

4. Let the noodles cool to room temperature; they will absorb more sauce as they sit.

5. ⟾ You can continue with Step 6 or see the Fork in the Road suggestions for add-ins, below.

6. Serve the noodles garnished with the scallions, sesame seeds, and/or cilantro, if desired.

⟾ Fork in the Road

The noodles can be slurped down unadorned and qualify as a main course because of the nutritious peanut butter, but they can easily be turned into a much more interesting and robust (and very attractive) one-dish meal with some add-ins and garnishes. Try any or all of the following vegetables mixed in with the noodles, and if you're not looking for a vegetarian meal, throw in a couple of handfuls of shredded chicken. The noodles make a great Fork in the Road dish for entertaining, as you can put out little bowls of anything you think is compatible with the noodles and let everyone make a customized bowl of pasta.

Add-ins: ½ seedless cucumber, peeled, cut in half lengthwise, and thinly sliced • 2 large carrots, peeled and thinly sliced or shredded • 1 cup cooked tiny broccoli florets • 1 cup slivered red, orange, or yellow bell pepper • 1½ cups shredded cooked chicken

Cooking Tip: Adding the sesame sauce to the noodles while they are still warm lets them better absorb all of it. You can make the sesame noodles ahead of time and let them sit at room temperature for up to three hours, but wait to toss in the add-ins until right before serving. If you refrigerate the noodles, you may want to give them a toss with a few tablespoons of water and then warm them up quickly in the microwave, as refrigeration does make the sauce thick and a bit sticky. If you don't have a microwave, toss the noodles with a few tablespoons of very hot water to help loosen things up.

What the Kids Can Do: They can peel the ginger with a spoon (see What the Kids Can Do, page 87), measure and dump the ingredients for the sesame sauce into the food processor, and toss the noodles with the sauce. Kids can also decide what add-ins they like, and cut or shred anything you feel good about, safety-wise.

. . . Then again, there ain't nothing wrong with plain sesame noodles.

NOBODY'S NEUTRAL ON CILANTRO

Cilantro is a notoriously love-it-or-leave-it herb, and not just for kids. People who don't like cilantro usually *loathe* it, finding it soapy tasting (this is actually due to a bona fide chemical response on the part of some people). You should definitely know your audience before adding it to a dish. You can also put out a tiny bowl of cilantro leaves on the side if that fits into your ability to get dinner on the table without that being the one last thing that makes you want to hurl something through a window. Then you can test your family's cilantro compatibility without risking the whole dish's appeal. You can do the same with scallions, sesame seeds, and any number of add-ins, *or* you can make executive decisions for the whole family.

PLAIN

ONION
+ RED PEPPER

BROCCOLI
+ BLACK OLIVE

PEPPERONI

Pick a topping, any topping.

Grilled Pizzas

Makes 2 approximately 12-inch pizzas; serves 2 to 4
A Fork in the Road Recipe
Vegetarian

Pizza is arguably The Best Food on the Planet, according to most kids (and most everyone else); sometimes even bad pizza is good. And, your family likely has its fair share of pizza in the given course of a month. But if you want to make your kids' heads explode, pizza on the grill has the capacity to amaze and dazzle like few other dinners.

Once you get the hang of it, you'll make this a summertime staple. You can stick with tomato sauce and cheese, or you can get inventive with the toppings (see the Fork in the Road). This recipe looks long (well, it is long) but only because it has lots of advice and options—the actual time it takes is quite reasonable.

I ball (I pound) pizza dough, store-bought (see I Heart Store-Bought Pizza Dough, this page), or Homemade Pizza Dough (recipe follows), thawed if frozen

Olive oil, for coating the dough and baking sheets

Coarsely ground cornmeal or all-purpose flour, for rolling and stretching the dough (see Note, page 189)

I cup store-bought or homemade tomato sauce (page 174), or pizza sauce

2 cups (8 ounces) shredded mozzarella cheese, preferably fresh

1½ cups toppings (see Fork in the Road, page 189)

¼ cup slivered fresh basil leaves (optional)

1. If you're using the Homemade Pizza Dough, follow the recipe directions. If you're using store-bought dough, divide the dough into two balls, gently coat each with olive oil, and let the dough come to room temperature either in a large bowl or on the counter, covered with a dish towel, about 1 hour.

I HEART STORE-BOUGHT PIZZA DOUGH

I almost always buy premade pizza dough. Most pizza restaurants will gladly sell you a ball of dough to take home, and it's also available at many supermarkets in the bakery section or near the refrigerated tortillas. I consider this, along with the enormous strides made in the world of medicine, to be one of the best reasons to rejoice in being alive in the twenty-first century. However, if you're in the market for a good project for kids in the kitchen, making pizza or bread dough is a great one (you'll find the pizza dough recipe on page 189).

Make Ahead:
Whether you are using store-bought pizza dough or making your own, you'll want to allow enough time for it to rise and relax before you start the grilling process, so plan accordingly.

What the Kids Can Do: Top their own pizzas! But have the kids do it off the grill, then you return the pizzas to the grill grate.

Vegetarian Note:
Depending on your choice of toppings, these pizzas can be as vegetarian as you like.

2. Lightly coat two baking sheets with olive oil. Sprinkle a work surface with cornmeal or flour. Gently begin to stretch or roll each ball of pizza dough into a 12- to 14-inch circle or a rectangular shape. You will need to stretch or roll the dough a bit, then give it a few minutes to relax before stretching it again, so that it doesn't keep springing back into a smaller shape. The goal is to make the dough less than 1/4-inch thick (it puffs up on the grill). Give the dough one final stretch. Don't worry about a small hole or two and definitely don't worry about an uneven shape; that's part of the pizzas' charm. Transfer the shaped dough to the prepared baking sheets.

3. Preheat the grill to medium-high (see Wait! I Have a Charcoal Grill, facing page, if you are grilling with charcoal).

4. Put the tomato sauce in a small bowl. Bring it along with a pastry brush, some olive oil, the mozzarella, and the dough on the baking sheets.

5. Pizza with tomato sauce and mozzarella is delicious, but if you're adding other toppings (see the facing page), bring them to the grill, too, so they are prepared and ready to go.

6. Brush the top of each stretched pizza dough with olive oil. Using a swift motion, pick up each circle or rectangle of dough by one edge and flip it oiled side down onto the grill grate. Close the grill lid and don't open it for 3 minutes, which gives the dough a chance to rise a bit and firm up.

7. Open the lid, peek at the underside of the dough, and check to see that nice grill marks have formed. Lightly brush the uncooked tops of the crusts with olive oil and turn over each crust. Reduce the heat to medium-low. Carefully brush the entire surface of each crust with 1/2 cup of the tomato sauce and sprinkle 1 cup of the mozzarella evenly over each top. Sprinkle any toppings, if you are using them, evenly over the pizzas. Close the lid of the grill and let the pizzas cook for 4 minutes, then begin checking to see if they are done. The cheese should be completely melted and the crust should have a nicely browned underside and be stiff when you lift it with tongs.

8. Remove the pizzas from the grill, sprinkle them with the fresh basil, if using, and cut the pizzas into pieces. Now you get to relax.

Cooking Tips: Here are the three major tips to remember when grilling pizzas.

1. Let the dough "relax," and handle it gently. Realizing that word *relax* is so alien to moms in general, in this case it should be interpreted as letting the dough rest, so that the gluten in the dough that has been activated by handling it or punching it down is given a chance to unclench, making the dough more pliable and supple. (Note to family: If we moms were given more chances to relax and unclench we would likely be more pliable and supple, too.)

2. Adjust the heat as needed. Watch the grill temperature. If it's too hot, the pizza can scorch and if it's too low it might stick or come out soggy.

3. Turning the crusts over after three minutes or so means that the firmed-up bottom becomes the top crust, and now you can layer on your sauce and cheese and toppings and not end up with an undercooked layer of dough underneath the toppings.

Once the bottom crusts are ready to be turned over, you can do this right on the grill and add the sauce and toppings there or, if the heat is too much for you, turn them cooked side up onto oiled baking sheets, load on the toppings, and carefully transfer the pizzas back to the grill.

Note: If you think your kids will be annoyed by the nicely rustic texture that cornmeal gives the dough when you use it to form the dough into the crust shape, you can use plain flour, but it's nice to have that bit of pleasing crunch in the crust.

Homemade Pizza Dough

Makes enough dough for two 12-inch pizzas or four 6-inch pizzas

For when you're feeling inspired.

- 1 package (¼ ounce) active dry yeast (2¼ teaspoons)
- 1 teaspoon granulated sugar
- 1 teaspoon kosher or coarse salt
- 2 tablespoons olive oil, plus extra for coating the bowl
- 3 cups all-purpose flour

1. Place the yeast and sugar in a large bowl, add 1 cup of warm water, and let sit until small bubbles form, about 10 minutes. Mix in the salt and olive oil. Add the flour gradually, mixing until the dough pulls away from the side of the bowl. Turn the dough out onto a lightly floured work surface and knead it until smooth, about 4 minutes (you can also use a standing mixer with the dough hook attachment to do this). Place the dough in a well-oiled bowl and cover it with a damp dish towel or with plastic wrap.

2. Let the dough sit undisturbed in a warm place until it is doubled in size, 1 to 1½ hours. Punch down the dough, divide it into 2 balls, and proceed with the Grilled Pizzas recipe; there's no need to let the dough rest again if it is at room temperature.

WAIT! I HAVE A CHARCOAL GRILL . . .

The directions for grilling pizza assume you are cooking on a gas grill, but if you are using charcoal, once the coals are hot create two zones on the grill, one with more of the hot coals under the grate (direct heat), the other with fewer (indirect heat), so the temperature on that side will be lower. Start the dough on the hotter side, then instead of lowering the temperature when you flip the pizza crusts, transfer them to the side with fewer coals before adding the sauce and toppings. That way the pizzas will cook and the cheese will melt without the bottoms of the crusts charring. With a charcoal grill you'll want to check for doneness even more frequently. This is a useful tip for cooking many things on a charcoal grill; creating two temperature zones lets you move food from one area to another as needed so that it cooks more evenly without burning.

✦ Fork in the Road

Chopped cooked broccoli, pepperoni, sliced black olives, sautéed sliced mushrooms, sautéed chopped onions, roasted or sautéed bell peppers, in strips or pieces—all are delicious on pizza. Or how about sausage and provolone? Blue cheese and figs? Greek olives and feta? Broccoli and fontina? Bacon, scallions, pepperoncini, and mozzarella? Chopped fresh tomatoes instead of sauce? Homemade pizza is the poster child for Fork in the Road cooking; let the kids—and your friends—invent their own combos. You will want to precook some of the more dense raw topping ingredients, like broccoli, onions, or sliced red peppers, and have all of the toppings sliced, slivered, or grated and ready to go before you begin the grilling. You can do this a day ahead of time and store everything in the fridge. For a crowd, you can double, or even triple, the recipe as desired.

Stir-fries are excellent springboards for meatless meals.

Chapter 12

Vegetarian Mains

Some of my best friends are vegetarians. Seriously, no sarcasm intended. In addition, my sister is a PETA card–carrying, non-leather-wearing vegetarian who is raising her two daughters as vegetarians and therefore fighting not to fall into a daily routine of soy nuggets and frozen veggie burgers. And once your kids get to a certain age, they will definitely have friends who one day announce "I am no longer eating meat." You may in fact hear that statement from your own kid and find that much of what you've been serving for the past eight, ten, or thirteen years is no longer a viable

THE PREDICAMENT

Really? But you ate meat yesterday . . .

option. Even those of us who aren't vegetarians are aware that the notion of getting meat to be less center stage on our plates is a good one for lots of reasons.

Many, many recipes in this book besides the ones in this chapter are vegetarian. There is a whole list on pages 336 to 337. And when you count in vegetarian variations of other recipes throughout, the total number of vegetarian options soars.

Finally, although each of the five recipes in this chapter is totally vegetarian, in a few cases there are some variations that do include meat as an option, such as the Mexican Tortilla Casserole (page 203), the quesadillas (see page 199), and the Black Beans and Rice (page 196). I hope this doesn't offend; my sister said it was okay (she has a mixed marriage; her husband is a carnivore . . . he's also Catholic, but that has been way less knotty).

Honey-Hoisin Tofu

Serves 2 to 4

Everyone loves tofu. No wait, that's not right, many people don't like tofu at all. Reservations usually center upon issues of texture and blandness, and an embarrassing number of us (not just kids; you know who you are, Gary) don't even want to give it the time of day. In describing tofu to his friend, my son Charlie said, "It's not something to hate; it's not something to love; it's just tofu."

Well, if you are trying to eat more vegetarian meals then you are going to have a pretty rough go of it if you don't find one or two tofu recipes to embrace. In this chapter you'll find Tofu-Veggie Stir-Fry in addition to this slightly sweet, robustly flavored tofu, which can be broiled or grilled. Serve it with rice and maybe some roasted asparagus (see page 262) or broccoli (see page 264). You could also serve slabs of this atop the Japanese Restaurant Salad (page 86) for a unique and delicious lunch, and check out the Creamy Tahini, Tofu, and Avocado Pitas (page 26).

You can sprinkle on additional scallions for color . . . or not.

¼ cup hoisin sauce (see Sauce it Up, page 151)

2 tablespoons honey

1 tablespoon canola or vegetable oil

2 teaspoons fresh lemon juice

1 scallion, both white and light green parts, finely chopped

½ teaspoon finely minced garlic

1 package (14 to 16 ounces) firm or extra-firm tofu, pressed and drained (see Pressing Tofu, page 195)

Nonstick cooking spray (optional)

Hot cooked rice (optional), for serving

Chopped scallions (optional), for serving

1. Place the hoisin sauce, honey, oil, lemon juice, scallion, and garlic in a sturdy zipper-top plastic bag or a plastic container and shake or squish to blend well.

2. Cut the tofu in half, horizontally, into 2 thinner flat slabs. Cut the 2 slabs into quarters, so you have a total of 8 pieces. Place the pieces of tofu in the plastic bag or the plastic container, gently flipping the tofu around so that it is completely coated with the marinade.

3. Refrigerate the tofu for 4 to 12 hours, turning it in the marinade several times to make sure it marinates evenly. If you don't have time to marinate the tofu, that's okay; it just won't be so deeply flavored. You can also marinate the tofu at room temperature for an hour, if that works.

4. Preheat the broiler or preheat a grill to medium-high. If you are broiling the tofu, spray a rimmed baking sheet with nonstick cooking spray or brush it with vegetable oil, or oil the grates of the grill.

5. Remove the tofu from the marinade, setting aside the marinade to use as sauce, if desired. Broil or grill the pieces of tofu 4 inches from the heat source, until one side is nicely caramelized, 5 to 8 minutes. Then, using a spatula, turn the tofu over, spoon a little more of the marinade on top, and cook the tofu until caramelized on the second side and hot throughout, 5 to 8 minutes longer.

6. Serve the tofu with hot rice, if desired. You can warm up the reserved marinade in a small saucepan or in a microwave oven and serve it over the rice.

Make Ahead: The tofu can marinate for up to twelve hours, so it's a great thing to make in the morning and broil when you get home.

What the Kids Can Do: They can combine the marinade ingredients and, maybe slice the tofu with an age-appropriate knife.

Tofu-Veggie Stir-Fry

Serves 4 to 6

For many of us it's an ongoing struggle to get a little more meat-free action going on at the dinner table. And in my house, even before I get to the part where I'm trying to make my kids embrace tofu, I have to get my meat-loving husband to let go of his tofu prejudice and stop thinking of it as the food of Birkenstocks-with-socks-wearing, macramé-weaving tree huggers (not that there's anything wrong with that). And, conversely, my sister, who is a vegetarian and raising her kids veggie too, is essentially obligated to find ways to introduce tofu into her family's diet in forms other than soy nuggets and patties. This recipe should help. What's key is the sesame oil, which is so toasty and irresistible that it distracts the skeptics from the bean curd and just tastes exotic and comforting at the same time.

This is not as viscous a stir-fry as some. There's no cornstarch thickening up the sauce, which is very simple and clean tasting. Serve this stir-fry over mounds of rice to soak up its nice light sauce. If you can, use brown rice, but in my house tofu *and* brown rice on one plate is pushing it a bit too far most nights.

You can easily switch up the veggies.

1 package (14 to 16 ounces) firm or extra-firm tofu, pressed, drained, and cut into ½-inch cubes (see Pressing Tofu, this page)

3 tablespoons vegetable or canola oil

¼ cup chopped onion

1 tablespoon minced peeled fresh ginger

1 teaspoon minced garlic

3 cups small broccoli florets

2 large carrots, peeled and thinly sliced

1 cup sugar snap peas, trimmed and strings removed

1 cup low-sodium vegetable broth

¼ cup low-sodium soy sauce or tamari, or 3 tablespoons regular soy sauce

1 tablespoon fresh lemon juice, or 1 tablespoon rice vinegar

2 tablespoons Asian (dark) sesame oil

3 scallions, both whites and light green parts, thinly sliced

Hot cooked rice, for serving

1. Using paper towels, pat the tofu as dry as you can.

2. Heat a wok or a large skillet with a lid over high heat. Add 2 tablespoons of the vegetable oil. When hot, add the tofu and cook, stirring occasionally, until the tofu is lightly browned in places, about 5 minutes. Transfer the tofu to a plate and set it aside.

3. Heat the remaining 1 tablespoon of vegetable oil in the wok or skillet over medium-high heat. Add the onion, ginger, and garlic and cook, stirring, until the garlic starts to turn golden, 1 to 2 minutes. Add the broccoli and carrots and cook, stirring, until coated with the ginger-garlic mixture and starting to become tender, about 2 minutes. Add the sugar snap peas and stir to combine. Add the vegetable broth and let come to a simmer, then cover the wok or skillet and cook until the vegetables start to become crisp-tender, about 3 minutes. Add the browned tofu, stir to combine, and cook until just beginning to heat through, 1 to 2 minutes.

4. Add the soy sauce, lemon juice or vinegar, sesame oil, and scallions and cook, stirring, until everything is heated through and you can really smell the sesame oil, about 2 minutes. Transfer the stir-fry to a serving platter and serve with the rice.

What the Kids Can Do:
If you're pressing the tofu, they'll have fun setting this up—it's like a teeny-tiny science experiment. Using a butter knife they can cut up the tofu (the cubes do not have to be perfect). They can remove the strings from the sugar snap peas. If they can handle a vegetable peeler, they can peel the carrots.

PRESSING TOFU

Tofu is sold packed in water, so it's hard to get it to really brown in a skillet. If you have the time and proclivity, pressing it to drain out excess moisture will help it brown a bit more when you cook it. This also gives the tofu a texture some people find more appealing (even extra-firm tofu is pretty soft). Place the block of tofu on a large flat plate, place a second plate on top, with the bottom against the tofu (use plates flat enough to sit evenly against the top and bottom of the tofu). Place a heavy book or a couple of cans of beans on top of the top plate and let the tofu drain for about forty-five minutes. Pour off the liquid that seeps out onto the bottom plate, and cut up the tofu following the directions in the recipe. You can drain the tofu for longer (and also leave it draining in the fridge for a day or night) but not much more liquid will be released.

Black Beans and Rice

Serves 6 to 8

My younger son, Charlie, was Cuban in a previous life. Oh, probably not, but it is a bit funny and disarming to watch this little Jewish, blue-eyed, blond child hunker down over a plate of black beans and rice as though it were mother's milk.

This is one of those recipes that is delicious hot off the burner, but even better one or two days after you first make it, because the flavors have a chance to meld and become one with the universe.

FOR THE BEANS AND RICE

2 tablespoons olive oil

2 large onions, chopped

I teaspoon finely minced garlic

½ cup chopped carrots (about 2 large carrots)

½ cup chopped red bell pepper (about I small pepper)

2 teaspoons dried oregano

I teaspoon ground cumin

I teaspoon chipotle puree (see page xx), or 2 teaspoons chili powder (optional)

4 cans (15.5 ounces each) black beans, rinsed and drained

I can (28 ounces) crushed tomatoes, preferably in puree (see Juice vs. Puree, page 175)

¼ cup tomato paste (see Cooking Tip)

1½ cups low-sodium vegetable broth or water

I bay leaf

Kosher or coarse salt and freshly ground black pepper

8 cups hot cooked white or brown rice

Cooking Tip: Are you wondering, "Hey, Ms. Full-of-Advice, what should I do with the rest of the tomato paste, other than leaving it partially covered in the back of my fridge, waiting for it to get moldy so I can toss it out and feel resentful that I wasted it?" Here's what you do: Scrape the rest of the tomato paste out of the can, put it into a small sandwich-size zipper-top plastic bag, flatten it out to fill the bag, write "Tomato Paste" and the date on it, and throw it in the freezer. The next time you need an annoyingly small amount of tomato paste, pull it out, and break off a piece that's about the size of one tablespoon or whatever amount the recipe calls for (don't fret about being exact; tomato paste isn't one of those ingredients you need to measure perfectly, like baking powder or something). And remember, if you don't have tomato paste, you can also use ketchup.

Non-Vegetarian Note: A handful of crumbled sautéed bacon is a wonderful addition and you could easily use chicken broth instead of vegetable broth.

There's more than one way to top a bowl of rice and beans.

FOR SERVING (OPTIONAL)

Grated cheddar cheese

Lime wedges

Sliced scallions, both white and green parts

Chopped fresh cilantro

Diced avocado

Diced tomato

Sour cream

Hot sauce

1. Heat the olive oil in a large pot over medium heat. Add the onions and cook until translucent and tender, about 5 minutes. Add the garlic, carrots, and red bell pepper, and cook until you can smell the garlic, and the carrots and bell pepper start to become tender, about 2 minutes. Add the oregano, cumin, and chipotle puree or chili powder, if using, and stir until everything becomes very fragrant, about 1 minute.

2. Add the black beans, crushed tomatoes, tomato paste, vegetable broth or water, and bay leaf. Season with salt and black pepper to taste. Let the beans simmer, uncovered, for 20 minutes. Taste to see what seasonings you want to add. Remove and discard the bay leaf.

3. Serve the beans over hot cooked rice, with grated cheese and a squeeze of lime, some scallions, cilantro, sour cream, and hot sauce, if desired.

Make Ahead: As mentioned, the beans are even better made a day or two ahead of time. As the beans sit in the fridge, they will thicken. When you reheat them, or a portion of them, you may want to add more broth or water to loosen them up.

What the Kids Can Do: They can drain and rinse the beans, add the ingredients to the pot if they are old enough to respect the hot stove, and choose garnishes to top their own bowls of beans.

CHEDDAR, TOMATO, OLIVE + FETA

MONTEREY, CHEDDAR, PEPPERS + ONION

MONTEREY

CHEDDAR, BROCCOLI + PEPPER

MONTEREY + ASPARAGUS

MONTEREY, CHEDDAR, SQUASH + TOMATO

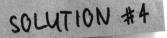

The Basic Quesadilla
(and Its Infinite Variations)

Makes 4 quesadillas
A Fork in the Road Recipe

Even really finicky kids seem to love quesadillas. It's just hard *not* to like melted cheese between two carbs. Cooking the first batch of tortillas on their own before you fill the quesadillas saves you the skilled chore of flipping them, which can result in a quesadilla piñata, meaning the filling flies out all over the place. Not fun. Make sure to really chop up any ingredients you use for filling so that they stay put inside the quesadilla.

If it's grill weather, quesadillas are luscious made that way, with their enticing grill marks on each side. But under the broiler is great, too—just don't choose this minute to tackle that pile of bills or reorganize your spice drawer. I have often been reminded that quesadillas are in the oven by the too–late smell of burning tortillas.

A salad or some steamed broccoli or some cut up veggies is all you need to make a favorite Mexican restaurant appetizer into a weeknight dinner at home. Speaking of which, quesadillas make great appetizers.

Another perfect opportunity to use up vegetable odds and ends.

FOR THE QUESADILLAS

8 medium-size (8-inch) flour tortillas
(see Tortilla vs Tortilla, page 199)

2 cups (8 ounces) shredded cheese, such as cheddar, a Mexican
blend, Monterey Jack, or a combination of any of these

FOR THE FILLINGS

See the Fork in the Road box, facing page

FOR SERVING (OPTIONAL)

Salsa

Sour cream

Guacamole (see page 54)

Chopped fresh cilantro (see Nobody's Neutral on Cilantro,
page 185)

If you're using the broiler

1. Preheat the broiler.

2. Place 4 tortillas under the broiler, right on the rack, and keep checking them until they turn golden brown on top, 2 to 3 minutes. A dark brown bubble here or there is fine. Remove the tortillas and place them uncooked side up on a work surface. Evenly sprinkle ½ cup of the cheese over each of the 4 tortillas.

3. ━━◀ You can either continue with Step 4 or top the cheese, if desired, with whatever filling your gang likes, either alone or in combination (see the facing page).

4. Place the 4 uncooked tortillas on top of the filling. Carefully transfer the tortillas to a baking sheet and place it under the broiler. Broil the quesadillas until the cheese is melted and the top tortillas are golden brown, about 3 minutes. Let the quesadillas sit for a minute before you slice each into 6 wedges and serve them with salsa, sour cream, guacamole, and/or cilantro, if desired.

What the Kids Can Do:
If you give each kid the first tortilla on a plate, with the fillings laid out for them to choose from, they can create their own quesadilla masterpiece, then you can finish it off under the broiler or on the grill. Remember, if you are grilling the quesadillas, you'll give your kid an uncooked tortilla to top, since it will go directly on the grill. If you are using the broiler, give your kid an already broiled tortilla, cooked side down to top, since it will go under the boiler with an uncooked tortilla on top.

Non-Vegetarian Note:
Once again I feel compelled to mention that while this recipe is situated in the vegetarian chapter, you may certainly choose to make a nonveggie version by including a handful of shredded cooked chicken or beef, some thinly slivered ham, or some coarsely chopped cooked shrimp.

If you're using a grill

1. Preheat the grill to medium.

2. Place 4 tortillas on the grill, right on the grill grate, and watch them carefully until they turn golden brown on the underside, 1 to 2 minutes. A dark brown bubble here or there is fine. Remove the tortillas and set them aside. Place the 4 uncooked tortillas on a flat surface. Evenly sprinkle ½ cup of the cheese over each of the 4 tortillas.

3. ━━━ You can either continue with Step 4 or top the cheese with whatever filling or fillings you like.

4. Place the 4 cooked tortillas on top of the filling, uncooked side down. Carefully transfer the tortillas back to the grill and grill the quesadillas until the cheese is melted and the bottom tortillas are golden brown, 2 to 3 minutes. Let the quesadillas sit for a minute before you slice each into 6 wedges and serve them with salsa, sour cream, guacamole, and/or cilantro, if desired.

━━━ Fork in the Road

This a perfect fork in the road dish because your kids can opt for the simplest of quesadillas while you go to town and create your own black bean/scallion/chopped fresh cilantro/asparagus/hearts of palm/feta cheese work of art. The list of options is but a start.

You'll want between ¼ and ½ cup total of the filling ingredients per quesadilla; use one or any combination of the following:

Chopped olives

Chopped cooked broccoli or asparagus

Thinly sliced zucchini or yellow squash

Rinsed and drained canned beans, such as black beans or kidney beans, lightly mashed if desired

Chopped tomatoes

Chopped artichoke hearts

Cooked chopped or sliced onions

Sliced roasted or sautéed bell peppers

Thinly sliced scallions

The fork is just for show — this is finger food all the way.

If you want to serve this on a board or platter, a springform pan makes it easier.

Mexican Tortilla Casserole

Serves 4 to 6
Vegetarian

Essentially a lasagna with tortillas standing in for noodles, this is one of those dishes that can miraculously be on the table in short order, made from things you most likely have in your pantry and fridge. If you don't like, or you don't have, one of the ingredients, skip it. Or, if you have something else that you think might be appealing all layered in (like slivered bell peppers to sauté with the onions, kale, chopped cooked broccoli—whatever the people in your home will eat), then fling it on in.

Nonstick cooking spray

I tablespoon olive, vegetable, or canola oil

I onion, chopped

I teaspoon ground cumin

I½ teaspoons chili powder

I teaspoon minced garlic

I can (14 ounces) chopped tomatoes, drained, with ⅓ cup juice reserved

¼ cup tomato paste (see Cooking Tip, page 196)

2 cans (15.5 ounces each) white, black, or kidney beans (or a mixture of any two), rinsed and drained

Kosher or coarse salt and freshly ground black pepper

I can (15 ounces) sweet corn kernels, drained, or I½ cups frozen corn, thawed

3 cups coarsely chopped spinach

4 medium-size (8-inch) flour tortillas

2 cups (8 ounces) shredded Monterey Jack or cheddar cheese

Chopped fresh cilantro (optional; see Nobody's Neutral on Cilantro, page 185), for garnish

Sour cream (optional), for serving

Salsa (optional), for serving

This is one of those lifesaving blueprint recipes you can go to on rushed weekday evenings.

Make Ahead: This can be assembled up to a day ahead of time, then covered and refrigerated. Bake before serving. It can also be baked, then refrigerated, and reheated in a 350°F oven for 20 minutes until warm.

1. Preheat the oven to 400°F. Spray a 9-inch round cake pan, springform pan, or baking dish with nonstick cooking spray.

2. Heat the oil in a large skillet over medium heat. Add the onion, cumin, chili powder, and garlic and cook until you can smell the spices and the onion is softened, about 3 minutes. Stir in the tomatoes with the 1/3 cup of reserved juice and the tomato paste, then stir in the beans. Season with salt and pepper to taste. Let the bean mixture simmer until everything is hot, about 3 minutes. Add the corn and spinach and stir until the spinach has wilted and everything is well blended and hot, about 3 minutes. Taste for seasonings, adding more salt and/or pepper as necessary.

3. Place 1 tortilla in the prepared cake pan. Spread one fourth of the bean and vegetable mixture evenly over the tortilla, then sprinkle 1/2 cup of the shredded cheese evenly over the top. Repeat with 3 more layers, ending with the last quarter of the bean mixture and then the last 1/2 cup of shredded cheese.

4. Bake the tortilla casserole until it is hot throughout and the top is lightly browned, about 20 minutes. Let the casserole sit for about 5 minutes, then cut it into wedges using a sharp knife and serve it with a spatula or better yet a pie server. Sprinkle the top with cilantro, if desired, and serve with sour cream and/or salsa on the side, if you like.

BAGGED PREWASHED SPINACH—BIG FAN

Prewashed baby spinach is a fantastic time-saver, since bunches of regular spinach can be extremely dirty, and rinsing those bunches of spinach is right up there with scrubbing the shower grout in terms of joyless tasks. With that said, if you get fresh spinach from a farmers' market or a garden, clearly it's worth the effort to clean it.

A nice wedge of what is basically Mexican lasagna.

Cooking Tip: You can make the tortilla casserole a day ahead of time, cover it with plastic wrap or aluminum foil, and put it in the fridge overnight; just take it out and let it sit at room temperature for about 20 minutes while the oven preheats to 400°F. Bake the casserole uncovered. You can also reheat the cooked casserole at 350°F for 15 to 20 minutes, until warm.

What the Kids Can Do: They can layer the tortillas, bean mixture, and cheese. Encourage them to distribute the filling evenly across each tortilla and portion everything equally over all four layers.

Non-Vegetarian Note: I'm sorry to be mentioning the "M" word yet again in the vegetarian chapter, but if you wanted to add some shredded cooked chicken or beef or chopped cooked shrimp to this, it would be delicious. Another brilliant add-in is leftover taco meat, either beef or turkey, from the Taco Night recipe (page 114). Use about two cups of any of these options, and when you make the bean mixture use only one can of beans instead of two. Then, when you are spreading the beans over the tortillas, you'll use a smaller amount of the bean mixture for each layer, followed by a half cup or so of any of the other aforementioned additions over each layer, and then the cheese.

Honey Ginger Soy Chicken (page 208) with loads of sauce and mashed potatoes.

Chapter 13

Potluck

There are other three-word phrases as pretty as "one-pot dish" ("baby–sitting niece," "massage gift card," "I'll walk Cooper," and "my homework's done" are a few that pop into mind), but at dinnertime there's just a certain ring to "one-pot dish."

The idea behind this one-pot/potluck arena is a slight mishmash of things, all with the common denominator that these are dishes you can put on the table and, with the possible addition of a salad, dinner is done. And all of them are also designed to be greeted with enthusiasm, and possibly elation, at a big gathering.

These dishes are also all: portable, hardy, comforting, homey, and beautifully reheatable.

The arroz con pollo is a flavorful (but not intimidating) chicken and rice medley cooked on the stovetop,

THE DILEMMA

How'd I get stuck with making the main dish?

with chunks of turkey sausage to liven things up. Turkey chili and beef stew are cold-weather (and imminently freezable) panaceas you will turn to again and again, and the Pulled Pork makes a lot of people euphoric. Finally, there's a roast chicken, burnished with a honey ginger soy glaze.

There are plenty of other dishes that could have landed in this chapter; for a full list see page 337. A few that are worth singling out for special recognition are the Mexican Tortilla Casserole (page 203), Cheesy Chicken Enchiladas (page 164), Macaroni and Cheese (page 169), Moist Make-Ahead Parmesan Turkey Meat Loaf (page 157), One-Skillet Cheesy Beef and Macaroni (page 155), Lasagna with Turkey Meat Sauce (page 160), and the soups, the chicken noodle soup (page 70) and Lentil, Tomato, and Rice Soup (page 68) in particular.

Honey Ginger Soy Chicken

Serves 6 to 8

That Ina Garten, she is one damn fine cook. Also known as the Barefoot Contessa, she has written more than half a dozen cookbooks, each one brimming with recipes you want to cook over and over and over again. I remember getting her first book and sticking Post-its on the recipes I liked best, and soon realizing this was a squandering of Post-its.

This is an unabashed adaptation of Ina Garten's famous Indonesian chicken. My kids and my husband adore this dish, as does anyone else I've ever served it to. It's sweet and salty and get its punch from the garlic and ginger. It's got a super-short ingredient list; it can marinate for one day or two; it's great hot; it's good cold; it's great for white meat; it's great for dark. In short, it's the kind of dish we are all looking for.

This chicken is in that category of deliciously saucy dishes that you'll want to serve over or near a heaping pile of rice, Mashed Potatoes (page 253), quinoa, or what have you.

I cup honey, at room temperature

¾ cup low-sodium soy sauce

½ cup very finely minced or grated peeled fresh ginger
(from about one thick 4-inch piece)

¼ cup minced garlic (8 to 12 cloves)

2 chickens (3 to 3½ pounds each), trimmed of excess fat and
cut into 8 pieces each

5 scallions, trimmed and cut into I inch pieces, from the white to
about halfway up the green (optional)

1. Place the honey, soy sauce, ginger, and garlic in a small bowl and whisk until well blended.

2. Arrange the chicken in a single layer in a large shallow baking pan (lined with aluminum foil, if you wish), skin

Cooking Tip: There is enough garlic and ginger here to warrant taking out your food processor, regular or mini size. Whirl up the ginger and the garlic together to mince them.

Make Ahead: This dish is make ahead by nature, as the chicken needs to marinate for a day or so. It makes great leftovers. If you are cooking the chicken ahead of time and refrigerating it, scrape off any fat that has accumulated on the surface of the sauce before serving or reheating.

What the Kids Can Do: Let the kids whisk together the sauce and pour it over the chicken.

side down. Add the scallions, if using, evenly scattering them over the chicken. Pour the honey ginger sauce on top and stir to mix so the marinade coats the chicken completely. Cover the pan tightly with aluminum foil. Let the chicken marinate overnight in the refrigerator.

3. Preheat the oven to 350°F.

4. Bake the chicken in the covered baking pan for 30 minutes. Uncover the pan, turn the chicken skin side up, and increase the oven temperature to 375°F. Continue baking the chicken until the juices run clear when you cut into a piece and the sauce is a rich, dark brown, 30 to 40 minutes longer. Serve the chicken with the pan sauce.

Lining the pan with foil makes cleanup fairly painless.

Simplest Beef Stew

Serves 6, but doubles or triples easily;
just use a bigger pot

A big pot of stew in the fridge is like having the most delicious secret in the world. You can walk around smiling a little Mona Lisa smile and humming, knowing that your delicious dinner is getting even better while you go about your business, and then come home and just whip it out and heat it on the stove. It's not a pretty dish, not a "look at me!" kind of dish. That's okay. It's stew.

Simple and unfussy, the stew does take a couple of hours of simmering, but there is very little hands-on work involved. And, you will have the added perk of a home that smells like some serious dinner is cooking. Once when I was making it, I went out in the hallway to take out the trash. A friendly neighbor was standing down the hall, a glass of wine in her hand, just hanging out outside her apartment. "My husband told me I had to come check out what smelled so wonderful, coming from down the hall," she said, with no evidence of irritation whatsoever. I am not sure I would have been as amenable to such a suggestion from my husband. I might have suggested that my husband spend as much time in the hall inhaling the aroma of our neighbors' dinner as he wished while I slid the deadbolt into place behind him.

Double this recipe. Triple it. Freeze half of the stew. Bring it to new neighbors, to parents of new babies, to friends who have had a tough week. Serve it with Mashed Potatoes (page 253), Roasted Potatoes (page 250), or hot, lightly buttered egg noodles.

Few dishes transform a handful of humble ingredients like a stew.

I tablespoon olive oil

¼ cup chopped bacon or pancetta (see Pancetta, below)

2 pounds boneless beef chuck, brisket, or round, cut into I-inch cubes

Kosher or coarse salt and freshly ground black pepper to taste

I large onion, chopped

2 carrots, peeled and diced

2 ribs celery, diced

I teaspoon minced garlic

I teaspoon dried thyme, or 2 teaspoons chopped fresh thyme leaves

½ cup red wine, preferably a robust one

1½ cups low-sodium beef broth, or more as needed

Chopped fresh Italian (flat-leaf) parsley (optional), for garnish

1. Heat the olive oil in a large Dutch oven or pot over medium heat, then add the bacon or pancetta, and cook, stirring occasionally, until it is browned and crisp, about 5 minutes. Using a slotted spoon, transfer it to a large plate, leaving the remaining fat in the pot.

2. Season the beef with salt and pepper to taste, increase the heat to medium-high, and add half of the meat (see the Cooking Tip), turning it so that it browns on all sides, about 5 minutes. Using the same slotted spoon, transfer the browned meat to the plate with the bacon and repeat with the remaining meat.

3. Pour off all but 1 tablespoon of fat from the pot. Reduce the heat to medium and add the onion, carrots, celery, garlic, and if you are using dried thyme, add it as well. Cook, stirring often, until the vegetables soften, about 3 minutes. Add the wine to the pot and let it simmer while you stir to scrape up the little browned bits stuck to the bottom of the pot. Add the broth and beef, bacon, and any accumulated juices. Let come to a simmer, then reduce the heat to medium-low and cover the pot. Simmer gently for about 2 hours, adding more broth or water if the stew is getting too dry.

4. Add the fresh thyme, if using, just as the meat becomes tender to your liking. You can serve the stew right away or refrigerate it and serve it a day or two later. If you wish, sprinkle parsley on top of the stew before serving.

Cooking Tip: Cooking the meat in two batches avoids crowding the beef in the pot, which would keep it from browning nicely; put too much in and the meat will just steam. Don't worry if you see a pink spot here or there—the meat will be quite thoroughly cooked during the two hour braising time.

Make Ahead: Like all stews this one is better made in advance, then reheated the next day or a few days later. You can also freeze it in a well-sealed container or freezer-proof zipper-top bag for up to four months. Thaw the stew in the refrigerator, and reheat it gently.

What the Kids Can Do: Kids can help measure and add things to the stew pot, and they can stir if they are old enough to be near the stove.

PANCETTA

Pancetta is a kind of Italian bacon (although it can also be made in other countries). It is seasoned with salt and pepper and often some herbs and spices, and unlike bacon, it isn't smoked, just cured for several months. Pancetta often comes sliced in a spiral form.

There's a certain built-in entertainment in watching a little kid grapple with a big sandwich.

Pulled Pork

Serves a big honking crowd of like 10 to 12 people (but it's the kind of food you have to make in quantity)

I f you are looking for a fast recipe, move along, my friend. This recipe requires at least four hours (Four! Crazy, no?) of cooking time, because that is simply what it takes to make a big piece of pork butt turn into a pile of steaming, aromatic, zesty, mouthwatering, unctuous, barbecue sauce–soaked, pulled pork, waiting to be heaped on a big roll and made into the best sandwich ever, or just eaten with a fork. Don't even bother to look at the meat for three hours; there is no point. It is slowly cooking, doing its thing, and you will only be disturbing it for absolutely no reason, since it will be nowhere near done, and there's not a thing you can do to hasten the process. Many other pulled pork recipes call for even longer cooking times than this one, but we have lives to lead.

The good news is that the recipe is amazingly simple, requiring nothing but time; no skill, no fussing, just time. If you have barbecue sauce already made, or use bottled sauce, it's even simpler. Either way, if you prefer your pulled pork with a bit more tanginess than sweetness you may want to add a splash of cider vinegar to the sauced pork mixture.

The reason this recipe makes so much is because you can't really get the kind of gently, richly braised shredded meat you want with a smaller cut. It takes a large piece of meat to create this kind of texture, and frankly once you are braising something for practically half a day you will want to make sure you have lots of leftovers to look forward to. Also, it's such a fun dish, such a jolly food, and so many people are crazy for it that it really seems like the kind of dish to make when you are getting together with friends. And you get to let your kids say "pork butt," which is a gift that keeps on giving.

Having a party is an excellent reason to make pulled pork. Not coincidentally, making pulled pork is a fabulous reason to have a party.

I bone-in pork butt (5 to 6 pounds)

Kosher or coarse salt and freshly ground black pepper

About 3 cups low-sodium chicken or beef broth

I tablespoon liquid smoke

4 cups barbecue sauce, either homemade (page 108) or store-bought

About ½ cup cider vinegar, or more to taste (optional, but recommended)

Sliced rolls (optional), soft or toasted for serving

Coleslaw and pickles (optional), for serving

1. Preheat the oven to 350°F.

2. Place the pork butt in a large pot with a lid and season it with salt and pepper to taste. Pour the broth around the pork until it comes about one quarter of the way up the sides of the meat. Add the liquid smoke to the broth. Cover the pot and put it in the oven.

3. The meat is done when it is falling apart, 3½ to 5 hours; use a fork to pull at the pork, and it will really start to come apart. The internal temperature will register 190° to 200°F on an instant-read thermometer inserted into the pork but not so that it touches the bone. Remove the pork butt from the oven. Let it sit for 15 to 20 minutes in the pot (see Carryover Cooking on page 136). Remove the pork from the pot and discard the cooking liquid. Cut the fatty parts off the meat, then use 2 forks to pull the meat apart, shredding it into small pieces. Place the shredded meat in a large bowl.

4. Warm the barbecue sauce in a small pot over medium heat. Mix the shredded meat well with the barbecue sauce. Taste, and if you think the pork could use a bit more zing, add cider vinegar to taste. You will also probably want to season the pork with additional salt and pepper.

5. Pile the pulled pork on rolls or just serve it with a big spoon, with coleslaw and pickles, if desired.

Cooking Tip: You can dress the entire pile of shredded pork with all of the barbecue sauce, or you can set some of the meat aside and use it in dishes like the Mexican Tortilla Casserole (page 203), Quesadillas (page 199) or instead of the chicken in Cheesy Chicken Enchiladas (page 164), which is amazing. Also, with or without the sauce, the pork makes a great ingredient for a wrap (see page 24).

Make Ahead: Are you kidding? By the time the pork is done I'm usually trying to stay up by watching reruns of (fill in any favorite old show here). This is make ahead and reheat nirvana. You can reheat the sauced shredded pork in a 300°F oven, covered, until it is hot, or heat it in a pot over medium-low heat, or even microwave it if you're in a hurry, but don't overdo it.

What the Kids Can Do: Add the rest of the ingredients to the pot with the pork butt and, if the pork is cool enough, pull it into shreds. If you are making sandwiches, they can heap the pulled pork on rolls.

Turkey or Chicken Chili

Serves 10 to 12

Every time I think I've made a ridiculously large amount of this chili, and my husband wonders loudly and pointedly if we're having a big crowd for dinner, we surprise ourselves by eating it all. Not in one sitting, unless we are in fact having a big crowd for dinner, but over the course of several pleasurable days.

This falls into the blissful, classic category of soups and stews that are even better after a few days. It also falls into the category of meals that make you glad to have in the fridge on a weeknight, especially when work or soccer practice means you're walking in the door at 6:00 P.M.

Serve the chili with rice, of course, and you don't even have to bother with salad or a vegetable unless you're feeling frisky. This chili's got the veggies built right in.

In some parts of the world, and especially the good old U.S. of A., the definition of chili is the subject of heated discourse. This version could anger the *con carne* sect, especially those from Texas. There are copious amounts of beans in this chili, and the meat is turkey, not beef. I make no claims to chili authenticity and will just humbly submit the words of chili expert Jane Butel: "Whenever I meet someone who does not consider chili a favorite dish, then I've usually found someone who has never tasted good chili."

FOR THE CHILI

2 tablespoons olive oil

2 onions, chopped

2 large red bell peppers, stemmed, seeded, and chopped

3 cloves garlic, minced

I tablespoon dried oregano

I teaspoon dried basil

I tablespoon chili powder

2 teaspoons ground cumin

3 pounds ground turkey or chicken and/or fresh turkey sausage removed from the casing (see Cooking Tip)

I teaspoon kosher or coarse salt, or more to taste

½ teaspoon freshly ground black pepper, or more to taste

3 cans (28 ounces each) crushed tomatoes

2 teaspoons pureed chipotle chiles in adobo sauce (optional)

3 cans (about 15.5 ounces each) cannellini, kidney, or black beans, or a mixture of 2 or 3 kinds of beans, rinsed and drained

2 to 3 tablespoons minced fresh dill or parsley (optional)

Hot cooked rice, for serving

FOR SERVING, PICK AND CHOOSE

Sour cream • Shredded cheese, such as cheddar or a Mexican cheese blend • Diced avocados, or store-bought or homemade guacamole (see page 54) • Minced scallions • Chopped fresh tomatoes • Fresh lime wedges

1. Heat the olive oil in a large deep pot over medium-high heat. Add the onions, bell peppers and cook until softened, 4 minutes. Add the garlic, oregano, basil, chili powder, and cumin and cook for 2 minutes more.

2. Add the turkey, chicken, sausage, or whatever combination you are using, and the salt and black pepper, stirring to coat well with all of the spices. Cook, stirring until the meat loses its pinkness, about 6 minutes, then add the tomatoes, chipotles, if using, and the beans. Reduce the heat to medium and cook, stirring occasionally until the mixture tastes like chili, 25 to 30 minutes. Stir in the dill or parsley, if using, and add more salt and/or pepper as necessary.

3. Serve the chili with hot rice and any toppings you like.

Cooking Tip: I like to use a combination of half ground turkey and half turkey sausage (and a mixture of hot and sweet sausage is great). For the ground turkey or chicken, don't go for ultralean or white meat; you'll be happier with the moistness of the darker meat. You can also use finely chopped skinless, boneless chicken thighs.

Make Ahead: This does make a big batch of chili, but it will keep for up to five days in the fridge. And do yourself a favor: Pack a quart of this in a freezer-safe container or zipper-top plastic bag, and another dinner ready for the defrosting. It can be frozen for up to four months.

What the Kids Can Do: There is quite a bit of chopping and measuring and stirring involved when making this chili. If your kids are young, making them in charge of putting various toppings in bowls is a nice task to assign.

Plunk this pretty dish right onto the table to serve.

One-Pot Arroz con Pollo

Serves 10

An all-in-one dish is a thing of beauty and a gift in the clean up arena. Arroz con pollo is no exception. Sometimes the dish is made with whole pieces of chicken, with bone in and skin on, but this version is faster and also more kid-friendly; it's ready to eat without having to navigate skin and bones in the midst of a casserole. Arroz con pollo is one of those dishes where the more flavorful dark thigh chicken meat stays juicier and makes the whole dish taste richer. Luckily in small boneless chunks it won't turn off kids who might think of themselves as white meat kids.

This elicited one of my favorite kid comments: Grant, one of the most polite children on the planet, went home and told his mother all about it. "It had peas and chicken and rice and it was outstanding," he said. "And she really made it. . . . I didn't even see any take-out containers!"

This dish is one of those that functions as both a meal and a temporary centerpiece. Serve it right at the table, because as you lift the lid off the pan, the wonderful aromas billow out almost like those swirls of fragrance that you see in cartoons, the kind that you see transporting Tom and Jerry by the nostrils, gently floating them to the table. And it's really gorgeous. This is a knockout company dish.

Once you play around with this kind of sauté-then-braise technique you will realize how flexible this cooking method is and how much fun you can have with different combos, creating the very definition of one-pot comfort food (see also One-Skillet Cheesy Beef and Macaroni on page 155). Not to mention appreciating how useful it is for using up things like half a head of broccoli and stretching a few chicken breasts into a meal. See Skillet Meals, this page.

SKILLET MEALS

Basically, first you sauté some member of the onion family (shallots, leeks, scallions, garlic) in oil or butter, then stir in either rice or small pasta, and maybe some other ingredients like chopped carrots or peppers and seasonings. Then you add liquid (about two and a half times the amount of starch you use), cover the pot, and let everything start to simmer. Then you can add other things like shrimp, chicken, or meat (pre-sautéed or not), beans, other vegetables, other seasonings, thinking about the timing so they will be done when the rice is done. Toward the end you can add ingredients with short cooking times, like peas or sliced zucchini, and at the very end ingredients like fresh herbs or tomatoes.

Once you've made a few dishes this way you'll be looking at every leftover in your fridge as a candidate for your next one-pot meal. It's like having your own little reality show, right in your kitchen: "How Can I Make Dinner with What's in My Fridge?"

3 pounds skinless, boneless chicken thighs and breasts, preferably all thighs or a combination

Kosher or coarse salt and freshly ground black pepper

Nonstick cooking spray

3 tablespoons olive oil

I tablespoon unsalted butter

I cup finely chopped onion

I large shallot, finely chopped

2 large carrots, chopped

I red bell pepper, stemmed, seeded, and chopped

I clove garlic, finely minced

1½ cups short- or medium-grain rice

I cooked turkey or pork kielbasa (14 to 16 ounces), diced (see Notes)

I box or can diced tomatoes (28 ounces), with their juice

4 cups low-sodium chicken broth

2 bay leaves

½ teaspoon sweet paprika or smoked paprika

¼ teaspoon saffron threads (see An Ode to Saffron, facing page)

I cup frozen peas (no need to thaw)

I cup sliced roasted red peppers, store-bought or homemade (see Roasting Peppers, page 31), or piquillo peppers (optional, see Notes)

¼ cup chopped fresh Italian (flat-leaf) parsley (optional)

1. Cut the chicken into chunks about 2 by 2 inches. Season the chicken with salt and pepper to taste.

2. Spray a very large skillet with a lid with nonstick cooking spray and heat 1 tablespoon of the olive oil over medium-high heat. Add as much chicken as will fit in the pan without crowding. Cook the chicken until it is golden brown on the bottom, 3 to 4 minutes (see Cooking Tip). Turn the chicken over and cook until the other side is browned, 3 to 4 minutes longer; the chicken will still be pink inside. Transfer the chicken to a large plate. Repeat until all of the chicken is browned, adding another tablespoon of olive oil as needed. Don't worry if the bottom of the skillet gets little bits of the chicken stuck to it; but if

Cooking Tip: When you are searing chicken thighs, you'll probably want to go for the full four minutes on each side, and if you use breasts, three minutes on each side. Do not move the pieces around for at least 3 minutes once you put them in the pan; that's how they'll brown nicely, and it also prevents them from sticking to the pan.

Make Ahead: You can make the arroz con pollo ahead of time and reheat it, covered, in a preheated 350°F oven until warm or hot throughout, about twenty minutes. You may want to drizzle a bit more chicken broth on top before reheating the casserole so that it stays moist.

If you are planning to bring this to a potluck of some sort, it does stay nice and warm for a while and does not have to be served piping hot by any means. If you do know that you are going to reheat it at your destination, save the last step of adding the peas and the peppers until the dish is at the point where everything is hot again, then add those final ingredients.

the skillet starts to get too dark lower the heat a bit. Pour off the fat and pan juices from each batch of chicken into a heatproof bowl or pitcher.

3. Heat the remaining tablespoon of olive oil and the butter in the skillet over medium heat. Add the onion, shallot, carrots, and bell pepper and cook until the vegetables start to become tender, 3 to 4 minutes. Add the garlic and cook, stirring until you can really smell the garlic, about 1 minute. Add the rice and the kielbasa and stir until the rice starts to turn slightly translucent and is nicely coated with all of the vegetables and the fat, about 3 minutes. Add the tomatoes with their juice and the chicken broth, bay leaves, paprika, and saffron. Stir well. Cover the skillet, increase the heat to medium-high, let the liquid come to a simmer, then reduce the heat to medium, and let simmer until the rice has begun to absorb the liquid, about 8 minutes.

4. Arrange the chicken pieces on top of the rice and drizzle any juices that have accumulated on the plate over the chicken. Pour off any fat that has separated from the reserved pan juices, and add the darker liquid from the bottom of the bowl or pitcher to the skillet. Cover the skillet again and let simmer gently until the chicken is cooked through, the rice is tender, and most of the liquid has been absorbed, 12 to 15 minutes.

5. Remove the lid, sprinkle the peas on top, and drape the roasted peppers, if using, attractively over the top. Cover the skillet and cook until the peas and peppers are heated through, about 2 minutes. Sprinkle the parsley on top, if desired. Serve portions of the chicken with the rice and vegetables.

Notes: You can buy packaged turkey and pork kielbasa that's already cooked. Hillshire Farm's turkey variety or Butterball's Polska Turkey Dinner Sausage are readily available brands.

Piquillo peppers are pimiento-type peppers. They are sweet and flavorful, not hot. Jars of the roasted peppers can be purchased at many supermarkets and specialty food stores.

What the Kids Can Do:

Several of the ingredients in this dish are soft enough for young people to help cut them up, depending on their level of comfort with a knife: roasted peppers, kielbasa, parsley. There is plenty of measuring to do, and kids can always add things to the skillet if you're okay with them being near the hot stove. Once you have the basic technique under your belt and start to invent your own meals in a skillet (see the Skillet Meals on page 219), let your kids examine the contents of the fridge or wander around a farmers' market plotting their next one-dish creation.

AN ODE TO SAFFRON

The starring ingredient in One-Pot Arroz con Pollo is actually the smallest in terms of the amount used: saffron. Its flavor is almost impossible to put into words, but there is something rich and amazing about the taste that is absolutely irreplaceable. It also tints foods a beautiful golden yellow. It is the world's most expensive spice because of the crazy-difficult cultivation process, having to do with harvesting the stigmas of crocuses, but we won't go into that here. A little saffron does go a long way, and it makes dishes like paella, risotto, and this chicken and rice recipe very, very special.

Simplest Chicken or Shrimp Kebabs (page 237)

Chapter 14

Mixed Company Dinners

Well, you've gone and done it, you've invited people over to your place for a meal. And not just people, an entire family, maybe even more than one family, and now comes the $64 million question: What are you making?

By mixed company I mean a mishmash of kids and parents, by definition all with various likes and dislikes and food issues. You will definitely want to ask about any allergies and intolerances, but if you engage too deeply in conversations that include bulletins such as "Billy likes yellow peppers but not orange, and Lucinda has been really into shrimp lately, and I am trying to go easy on the carbs, and my husband hates lamb," then you are setting yourself up for hair-pulling frustration. Politely solicit the basic facts regarding actual concerns and make sure you have a few side dishes so everyone can fill a plate without making your menu planning for the evening an unsolvable Rubik's Cube.

Menu planning makes some people very happy and makes other people wish they were doing something more fun, like having a colonoscopy. If you love it then I hope you'll find lots to mix and match in this book, and of course, you'll concoct menus from recipes from hither and yon. If the word *menu* has just caused a trickle of cold sweat to run down your back, then quickly turn to page 341 for some inspiration.

These five recipes are some of the most company-worthy main courses in the book, designed to please both adults and kids. One thing that always seems to make a multi–age group meal fun is dinner served on skewers. In this chapter you'll find two recipes for food on sticks. One is for simple chicken or shrimp kebabs, with or without marinades, and the other is for either beef or chicken (or both) teriyaki skewers; possibly the biggest winners for a festive multifamily meal. Shrimp Risotto is a one-pot wonder and so easy it will explode any lingering myths that risottos are tricky.

Two Fork in the Road recipes round out this group of one-stop shopping meals for everyone from the picky to the gourmet: plainly cooked lamb chops on a bed of lemony white beans (for those who are into lemony white beans) and a simple sautéed chicken breast, with an optional tangy piccata sauce.

Other main dishes that I go to time and time again for large crowds are: Taco Night (page 114), Shrimp Scampi (page 148), Pasta with Meatballs and Sauce (page 122), Macaroni and Cheese (page 169), Lasagna with Turkey Meat Sauce (page 160), Turkey or Chicken Chili (page 215), Soy-Ginger Flank Steak (page 120), Cheesy Chicken Enchiladas (page 164), Grilled Pizzas (page 187), One-Pot Arroz con Pollo (page 219), and Lemon Chicken (page 104). And you'll discover your own go-to recipes throughout this book and hopefully find yourself entertaining mixed company more often.

My friend Christopher Idone says this of good cooks: "They invite you to dinner, give you a good time, and that's it. And that's what entertaining has always been and will always be."

This would be a pretty dazzling holiday main course.

Lamb Chops with Lemony White Beans and Spinach

Serves 4 to 6
A Fork in the Road Recipe

Rib lamb chops are a treat. Pricey, sure, but with a distinctive flavor and that unique benefit of being a food that kids can eat with their hands without the disapproving glares of their parents. These chops are cooked very simply, the key being salt and pepper, high heat, and a short cooking time. If you want to cook just the lamb chops and forgo the whole spinach-bean thing, then you'll have perfect, plain lamb chops. They'd be great with the couscous on page 248 or the Roasted Potatoes on page 250 or the Mashed Potatoes on page 253. The Roasted Butternut Squash on page 266 would be great, too, as would roasted broccoli or cauliflower (see page 264), or Roasted Asparagus (page 262).

However, it's the bed of flavorful white beans and spinach with a hint of rosemary that makes this dish company worthy, and it's a fact that some kids may need some coaxing to try this mixture. But it's absolutely delicious, and frankly in this particular case, your kids' loss is your gain—more for you. The final seasoning of the dish is called a *gremolata*. Ignore the fancy-pants nature of the word; gremolata is simply a minced blend of parsley, garlic, and lemon zest (see Note). It's used to add a burst of fresh, bright flavor to a dish, usually at the end of cooking. It's one of those tricks of the trade that cause people to be impressed by the cook's prowess but that is so easy that you just feel quietly clever to have discovered it.

You can also use loin chops, which are less expensive and still tender and delicious.

FOR THE GREMOLATA

2 tablespoons chopped fresh Italian
  (flat-leaf) parsley

1 teaspoon very finely minced garlic
  (see Note, page 91)

1 teaspoon grated lemon zest

Kosher or coarse salt and freshly ground black pepper

FOR THE WHITE BEANS AND LAMB CHOPS

1 tablespoon extra-virgin olive oil, plus more for brushing the skillet

1 large shallot, minced

½ teaspoon finely minced garlic (see Note, page 91)

1 teaspoon minced fresh rosemary, or
  ½ teaspoon crumbled dried rosemary

2 cans (15.5 ounces each) cannellini beans, rinsed and drained

1½ cups low-sodium chicken broth

12 rib lamb chops (¾ inch thick; about 1¾ pounds total)

Kosher or coarse salt and freshly ground black pepper

6 cups fresh baby spinach leaves, rinsed but still a bit damp

1. Make the gremolata: Place the parsley, garlic, and lemon zest in a small bowl and stir to mix well. Season the gremolata with salt and pepper to taste and set it aside.

2. Prepare the white beans and lamb chops: Heat the olive oil in a medium-size skillet over medium-high heat. Add the shallot and cook until tender, about 2 minutes. Add the garlic and the rosemary and cook until you can smell the garlic and herbs, about 1 minute. Add the beans and cook, stirring well, until well combined and heated through, about 3 minutes. Add the chicken broth and bring to a simmer. Cook until the liquid is reduced and everything is well combined, about 5 minutes. Use a fork to crush up some of the beans. Keep warm.

3. ☛ Season the lamb chops on both sides with salt and pepper. You can continue with Step 4 or see the Fork in the Road suggestions for another seasoning on the facing page.

4. Brush a large heavy skillet (such as cast iron) with olive oil and place over high heat until the pan is very hot. Add the lamb chops in a single layer; you may have to cook

Cooking Tip: If you want to make the white beans and skip the chops, you will have a nice side dish for all kinds of meat and fish dishes. And it actually could be a main dish (and a vegetarian one at that; see Vegetarian Note), served in more copious amounts along with some cooked orzo or rice or quinoa or wheat berries.

Make Ahead: You can make the bean mixture ahead of time through Step 2. Reheat the bean mixture just before serving, adding the spinach and the *gremolata* once the beans are hot, just before you're ready to serve.

What the Kids Can Do: Kids can help mix together the gremolata, smush the beans (while paying attention to the hot pot), and add the spinach to the beans, if they can be near a hot stove. And they can help arrange the lamb chops over the bean mixture, using a paper towel to grab the "handles."

Vegetarian Note: For a vegetarian dish, lose the chops and swap in vegetable broth for the chicken broth.

the chops in 2 batches to avoid crowding. Sear the lamb chops for 3 minutes, without moving them, then turn them and sear them until they are done to your liking, for another 2 to 4 minutes. Alternatively you can cook the chops under the broiler, making sure it's thoroughly preheated and the chops are placed very close to the source of the heat so they sear quickly. You can use an instant-read thermometer to test for doneness; when done to rare the internal temperature will be 120° to 125°F; for medium, 140° to 150°F. Transfer the chops to a plate and let them rest for a few minutes while you finish the beans.

5. Return the beans to a simmer, then add a handful of spinach to them, continuing to add batches as each wilts into the bean mixture. Once everything is blended, turn off the heat, add the gremolata, and stir to blend well. Taste for seasoning, adding salt and pepper as necessary. Spoon the bean mixture onto a serving platter. Arrange the lamb chops attractively on top or on a separate serving dish—if you've got no-beans-for-me eaters. You can also serve everything on individual plates, arranging 2 to 3 bean-free lamb chops for some and over a portion of the beans for others.

Note: There are different versions of gremolata, which is an Italian chopped herb condiment most often made with lemon zest, garlic, and parsley. Sometimes other herbs make an appearance, such as mint, rosemary, or sage, and occasionally anchovies enter the picture. Other cuisines have versions of the same condiment, called by different names.

Fork in the Road

Sprinkle some of the lamb chops lightly with cumin when you season them with salt and pepper. Also, your Fork in the Road may come at the serving stage—there are those who may not want their chops served atop the beans.

The beans would also make a fine crostini topping (page 49).

Teriyaki Chicken and Beef Skewers

Serves 4 to 6

When I asked the cook at my kids' school what the most popular dishes were, he said, "Pizza, meat sauce, breakfast for lunch, and this," and with "this" he picked up and thudded down the most enormous container of prepared teriyaki sauce I'd ever seen. "If I put this on everything they would love it."

Turns out, teriyaki sauce isn't hard to make at all, and you can, in fact, put it on almost anything. Here's the recipe, and you have the option of using the sauce with either chicken or steak, and also try it with shrimp, salmon, or tofu.

If you are having a bunch of people over and want to offer a choice, it's nice to make half the skewers with chicken and half with beef. Cutting the meat into strips takes the same amount of time, and the platter will look bountiful. You're still only making one batch of the teriyaki sauce, so it really doesn't require any extra work.

Teriyaki anything begs for rice, and if you're feeling all "theme-y" about the whole meal, you might want to whip up a quick Japanese Restaurant Salad (page 86) to go with, and maybe the sautéed beans and sugar snap peas (see page 270), or use snow peas instead. Some steamed or roasted broccoli (see page 264) or Roasted Asparagus (page 262) would work nicely, too (plus the dressing from the Japanese Restaurant Salad also makes a nice sauce for the veggies).

This is absolutely one of my favorite go-to entertaining dishes. →

2 tablespoons finely minced peeled fresh ginger

I tablespoon finely minced garlic

⅔ cup low-sodium soy sauce, or ½ cup regular soy sauce and 2 tablespoons water

2 teaspoons canola or vegetable oil, plus oil for the baking sheet (optional)

3 tablespoons mirin (optional, see Mirin, page 86)

¼ cup firmly packed brown sugar

I teaspoon cornstarch

2 pounds chicken tenders, or 2 pounds skinless, boneless chicken breasts or thighs, cut into ½ inch–wide strips, or 2 pounds sirloin steak, cut into ½-inch slices

Nonstick cooking spray (optional)

Toasted sesame seeds (optional; see Toasting Sesame Seeds, this page)

YOU'LL ALSO NEED

Eighteen to twenty 8-inch wooden or metal skewers

TOASTING SESAME SEEDS

Heat a small skillet over medium heat (do not use a nonstick skillet for this). Add the sesame seeds and cook, stirring frequently, until they are aromatic and golden in color, I to 2 minutes. Watch the sesame seeds carefully and transfer them from the skillet to a heat-proof bowl the minute they start to color; they can burn very quickly.

1. Place the ginger, garlic, soy sauce, oil, mirin, if using, brown sugar, and cornstarch in a small bowl or in a small container with a lid and stir well or shake to combine.

2. Pour the teriyaki marinade into a 1-quart heavy-duty zipper-top plastic bag or a larger plastic container with a lid. Add the chicken or steak and mix to coat well. Seal the bag or container and let the chicken or steak marinate in the refrigerator for 8 to 24 hours (the longer it marinates, the more pronounced the teriyaki flavor will be). You'll want to flip the baggie or toss the meat in the container a couple of times during the marinating process so that it marinates evenly.

3. If you are using wooden skewers, at least 30 minutes before cooking soak them in water to cover in order to prevent them from burning. Lightly oil a rimmed baking sheet or spray it with nonstick cooking spray.

4. Preheat the broiler (see Note).

5. Remove the chicken or steak from the marinade, setting aside the marinade. Skewer 1 or 2 pieces of chicken or steak on each skewer lengthwise, threading them so they are on securely. Place the skewers on the prepared baking sheet and broil until the teriyaki sauce turns a nice burnished color and the chicken is cooked through or the meat is cooked to your liking, 2 to 4 minutes on each side for chicken, another minute or 2 for medium steak.

6. Pour the reserved marinade into a small saucepan and bring to a boil over high heat. Reduce the heat to medium and let the marinade simmer until it becomes slightly reduced and glazelike, about 4 minutes.

7. Serve the skewers on a platter sprinkled with the sesame seeds, if desired. Pass around the boiled marinade in a small pitcher or bowl for drizzling over the meat or whatever starch or veggies you are serving alongside.

Note: You can also grill these skewers on a charcoal or gas grill over high heat for 2 to 4 minues per side.

Cooking Tip: If you want to use the teriyaki marinade as a sauce on the side, all you need to do is boil it for five minutes after you've removed the chicken, fish, or meat, and it will be safe to serve over rice or whatever else you like (if you've marinated tofu, this step is unnecessary). The boiled marinade will thicken and get a nice syrupy consistency.

What the Kids Can Do: They can help make the teriyaki marinade and toss the chicken or meat with the sauce, and if they are old enough to skewer the chicken or steak, they can do that as well.

Chicken Piccata-ed or Plain

Serves 6
A Fork in the Road Recipe

This is absolutely one of my fallback dishes for entertaining families when I don't know how finicky the kids' palates are. My kids usually eat the grown-up version *but* occasionally one of them has a relapse of sorts and declares the sauce (which he loved the week prior) to be unfit for human consumption. Suddenly the simplified version of chicken breasts and rice or potatoes with no sauce is all he will touch. This is exactly the kind of flexible option that doesn't make the cook (aka you) nuts and vaguely irritated since you will make one dish, just one, that allows the blander eaters to enjoy the meal without rendering the adults bored out of their skulls.

Serve this with rice or Mashed Potatoes (page 253), or any starch you love. A simple salad and some sautéed green beans will round it out nicely.

⅔ cup all-purpose flour

Kosher or coarse salt and freshly ground black pepper

6 skinless, boneless chicken breasts, pounded thin
    (about 2 pounds total; see Note, page 235)

2 to 3 tablespoons olive oil

3 tablespoons minced shallots, or ⅓ cup minced onion

½ teaspoon minced garlic

½ cup dry white wine (optional)

1½ cups low-sodium chicken broth

2 tablespoons freshly squeezed lemon juice

2 teaspoons unsalted butter

1 tablespoon rinsed and chopped capers (see Kids and Capers?
    Salty Little Bites, this page)

Chopped fresh Italian (flat-leaf) parsley (optional), for serving

---

KIDS AND CAPERS? SALTY LITTLE BITES

Capers? Yuck! Gross! Well, maybe. Maybe not. Not to be too repetitive, but some kids are prone to liking salty things, and capers (which are salted and/or pickled little berries from the caper bush) are like little tiny bursts of briny flavor and add great flavor to the piccata sauce.

If you think your kid *might* like the sauce, but might be thrown off by the capers, leave them whole. You can pretty easily pluck out whole capers, but once they are chopped up into the sauce they are quite hard to retrieve.

PLAIN

PICCATA-ED

This is a quintessential example of a Fork in the Road dish—one dinner, two versions.

1. Place the flour, 1½ teaspoons of salt, and ½ teaspoon of pepper in a wide shallow bowl and use a fork to mix them together. Coat the chicken breasts in the flour mixture.

2. ●━━━◀ Heat a very large skillet over medium-high heat and add 1 tablespoon of the olive oil. When the oil is hot, add 2 or 3 of the chicken breasts, whatever will fit comfortably in a single layer in the skillet, and cook them until golden brown and almost cooked through, 2 to 3 minutes on each side. Transfer the browned breasts to a plate and repeat with another tablespoon of oil and 2 or 3 more breasts until all of the chicken is cooked to this stage. If you are planning to serve some of the chicken breasts without any sauce, see the Fork in the Road box below.

3. Don't clean the skillet! Add the shallots and garlic and cook over medium heat until they are tender, about 2 minutes. Add the wine, if using, and the chicken broth and stir to scrape up any browned bits on the bottom of the skillet. Simmer until the liquid reduces slightly, about 2 minutes. Add the slightly undercooked chicken (any pieces that are going to be served with the sauce) to the pan and let them simmer to finish cooking, 2 to 3 minutes.

4. Transfer the chicken to a serving platter. Add the lemon juice, butter, and capers to the skillet and stir until the butter is melted. Taste for seasoning, adding salt and pepper to taste. Pour the sauce over the chicken and sprinkle it with parsley, if desired.

Note: To pound chicken breasts place them between 2 pieces of plastic wrap and use a rolling pin or a mallet to firmly but gently pound the breasts until they are about ½-inch thick throughout.

●━━━◀ Fork in the Road

Any amount of the chicken can be removed from the pan before it gets all sauced up, so whoever wants a plain piece of chicken will get one. Cook them through for about 4 minutes on each side, and set those breasts aside on a different plate. Keep warm.

Cooking Tip #1: So, you can either pound the hell out of some chicken breasts or buy thinly sliced chicken cutlets and save yourself the whacking. Having said that, if you were to make this with regular skinless, boneless chicken breasts without pounding them thin, that's very fine, too. Just cook the thicker breasts for about 5 minutes on each side and make sure they finish cooking all the way through, with or without the sauce. It's nice to slice the chicken on the diagonal before serving since most kids won't tackle a whole chicken breast, and it just looks very appetizing in general.

Cooking Tip #2: You don't have to add the little bit of butter at the end, but it pulls the sauce together deliciously, adding flavor and silkiness. And two teaspoons of butter is negligible when divided among six people, so no stressiness there.

What the Kids Can Do: Kids can help pound the chicken breasts, which is a nice change of pace from trying to keep them from pounding each other. They can mix up the flour mixture, dredge the chicken breasts in the flour mixture, and sprinkle on the parsley, if desired. (Wash hands!)

Mix and match ingredients to create
a colorful platter.

Simplest Chicken or Shrimp Kebabs

Serves 6
A Fork in the Road Recipe

Grilling things on sticks is one of the most primal and satisfying ways to cook dinner during the summer months, and frankly during any month you can stand to be outside for the ten minutes it takes to get it done. Broiling is also an excellent option for kebabs. The reason kebabs are so quick, of course, is because the food you're cooking has been cut into small pieces. The only real consideration is whether what you're "kebabing" is the kind of food that cooks well with a fast sear. And the choices are vast. This recipe is for chicken or shrimp, but you can also use scallops, or cubes of firm fish, or turkey, or tender cuts of meat.

These kebabs don't reinvent the wheel. Cavemoms skewered hunks of primitive beasts on sticks for their children. But what I do know is that chicken on a skewer often gets eaten with fewer protests and more cheer than chicken *not* on a skewer (you'll decide if the kids are old enough to eat right off the skewer).

You can season kebabs very simply or have your way with them. At their most basic you can toss the meat and veggies with a bit of olive oil, salt and pepper, and perhaps squeeze a lemon or lime after they are cooked, or just add a few simple seasonings and you'll have something special. Of course you can keep some kebabs plain and simple and brush others with the sauce of your liking; this is a quintessential Fork in the Road recipe. If time is a factor you can just toss everything with the sauce before grilling, but marinating definitely deepens the flavor.

Make Ahead: You can marinate the shrimp or chicken and vegetables in oil or the Asian marinade for up to one day. Leftover cooked skewers can be eaten cold, at room temperature, or gently rewarmed in the oven.

What the Kids Can Do: Let the kids help thread everything on the skewers, as long as you feel comfortable with them handling pointy sticks. They will love customizing their own kebabs. Remind them to wash hands well. They can also help make the marinades.

1½ pounds skinless, boneless chicken breasts or thighs, cut into 1-inch chunks, or 1½ pounds peeled extra-large (21 to 25 count) or jumbo (16 to 20 count) raw shrimp, or a combination of shrimp and chicken

3 cups mixed vegetables, such as red onions, bell peppers, zucchini, yellow squash, and briefly cooked cauliflower or broccoli, cut into 1½-inch pieces, or whole cherry tomatoes

½ cup olive oil or a grilling sauce (see Step 1)

Kosher or coarse salt and freshly ground black pepper

Lime or lemon wedges (optional), for serving

YOU'LL ALSO NEED

Fourteen 6-inch or eight 12-inch wooden or metal skewers

1. Place the chicken and/or shrimp in a large bowl. Add the vegetables, then toss with the olive oil or one of the grilling sauces (see the Fork in the Road suggestion on the facing page). Let the chicken and/or shrimp marinate for at least 1 hour at room temperature or refrigerate it, covered, for 2 hours or up to a day, depending upon the marinade.

2. If you are using wooden skewers, at least 30 minutes before cooking soak them in water to cover in order to prevent them from burning.

3. Thread the chicken or shrimp and veggies on skewers, creating appealing patterns (the 6-inch skewers will hold about 5 pieces of chicken, alternated with veggies; for 12-inch skewers double that amount). Lightly salt and pepper the skewers.

4. Preheat the grill to medium-high.

5. Grill the kebabs 4 inches from the heat source until the chicken or shrimp is cooked through and everything has a nice grill-marked exterior, 2 to 4 minutes per side (longer for dark chicken meat, shorter for shrimp, and in the middle for white chicken meat), 4 to 8 minutes in all. Serve the kebabs hot, with wedges of citrus, if desired. If you used metal skewers they will be hot so slide the chicken or shrimp off the kids' skewers so they don't burn themselves and remind the others not to eat directly off of them.

Use quick-cooking vegetables with quick-cooking shrimp.

Asian Grilling Sauce

Makes about ½ cup

A simple marinade, this features the most basic popular Asian flavors.

- ¼ cup low-sodium soy sauce, or 3 tablespoons regular soy sauce and 1 tablespoon water
- 3 tablespoons vegetable or canola oil
- 1 teaspoon minced garlic
- 1 teaspoon minced or grated peeled fresh ginger
- A pinch of red pepper flakes

Place the soy sauce, oil, garlic, ginger, and red pepper flakes in a small bowl or plastic container and mix well.

Citrus-Basil Sauce

Makes about ⅔ cup

The chicken or shrimp should marinate in this sauce for only one to two hours or the citrus will start "cooking" the proteins with the acids in the juices—no big deal, but it alters the texture a bit.

- ¼ cup fresh orange juice
- 2 tablespoons fresh lemon or lime juice
- ½ teaspoon grated fresh orange zest (optional)
- ½ teaspoon minced garlic
- 3 tablespoons olive oil
- 1 tablespoon chopped fresh basil

Place the orange juice, lemon or lime juice, orange zest, if using, garlic, olive oil, and basil in a small bowl or plastic container and mix well.

⫘ Fork in the Road

If you want to use a combination of chicken or shrimp, and/or if you want to use a grilling sauce to marinate some of the skewers, then just divide things up into the appropriate number of different bowls and distribute the vegetables proportionately. Each grilling sauce recipe makes enough for the whole 1½ pounds of chicken or shrimp, but you can divide either of the sauce recipes in half and use it on half of the chicken or shrimp. Then, marinate the rest of the chicken or shrimp in ¼ cup of olive oil.

Best to keep white meat and dark meat on separate skewers because of different cooking times.

Shrimp Risotto

Serves 6

RISOTTO RICES

You need to use a starchy short-grain rice to make a proper risotto, and Italy produces lots of them. Arborio is the most common, from the town of Arborio in the Po Valley of Italy; it's available at many supermarkets and Italian or specialty food markets. Carnaroli, which has a slightly longer grain and even higher starch content, and Vialone Nano are two other often available desirable varieties.

No matter how many times someone will reassure you that risotto is not at all hard to make, not nearly as time-consuming or tricky as you might think, you won't believe it until you've tried it yourself. Once you've gotten the hang of risotto it becomes like a blueprint or even more like a sport of sorts. It's similar to the One-Pot Arroz con Pollo on page 219 because once you get comfortable with the fundamental concept, the possibilities are unlimited.

The basic technique is this: You sauté some type of onion in a bit of oil or butter, add the rice, and stir, and then usually put in a splash of wine (all the alcohol will cook off). Then you slowly add broth as you stir frequently—the stirring helps the starch transfer from the rice into the liquid, so everything binds together in a creamy, soulful dish. Risotto may be my favorite dish to make because it is so accommodating, and I find the stirring therapeutic, waiting for the moment when the rice gives up its starch and all the little bits and pieces start to become one. Along the way you can add other ingredients, ending with a little more butter, and often cheese, for a rich and creamy finish.

You don't want the rice to be too soft; it should be *al dente* when it comes off the stove, as it will continue to cook in its own heat. Also, make sure the rice ends up a little more liquidy than you want because it will continue to absorb the liquid even as you serve it and so it will thicken a bit more (think oatmeal). The Italians call the ideal texture *all'onda*, which means "flowing in waves" and is such a romantic and expressive description I have to mention it here, even though it's practically the only Italian phrase I know besides *al dente*.

W/SHRIMP

PLAIN

W/SHRIMP, PARM + PARSLEY

You can also leave out the shrimp for a simple plain risotto.

Shrimp is featured in this recipe, but just about any kind of seafood will work in risotto, as will diced chicken and various vegetables (see the Vegetarian Note). The saffron adds a very classic and very tantalizing element to the dish. You can also use other kinds of broth, depending on what goes with the rest of the ingredients in the risotto.

The parsley or chives added at the end are optional but they contribute a freshness and a burst of color. Sprinkle some on your own portion if the little ones won't have any of it.

6 cups low-sodium chicken broth

Generous pinch of saffron threads
(see An Ode to Saffron, page 221)

2 tablespoons olive oil

2 tablespoons (¼ stick) unsalted butter

1 large shallot, minced

1 clove garlic, minced

1½ cups Arborio rice (see Risotto Rices, page 240)

Kosher or coarse salt and freshly ground black pepper

½ cup dry white wine (optional)

1 pound uncooked large (31 to 35) shrimp, peeled and deveined

¼ cup freshly grated Parmesan cheese, plus more for serving
(optional)

2 tablespoons chopped fresh Italian (flat-leaf) parsley or chives
(optional)

1. Place the chicken broth in a medium-size saucepan and bring to a simmer over medium heat. Stir in the saffron and reduce the heat to medium-low.

2. Heat the olive oil and 1 tablespoon of the butter in a heavy medium-size saucepan over medium heat. Add the shallot and garlic and cook, stirring until just tender, about 2 minutes. Add the rice, season with salt and pepper to taste, and stir until all of the grains are well coated with the fat and the rice is turning slightly translucent, about 2 minutes.

3. Add the white wine, if using, and stir until it is almost completely absorbed into the rice, 1 to 2 minutes. Add 1 cup

What the Kids Can Do: Grate cheese, if they can watch their knuckles, and stir the risotto if they can be near a pot on the stove.

Vegetarian Note: If you use vegetable broth instead of the chicken broth and substitute coarsely chopped broccoli or asparagus pieces or peas or cooked sweet potatoes or winter squash (see Roasted Butternut Squash, page 266), or really almost any kind of vegetable for the shrimp you can make a vegetarian version of risotto. This is a great dish to have in your repertoire if you're on the prowl for more meatless dinner options.

of the hot broth and let simmer, stirring frequently, until the liquid is almost absorbed, about 3 minutes. Continue adding the broth 1 cup at a time, stirring often and letting it simmer until the liquid is almost absorbed before adding more (you can add some water to the pan with the broth if it looks like you might run low). When the rice is still fairly al dente, after 15 to 18 minutes, stir in the shrimp and another cup of the broth and cook, stirring frequently, until the shrimp are almost cooked through and the rice is al dente, about 4 minutes. Add another $1/2$ cup of liquid if the mixture is too thick (you want it to be quite loose).

4. Remove the risotto from the heat and stir in the remaining tablespoon of butter and the Parmesan, if using. Taste for seasoning, adding more salt and/or pepper as necessary. Transfer the risotto quickly to a serving bowl or individual bowls, sprinkle the parsley or chives, if using, on top, and serve immediately with more Parmesan cheese on the side, if desired.

PARMESAN CHEESE IN SEAFOOD RISOTTO (GASP)

Purists may scoff at the notion of including cheese in any dish with seafood; in Italy this has been traditionally frowned upon. You may decide for yourself. I think a little Parmesan adds a lot of flavor, and most everyone who has inhaled risotto in my house agrees. Furthermore, Ed Brown, an extremely talented New York chef, had a dish on one of his restaurant's menus that brought him much fame and repeat business: a grilled cheese sandwich crammed with lump crab meat. Over lunch it was hard to debate the pros and cons of cheese with seafood because your mouth was always pretty full. In any case, you don't have to invite the purists over for dinner.

High heat = crispy brown edges.

Chapter 15

Let's Call a Carb a Carb!

Potatoes, rice, and pasta are certainly some of the most embraceable foods for young eaters. These are the foods that even the "white food only" eaters find attractive, and there are so many ways to prepare them (not just with butter and cheese), and they are for the most part so easy to get onto the table, that they are often the happiest (read: least contentious) part of any meal. Most of the recipes in this chapter have a spate of variations. They are so malleable you can play with them all week long and use them as a canvas to introduce hints of new flavors to selective eaters.

THE DILEMMA

I need something new for my "white food only" kid.

Some other white foods—or practically white foods—found throughout the book can also serve happily as side dishes or buffet or potluck offerings. Check out the pasta chapter, of course, or the Shrimp Stir-Fried Rice (page 150) and its vegetarian variation on the same page, or even the sautéed corn on page 268, which has one foot in the vegetable camp, one in the starch camp.

So, just because your kid may be a "white food" kind of kid it doesn't mean you need to throw in the towel and ladle out plain ziti night after night. Embrace the light; walk toward it. Remember that there are lots of shades of white. Anyone who has ever tried to pick out a white paint at the paint store knows that.

Cheesy Rice with Broccoli

Serves 4 to 6 as a side dish
A Fork in the Road Recipe

Rice is the optimal sidekick to so many dishes, and a good, cheesy version of it will round out your dinner with flair on many occasions. If you are looking for a purely plain version, a picky-eater version, then you may well want to skip the broccoli and deal with the vegetable part of the meal all on its own, without tainting the otherwise satisfactory rice side dish. You can also just add vegetables to the portions of those who like them (see the Fork in the Road).

With the broccoli this dish is essentially two side dishes—a starch and a veggie—in one. If you choose to add the whole amount, you'll get a very broccoli-rich rice dish, unlike some of those bagged or boxed rice mixes that yield a lot of heavily sauced rice with microscopic bits of veggies.

I tablespoon olive oil

¼ cup chopped onion

I cup long-grain white or brown rice (see Note)

2½ cups low-sodium chicken or vegetable broth

Kosher or coarse salt

2½ cups coarsely chopped broccoli (optional)

½ cup (2 ounces) grated yellow or white cheddar cheese, preferably sharp

I tablespoon unsalted butter

Freshly ground black pepper

Chopped fresh Italian (flat-leaf) parsley (optional), for garnish

Hot sauce, such as Sriracha or Tabasco (optional), for serving

1. Heat the olive oil in a medium-size saucepan over medium heat. Add the onion and cook until tender and golden, about 4 minutes. Add the rice and stir until it is well

Cooking Tip: Sharp cheddar offers more flavor bang for the buck than mild cheddar, and when it is stirred into the pot of rice and broccoli the flavor is disseminated throughout the whole dish, so the stronger flavor won't alienate apprehensive palates. If you use mild cheddar the flavor of the cheese will be much more muffled.

What the Kids Can Do: Kids can chop the broccoli with an age-appropriate knife and carefully grate the cheddar, if they can handle the grater. They can also stir the cheese and butter into the rice and taste it for seasoning.

Vegetarian Note: Use vegetable broth and you've got yourself a vegetarian rice dish.

You can skip the broccoli if you're in the market for just cheesy rice.

mixed with the onion and is glistening and somewhat translucent, about 2 minutes.

2. Add the broth and season the rice with salt to taste. Stir well, increase the heat slightly, and let come to a simmer. Cover the pan, reduce the heat to medium-low, and let the rice simmer gently until most of the liquid has been absorbed, about 15 minutes.

3. ⟜⟞ You can continue with Step 4 or stir in the broccoli, if using, and cover the pan again. Also check the Fork in the Road suggestions for other vegetable add-ins on this page.

4. Let the rice simmer until it is cooked through and the broccoli or other vegetable choice, if using, is crisp-tender, about 5 minutes. Remove the pan from the heat and let the rice sit, covered, for about 3 minutes. Stir in the cheese and butter. Taste for seasoning, adding more salt as necessary and pepper to taste. Garnish the rice with parsley, if using, and pass the hot sauce, if desired, on the side. Serve the rice hot.

Note: If you are using brown rice, increase the amount of broth to 2¾ cups and let the rice simmer for about 30 minutes.

⟜⟞ Fork in the Road

You can use pretty much any vegetable instead of the broccoli: chopped cauliflower, or carrots, sliced asparagus, even peas (with peas you may want to reduce the amount to 2 cups), or a combination. And, if you need to keep some of the rice vegetable-free, just sauté or steam a cup or two of a vegetable you like, and stir it into some of the rice before serving, leaving the rest plain. For some heat, add a shot of Sriracha or Tabasco sauce to your portion. For a change of pace, try ½ cup feta or ¼ cup freshly grated Parmesan cheese in place of the cheddar.

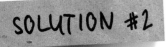
Israeli Couscous with Vegetables

Serves 4 to 6 as a side dish
A Fork in the Road Recipe

For a while I've been obsessed with Israeli couscous, also called Mediterranean couscous or couscous grande. These are tiny balls of toasted semolina pasta that when cooked plump up into toothsome, chewy, slightly less tiny balls of pasta. The brand I have been using of late is Marrakesh Express, and they describe their couscous grande as "creamy pearls of pasta," which I wish I made up, but I didn't.

Regular couscous is nice but I've never fallen in love with it, although I know there are lots of fans out there. This bigger version is great stuff. You can throw in whatever ingredients you have and add the flavors you like. As a bonus, it's kind of funny to see little kids chase the little pasta balls on their plates with a fork. If you want to be nice you could give them a spoon, but it's not as much fun to watch. Chopsticks would be hysterical.

FOR THE COUSCOUS

1 tablespoon unsalted butter

1 tablespoon olive oil

2 large shallots, minced

1½ cups Israeli couscous or couscous grande

3¼ cups low-sodium chicken or vegetable broth, or 3¼ cups water

FOR THE FORK IN THE ROAD ADD-INS

1 roasted bell pepper, peeled, seeded, and thinly sliced (see Roasting Peppers, page 31)

1 cup (4 ounces) crumbled feta, rinsed and drained

½ cup coarsely chopped pitted olives, such as kalamata

2 teaspoons fresh lemon juice

1 teaspoon grated lemon zest

2 teaspoons chopped fresh thyme, basil, oregano, or parsley, or a mixture of herbs

Kosher or coarse salt and freshly ground black pepper

2 scallions (optional), both white and light green parts thinly sliced

¼ cup chopped cooked bacon (optional)

1. Melt the butter in the olive oil in a large saucepan over medium-high heat. Add the shallots and cook until softened and translucent, about 4 minutes. Add the couscous and stir until the couscous is coated with the shallot mixture and starting to brown lightly, 3 to 4 minutes. Add the broth or water and stir well. Cover the pan and cook until most of the liquid has been absorbed, about 12 minutes.

2. Remove the pan from the heat and let it sit, covered, until the rest of the liquid is absorbed, about 5 minutes.

3. ✦ Set aside whatever amount of couscous you would like to keep plain. Also see the Fork in the Road suggestions for adding the ingredients to the couscous on this page.

4. Fold in the roasted pepper, feta, olives, lemon juice and zest, and the herb(s) and mix gently until well blended. Season the couscous with salt and black pepper to taste. Transfer the couscous to a shallow serving bowl and sprinkle the scallions and bacon on the top, if using. Serve warm or at room temperature.

✦ Fork in the Road

After the couscous is cooked, set aside however much you want to keep plain (you can toss in a bit of butter or olive oil, and maybe some grated cheese, if that works). Then add the rest of the ingredients to the remaining couscous, reducing amounts as necessary or desired. Even better, you might have one portion plain for your most finicky kid, another with some olives and lemon juice and zest added for a slightly more adventurous eater, and then throw in the whole kit and kaboodle for yourself.

To make the couscous a main course, you can add chunks of cooked chicken or shrimp. Or use it as a bed for sliced steak or a fillet of salmon.

What the Kids Can Do:

Kids can decide what add-ins they are interested in and add them. They can juice the lemon. Using an age-appropriate knife, they can slice the bell pepper and chop the olives or herbs. They can crumble the feta and/or bacon.

Vegetarian Note: Use vegetable broth or water (and no bacon—duh). A veggie version can serve as the main dish for the non-meat-eaters at your table and a side dish for everyone else.

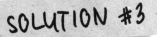
Roasted Potatoes

Serves 4 to 6 as a side dish
A Fork in the Road Recipe
Vegetarian

My mom is a talented intuitive cook. So I know it pains her a little bit to have to call me for this recipe, which is barely even a recipe. But call she does whenever she plans to make roasted potatoes. And every time I go over this with her on the phone she says, "Right, right, of course," and then doesn't bother to write it down because it's so ridiculously simple.

The secrets: a generous but not unconscionable amount of olive oil; high heat; a pretty liberal amount of salt; and nonstick cooking spray. You can also cut the potatoes like thick steak fries, if you are entertaining or just feeling ambitious, and these also make a nice appetizer. Try serving them with the Chipotle Mayonnaise (page 63).

Nonstick cooking spray

2 pounds (about 4 large) Yukon Gold, new potatoes, or other waxy potatoes, peeled or scrubbed

4 to 5 teaspoons olive oil

I to 1½ teaspoons kosher or coarse salt, or more if needed

1. Preheat the oven to 425°F.

2. Spray a rimmed baking sheet generously with nonstick cooking spray. Cut the potatoes into 1 or 1½ inch chunks (bigger chunks equal more creamy insides). Spread the potatoes out on the prepared baking sheet, drizzle the olive oil over them, sprinkle them with the salt, and toss with your hands to coat the potatoes well. Make sure the potatoes are in a single layer.

3. ➤ You can continue with Step 4 or see the Fork in the Road suggestions for seasoning the potatoes on the facing page.

These take 5 minutes of prep time, then the oven does all the work.

Fork in the Road

Before they go into the oven, slide portions of potatoes for the less intrepid palates to one side of the baking sheet. To spice up the remaining potatoes, sprinkle them with ½ teaspoon of paprika (sweet, smoked, or hot), chili powder or ground cumin, or a combination of any of the aforementioned. • To make rosemary potatoes, sprinkle the potatoes with a ½ teaspoon of crushed dried rosemary or chopped fresh rosemary. • For garlicky roasted potatoes, about 20 minutes after the potatoes have gone into the oven, pull them out and toss them well with a minced clove of garlic, then let them finish roasting. During the roasting, be sure to keep the plain potatoes separate from the flavored potatoes.

4. Bake the potatoes until they are nicely browned and crisp on the outside, 30 to 45 minutes, stirring them once toward the end of the baking time and spreading them out again. If the potatoes stick to the baking sheet, just leave them be! After a little more time in the oven, they will crisp up on the bottom and be easier to remove.

5. Add a sprinkling of additional salt if needed and serve the potatoes hot or warm. If you serve them right away, warn people that they are *hot*!

What the Kids Can Do:

Kids can toss the potatoes with olive oil and spread them in the baking sheet, then sprinkle them with salt.

CHEDDAR

MIXED HERBS

PARM

PESTO

GOAT CHEESE

DIJON

HORSERADISH

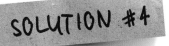

Mashed Potatoes

Serves 6 as a side dish
A Fork in the Road Recipe
Vegetarian

When my friend Pam's daughter was about six she said something so funny I will never forget it. Her younger sister, Phoebe, age three, was rhapsodizing about her imaginary Prince Charming and what he would say and do when he came to rescue her from . . . well, from what remains unclear, since her life was quite delightful. Maya chimed in with her own version of what the future looked like for her: "My prince will have a big, big butt and when he rides up he'll jump down off his horse and say, 'Hellllooooo, Sweetheart.'"

What does this have to do with mashed potatoes? Nothing, really. It's just that every time I see a beautiful blob of hot mashed potatoes I want to say, "Helllooo, Sweetheart," too. Charlie also often raises a forkful of mashed potatoes and gazes at them with unabashed affection, in a way that belies the fact that this is, in fact, a foodstuff, not a long lost family member. And Gary, upon hearing that mashed potatoes are on the menu, pulls out that old *Bewitched*-era chestnut, "Mashed potatoes? Honey, did you wreck the car?" Funny man. Actually, the line was amusing to him until the time that I actually wrecked the car and then made mashed potatoes for dinner. Who's funny now?

What do mashed potatoes go with? What *don't* they go with? Try them with the Soy-Ginger Flank Steak (page 120), any of the versions of the roast chicken (see page 98), the Lemon Chicken (page 104), the Asian Salmon (page 144), the Monday Night Brisket (page 127), Apple Glazed Pork Chops (page 134), and of course, meat loaf, like the turkey version on page 157.

MASHERS, RICERS AND FOOD MILLS

A potato masher is a flat disk with a wafflelike grid of holes and a handle attached, so that the metal grid can pound the potatoes (or other soft-cooked foods). You can do many things with an old-fashioned potato masher, including make these potatoes, although you will certainly have a lump or two left in the mix. (Many people not only don't mind that, they really love it.)

A potato ricer is a gizmo that looks much like an oversize garlic press. You put a cooked potato (or other thoroughly cooked root vegetable) in it, squeeze, and skinny spaghetti-like pieces come out (picture those Play-Doh kits that extrude the dough through various panels). Actually, the bits are more ricelike in shape, and when you mix them with hot milk and cream they blend perfectly into a smooth mash.

A food mill looks a little like a pot with a colander for a bottom and a hand crank to force the food underneath a metal blade and out through the holes in the bottom. The results are much like those of the ricer, but when you use a food mill to mash some soft foods it also acts like a sieve, leaving behind the seeds and skins of cooked tomatoes or berries, for instance, while the rest of the fruit goes through and becomes a sauce. Other items that take well to the food mill: cooked apples, cooked peppers and beans, and soups. And if homemade baby food is part of your world, it's the perfect tool.

Kosher or coarse salt

8 large Idaho or Yukon Gold potatoes (about 4 pounds total), peeled and cut in half

I cup milk, preferably whole

½ cup light or heavy (whipping) cream or half-and-half (see Note)

4 tablespoons (½ stick) unsalted butter, cut into pieces, at room temperature

Freshly ground black pepper

1. Fill a large pot with water and bring it to a boil over high heat. Add a generous amount of salt, let the water return to a boil, then add the potatoes (the water should cover the potatoes by at least 2 inches). Let the water come to a simmer, reduce the heat to medium, and cook the potatoes, partially covered, until they are very tender when pierced with a knife, 15 to 20 minutes.

2. Drain the potatoes, return them to the pot, and place it over medium-low heat. Heat the potatoes, tossing them occasionally, until the moisture is all gone and the potatoes have begun to dry out, but not to brown, about 3 minutes. Remove the pot from the stove and put the potatoes through a ricer or mash them with a potato masher until they are as smooth as you like them (see Mashers, Ricers, and Food Mills, page 253). Return the potatoes to the pot.

3. Place the milk and the cream in a microwave-safe bowl or pitcher and heat until hot, about 1 minute. (You can also heat the milk and cream in the pot over medium heat before you return the potatoes to it.) Add the butter and the hot milk and cream mixture to the potatoes and stir with a wooden spoon or a whisk until well combined.

4. ━━◀ You can continue with Step 5 or see the Fork in the Road suggestions for add-ins on this page.

5. Season the potatoes with salt and pepper to taste and stir over medium-low heat until everything is hot and well blended, about 2 minutes. Now you can wreck the car.

Note: If you don't feel like using the cream here, or you don't have it on hand, just add another ½ cup of milk and call it a day.

Cooking Tip: When you add the butter and the milk and cream mixture to the potatoes and stir at first it will look like the potatoes are way too liquidy. Don't worry, when the mashed potatoes are returned to the heat they will thicken up.

Make Ahead: If you make the mashed potatoes ahead of time you can hold them, covered in the pot, for up to three hours, then reheat them gently over low heat, adding some more hot milk as necessary and stirring frequently.

What the Kids Can Do: Kids might peel the potatoes, cut up the butter, measure the liquids, mash or rice the potatoes, and stir up the mashed potatoes

◀━━ Fork in the Road

Lots of things can be added to mashed potatoes to make them special. The amounts here are for the whole recipe. You may want to toss one or two peeled garlic cloves into the pot and simmer them with the potatoes, then mash them, too.

½ cup soft goat cheese or shredded hard cheese, such as cheddar or fontina • ¼ cup freshly grated Parmesan cheese • 1 to 2 tablespoons chopped fresh herbs, such as basil, oregano, thyme, tarragon, or chives • ¼ cup pesto • 2 tablespoons Dijon mustard • 1 tablespoon drained prepared horseradish.

Potato Pancakes

Serves . . . uh . . . well, this really depends; could be anywhere from 6 to 16, depending on what else you are serving and how long it's been since your family has eaten latkes

Vegetarian

The very best part of Hanukkah is the potato pancakes, also called latkes. Okay, the candle lighting is great, the present thing is certainly fun, but it's all about the latkes, really. On more than one occasion I have made eight to ten pounds of potatoes worth of latkes for twelve people and they were *gone*. (People who don't know me will think I am exaggerating. People who do know me will know that I am not.)

Serve the potato pancakes with both sour cream and applesauce, so people can choose or mix and match. If you're feeling a little lavish, you might serve them with some cheap caviar or smoked salmon or gravlax, and maybe swap out the sour cream for crème fraîche.

By the way, you don't have to be Jewish or actually celebrating the eight days of Hanukkah to think about latkes. There is no reason that little crisp potato pancakes wouldn't make a wonderful appetizer, a great side dish, or just a big old treat all year long.

5 pounds baking potatoes, peeled

3 large eggs

I large onion, finely minced

2 tablespoons matzoh meal or flour (optional)

Kosher or coarse salt and freshly ground black pepper

I to 1½ cups olive oil

4 tablespoons (½ stick) unsalted butter
    (optional, but recommended)

Applesauce and sour cream, for serving

CARBS: WHY CAN'T WE ALL JUST GET ALONG?

Remember, just a few minutes ago, when you were supposed to avoid all carbs, run from them at the speed of light as though the bread might actually jump out of the basket and affix itself to your rear end, the noodles wrapping themselves around your thigh like a toddler with separation anxiety? Ooh, watch out, those carbs are coming to get you!

This is not a diet book and I am not a nutritionist. Without treading too deeply into ever-evolving dietary guidelines, it seems as though we are getting a bit closer to the place where we accept that there are good carbs and starches, and there are carbs that should be consumed with a bit more restraint. Whole grains, which provide fiber, vitamins, nutrients, and energy in the form of glucose, are on the whole better for you than refined flours and sugars, so incorporating more whole grains into your meals is a great idea. Portion control is also a good idea.

And you know what else is a good idea? Not getting too crazy about all of this. I wish I could get away with more brown rice in my house, but my kids just like white rice better. So I try to go for whole grains in other areas, where the odds of the kids eating the food is better. Basically if you make food in your own kitchen and cut down on some of the stuff that comes in bags and has ingredients you can't pronounce and colors that aren't found in nature, you're doing okay.

1. Using a food processor or a handheld grater, grate the potatoes using the large-hole blade or side of the grater. Place the grated potatoes in a large bowl and let them sit while they release their liquid, about 10 minutes.

2. In another large bowl, mix the eggs and onion. Using your hands, grab a handful of the grated potato and squeeze it over the bowl of potatoes, pressing out as much liquid as possible. Put the squeezed potatoes in the bowl with the egg mixture. Repeat until all of the potatoes have been squeezed and added to the bowl with the egg mixture.

3. Stick your finger into the liquid left in the bowl that held the grated potatoes. You'll feel a firm layer of potato starch at the bottom. What you need to do is carefully pour off the liquid from the starch and then scrape up all of that valuable starch from the bottom of the bowl and mix it well

This isn't the moment to exercise self-restraint.

with the egg and potato mixture (best to use your hands). This natural starch helps bind the potatoes together. If there is only a tablespoon or two of the starch, you'll also want to blend in the matzoh meal or flour. Season the potato mixture with salt and pepper to taste (be liberal, the pancakes will be quite bland without enough seasoning).

4. Heat a couple of tablespoons of olive oil and a teaspoon or so of butter, if using, in a large skillet (or use two large skillets to make the cooking go faster) over medium-high heat until the butter has melted and the fat is hot. Swirl the pan and then add spoonfuls of the potato mixture, as big or small as you wish, and gently press them into round flat shapes. Cook the potato pancakes until they are golden brown and crisp, 4 to 5 minutes on each side. You'll need to keep a close eye on the heat; too low and the potato pancakes won't brown properly, too high and the oil will start smoking. Adjust the heat as needed.

5. Drain the potato pancakes briefly on paper towels and transfer them to a serving platter. Repeat with the remaining potato mixture, adding more oil and butter as necessary (you may want to dump out the pan, give it a quick wipe, and start over if you find that the oil is getting kind of dark and that too many bits of charred potato and onion are floating around). The potatoes will continue to release liquid as they sit; as you get to the bottom of the bowl, to avoid splattering give the potato mixture a quick squeeze before putting it in the hot pan. The potatoes will also start turning darker as they sit but when you cook them it won't be very noticeable.

6. Serve the potato pancakes warm with applesauce and sour cream.

Cooking Tip #1: It's a little indulgent, but I like to cook the pancakes in mostly pure olive oil, with a tiny bit of butter added for flavor, but you can use just olive oil. However, both olive oil and butter do burn at high temperatures, so keep an eye on the heat level; you want the fat high enough to cook up crisp pancakes, but not so high that it smokes and turns brown. And do not whip out the fancy bottle of extra-virgin olive oil for this purpose. Glug in the less expensive pure olive oil when you are frying. You can also use vegetable or canola oil; these work just fine.

Cooking Tip #2: Because of the way the heat is dispensed from the burner, you may notice that the potato pancakes near the edge of the pan cook faster than those in the center. When you flip the pancakes, shuffle them around a bit so they cook more evenly.

What the Kids Can Do: If they are older, kids can peel and grate the potatoes with a handheld grater; frankly, this is one of the delightful benefits of having more mature children. "Ability to safely grate potatoes" should be listed as a milestone in child-rearing books, right up there with "first tooth" and "takes first step." To prevent scraped knuckles tell your kids to stop grating before they get to the end of the potato. Of course, kids can crack the eggs, and they can mix up the potato mixture.

A little tiny party in a skillet.

Chapter 16

Best-Shot Vegetables

Maybe your kids are into vegetables, or maybe you think kids and vegetables don't even belong in the same sentence. Take a deep breath, cut yourself some slack, and let's discuss this calmly.

First of all, in this chapter there are five very simple vegetable side dishes that have met with repeated good cheer, so conceivably you will find something here that will provide both pleasure and nourishment. Some straightforward roasted vegetables like broccoli, cauliflower, asparagus, and squash offer up a bit of sweetness thanks to the caramelization of natu-

> ### THE REALITY
>
> *They can't eat only raw baby carrots for the rest of their lives.*

ral sugars that occurs when these are baked at high temperatures. A very simple sautéing/steaming technique, used for a combination of sugar snap peas and slender green beans (or many other vegetables) leaves these with a very lightly buttery glaze that has great kid appeal. And a sautéed corn dish, confetti-like in appearance, and with or without the addition of that not so secret ingredient bacon, is sweet and pretty and rounds out many meals quite nicely.

Now on to the more wearisome issues. Why do so many kids not like vegetables, or not like certain vegetables in particular? While moms around the globe are having standoffs with their offspring over plates of congealing peas, actual scientists have been conducting actual studies on this eternal

Sautéed Spring Vegetables

conundrum. Turns out there may be something genetic at play (this is probably by far the most science-y thing I have to share, but it's so interesting that as incongruous as it may seem, it's worth noting).

Each of us human beings carries two genes that cause us to have an aversion to bitterness. These genes (the TAS2R38 genes, in case you are curious) are present because long, long ago, when we were all hunters and gatherers, these genes developed in people as a protective mechanism to help us avoid poisonous berries and plants and so forth. There are two different versions of this gene, and one version is much more sensitive to bitterness than the other. If a person has one or both of these genes in the more sensitive category, that person will be very apt to be more sensitive to bitter tastes than someone with both these genes in the less sensitive category. And, studies show that a large majority of kids have at least one of the sensitive genes.

But wait, there's more. Even though most people have at least one of the more sensitive genes, they do seem to outgrow any heightened aversions to vegetables and bitterness in general. This may be the result of various cultural and ethnic influences over time. Another theory revolves around the fact that while we are all born with more than ten thousand taste buds, the number of these reduces dramatically to about three thousand once full adulthood is reached. This means that their greater number of taste buds causes kids to be hypersensitive to strong flavors, while adult palates aren't nearly as easily overwhelmed.

And aside from the science, there's just some pervasive expectation, on the part of both adults and kids, that children and vegetables are going to butt heads. Many of the tips that might help if you are trying to get more fish into your kids' diets (see page 139) are also applicable here. The most germane ones are not putting too much pressure on the situation and exploring the boundaries of your patience. My kids might snort if they heard me imparting this bit of sage wisdom and mutter whatever kids say when they are thinking "Those who can't do, teach." Still, I do know that urging kids to try things, without forcing them to gag down mounds of vegetables they don't like, is really the only way to go. Then there are always raw carrots. And the Serenity Prayer, if you find that helpful.

Roasted Asparagus

Serves 4 to 6 as a side dish
A Fork in the Road Recipe
Vegetarian

Come spring, this dish makes an appearance on our table a couple of times a week. Roasting is as easy a cooking method as there is; the high heat deepens the flavor of any vegetable, and all those nutrients stay right in the veggies where they belong.

Funnily enough, Charlie doesn't like the asparagus tips, so he chomps all the way up the stalk and leaves the perfect little pointed tops for one of us to pick off of his plate. I guess if I were smarter I would cut the tips off some of the asparagus before cooking them and save them to blanch and garnish a risotto. But this is the kind of thought that (a) only occurs to me as I look at the abandoned gnawed tips lying on Charlie's plate, and (b) has absolutely nothing to do with reality. Still it's fun to think about for a minute. I also like to think about having someone give me a manicure in my house.

Thick or thin? Your choice. I think for a while there was something very sexy and desirable about really skinny asparagus, but basically it's a matter of personal preference. The thin stalks just need the bottom two inches cut off, cook faster, and work nicely in sautéed or stir fried dishes. The fatter ones take longer to cook, but the thickness provides a much more satisfying bite.

1½ pounds asparagus

2 tablespoons olive oil

1 teaspoon kosher or coarse salt

½ lemon (optional), for serving

½ to 1 teaspoon minced capers (optional), for serving

Lean, green, and simple.

Cooking Tip: For thicker asparagus, it's nice to peel the lower parts of the stalks, which results in stalks that are very tender from stem to stern. After trimming off the bottom inch or so, you simply take a vegetable peeler and peel the green outer layer off the bottom three or so inches of the stalk. If you don't feel like doing this, just snap off three inches from the bottoms of the stalks instead of two.

What the Kids Can Do: They can trim the asparagus, if they're old enough to use a knife, and maybe peel the stalks. They can drizzle the olive oil and sprinkle the salt over the asparagus, tossing it to mix.

1. Preheat the oven to 450°F.

2. Trim the bottom couple of inches off of the asparagus (see Cooking Tip, facing page). Place the asparagus in a baking dish (the stalks can overlap a bit). Drizzle the olive oil over the asparagus and toss gently to coat the stalks evenly. Sprinkle the salt over the asparagus and toss it again.

3. Bake the asparagus until the stalks are cooked almost as done you like them, 7 to 10 minutes for thin stalks, 10 to 12 for thick ones. If the stalks overlap in the baking dish, just give them a little shuffle with a spatula halfway through the cooking time so they all have a chance to brown a bit. Remember the asparagus will continue to cook a bit after you remove it from the oven, so take it out while it's still a little too firm.

4. ➤ You can continue with Step 5 or serve all or some of the asparagus as is. Or see the Fork in the Road suggestion below for an asparagus vinaigrette.

5. If desired, squeeze the lemon juice over some or all of the asparagus and/or sprinkle the capers on top before serving warm or at room temperature.

➤ Fork in the Road

Vinaigrette for Simple Roasted Asparagus

Makes about ¼ cup

You might also enjoy the Olive Vinaigrette on page 265 drizzled over some individual portions of asparagus as desired.

> 1 tablespoon olive oil
>
> 1 tablespoon red wine vinegar or sherry vinegar
>
> 2 tablespoons finely minced shallots
>
> ½ teaspoon Dijon mustard
>
> ½ teaspoon minced fresh thyme leaves (optional)
>
> Pinch of kosher or coarse salt
>
> Roasted Asparagus (above), prepared through Step 3

Place the olive oil, vinegar, shallots, mustard, thyme, if using, and salt in a small bowl or a plastic container with a lid. Whisk or shake to combine well. Drizzle the vinaigrette over the portions of asparagus for anyone who wants to try it, and serve warm or chilled.

WHO IS AL DENTE?

One last thing I've been thinking about lately: For quite a while it's been the fashion to eat asparagus and many other vegetables al dente, while they're still quite crisp. Well-cooked vegetables are sneered at as old-fashioned and unchic. This is annoying; you should cook your vegetables to the degree of doneness you like to eat them. If you (and as important, your kids) are fans of slightly mushy veggies, then you should cook those vegetables until they are slightly mushy. You don't need undercooked vegetables to prove you're cool.

If you are boiling the vegetables, do be aware you may lose a bit of the nutrients in the water when they cook longer, but in the scheme of things, if it means your kids are going to eat their vegetables, then it's probably the better decision.

Roasted Cauliflower or Broccoli with (or without) Olive Vinaigrette

Serves 4 to 6 as a side dish
A Fork in the Road Recipe
Vegetarian

So, you've steamed or boiled enough cauliflower or broccoli to fill a minivan, and you need to change things up, at least a little bit. Roasting is the answer. Roasting concentrates flavor by caramelizing the natural sugars in the vegetables and provides a slight and very appealing sweetness. I'm not going to pretend that the first time you serve this your kids won't poke around a bit at the browned parts and voice concern—mine did, and not very politely, I might add. But one bite, two bites, and *sold* to the quirkiest eater. And the fact that Ben R. was over and dove right in certainly showcased the positive side of peer pressure.

You can use a mix of half broccoli and half cauliflower if you want more choice, and that's also a nice idea if you're entertaining. This is a Fork in the Road recipe because of the black olive vinaigrette, which is pretty grown-up on the face of it, although if your kids are salt junkies they may think this is a brilliant addition. Make sure to taste the dressing before you season it at the end because olives vary wildly in their saltiness.

PLAIN

W/OLIVE VINAIGRETTE

I big head cauliflower, or I½ large broccoli crowns
(about 2½ to 3 pounds total)

2 tablespoons olive oil

Kosher or coarse salt and freshly ground black pepper (optional)

1. Place a rack in the lower third of the oven and preheat the oven to 450°F.

2. Prepare the cauliflower or broccoli: Cut the cauliflower or broccoli into ¾ inch–thick slices and break them into pieces. Place the sliced vegetables on a large rimmed baking sheet and gently toss it with the 2 tablespoons of olive oil, about ½ teaspoon of salt, and a few grinds of pepper, if desired (your hands are really the best tools for tossing). Spread the vegetables in a single layer and bake until slightly browned and tender, turning gently with a spatula once or twice, 25 to 30 minutes.

3. ◄═ You can continue with Step 4 or serve all or some of the cauliflower or broccoli as is. Or see the Fork in the Road suggestion below for Olive Vinaigrette.

4. Serve the cauliflower or broccoli with the olive vinaigrette on the side, if desired, and let whoever is interested drizzle some on top. If you score a home run, you can drizzle vinaigrette over all of the veggies next time.

═◄═ Fork in the Road

Olive Vinaigrette

Makes about ⅓ cup

2 tablespoons extra-virgin olive oil

¼ teaspoon minced garlic

I tablespoon fresh lemon juice, or more to taste

¼ cup chopped pitted kalamata or other cured black olives

Kosher or coarse salt and freshly ground black pepper

While the vegetable is roasting place the 2 tablespoons of extra-virgin olive oil and the garlic, lemon juice, and olives in a mini food processor and puree until well blended. Alternatively, using a fork, you can mash everything in a small bowl until they become a paste. Taste for seasoning, adding salt and pepper to taste and more lemon juice as necessary.

Cooking Tip: Back to the vinaigrette: Any kind of black olives are great. Olives cured with herbs are also hunky-dory; you'll get the added whomp of whatever herbs the olives were marinated in. And feel free to add ¼ teaspoon of dried oregano or thyme to the vinaigrette or ½ teaspoon of fresh.

What the Kids Can Do: Kids can toss the sliced cauliflower or broccoli with the olive oil, help puree the vinaigrette if you are making it, and drizzle the vinaigrette over the vegetables, if desired.

Roasted Butternut Squash

Serves 4 as a side dish
Vegetarian

Roasting winter squash with a bit of brown sugar falls into the nothing-new-under-the-sun category, but frankly feeding children and searching for new things under the sun aren't always compatible endeavors. This is an easy side dish you can make all fall and winter long, and one that you will happily call upon when it comes time to find something orange to add to the holiday buffet and you can't face one more multistep recipe.

You can multiply this recipe easily, but you will want to make sure that the pieces of squash are distributed in a single layer on the baking sheet, without being at all crowded to get that nice browned, caramely exterior. If you make more than one batch you'll likely have to use more than one baking sheet and rotate them on the oven racks midway through roasting.

Nonstick cooking spray

I butternut squash (about 1¼ pounds), peeled and cut into 1½-inch pieces (see the Cooking Tip)

2 tablespoons (¼ stick) unsalted butter, melted

I tablespoon light or dark brown sugar

½ teaspoon kosher or coarse salt

1. Preheat the oven to 450°F. Spray a rimmed baking sheet with nonstick cooking spray.

2. Spread the pieces of squash on the prepared baking sheet. Drizzle the melted butter over the squash and sprinkle it with the brown sugar and salt. Toss the squash until it is evenly coated.

3. Bake the squash until it is nicely browned and tender, 35 to 45 minutes, stirring it once halfway through the cooking time.

Cooking Tip: Peeling butternut squash is a bit of a drag (and you can buy cleaned and halved or cubed squash if you're not in the mood). First you'll want to trim off the bottom and the top of the squash, so it will stand upright on the counter. Then, using the best vegetable peeler you have, peel off the very thick outer skin. It usually takes a couple of swipes with the peeler to get all the way through the skin, past the greenish part and into the really orange part. Then cut the squash in half from top to bottom. Each side will have a pocket full of seeds in its bulbous bottom; scoop those out with a spoon, along with any stringy bits, and discard them. Cut the bright orange squash flesh into chunks.

What the Kids Can Do: Kids can scoop the seeds out of the squash and measure the brown sugar and salt. Once you have cut up the squash they can spread it out on the baking sheet, drizzle the butter over it, and toss it with the brown sugar and salt.

sweet, buttery, and (almost) embarrassingly simple.

Sautéed Corn, Spinach, Bacon, and Scallions

Serves 4 as a side dish

You'll want to try this in peak corn months, after you've had your fill of plain steamed ears of corn and are looking for a side dish with a little more something something. It is a very flexible dish, so have fun with it after you lug home booty from the farmers' market (see Where Do Groceries Come From? on page 271). The spinach wilts down, but makes the dish so pretty and adds a right hook of vitamins and iron. If you're in need of a vegetarian side, leave out the bacon.

In the winter months the recipe works perfectly well with frozen corn and is a cheery, if off-season, accompaniment for many main dishes. The seasonings are quite mild, so the dish will go with lots of different flavors and foods—anything from Soy-Ginger Flank Steak (page 120), chicken and shrimp Kebabs (page 237), pulled pork sandwiches (see page 213), Apple Glazed Pork Chops (page 134), Teriyaki Chicken and Beef Skewers (page 230), Ribs with a Rub (page 131), Flaky Fish with Balsamic Glaze (page 142), roast chicken (see page 98), to Asian Salmon (page 144), and beyond.

4 slices bacon, cut into 1-inch strips (optional)

1 tablespoon unsalted butter

1 shallot, minced

3 cups fresh or frozen corn kernels (from about 4 ears corn)

½ cup chopped red bell pepper (optional)

Pinch of red pepper flakes (optional)

Kosher or coarse salt and freshly ground black pepper

2 to 3 scallions, both white and light green parts, sliced

4 cups baby spinach leaves

What the Kids Can Do:
Kids can cut the bacon or bell pepper with an age-appropriate knife, and if they are old enough, with supervision they can stir together the mixture on the stove.

Cooking Tip: You can use orange or yellow bell pepper in place of the red. You can add sliced or diced zucchini or yellow squash; you can skip the spinach or only add it to some of the mixture; you can sauté some chopped carrot with the shallots. You can add halved cherry or grape tomatoes and slivered fresh basil or other herbs to all or part of the corn mixture at the end for an additional punch of color and flavor. You can do pretty much anything you like to keep changing up this vegetable medley.

Vegetarian Note:
To make this corn dish vegetarian, skip the bacon.

1. Cook the bacon, if using, in a large skillet over medium-high heat, turning occasionally, until browned, 4 to 6 minutes. Using a slotted spoon, transfer the bacon to paper towels to drain. Pour off all but 1 teaspoon of the fat from the skillet.

2. Add the butter to the skillet and melt over medium heat. Add the shallot and cook, stirring occasionally, until tender, about 2 minutes. Add the corn and the red bell pepper and red pepper flakes, if using. Season with salt and black pepper to taste. Cook, stirring often, until the corn is tender, about 5 minutes. Crumble the bacon and add it along with the scallions and the spinach, 2 cups at a time. Stir until the spinach leaves have wilted and combined with the corn, about 1 minute.

Add whatever veggies you have hanging around.

Sautéed Spring Vegetables

Serves 4 to 6 as a side dish
Vegetarian

When making this dish, you can use whatever vegetables speak to you at the supermarket—or better yet at the farmers' market. I often make this with all haricots verts (which is basically French for string beans). These are thinner and more tender than regular string beans, but you can absolutely use any variety of string beans here, or all sugar snap peas or snow peas, or some asparagus cut up into two-inch pieces. A vegetable combo is just slightly more festive. Sautéing in butter and then adding some water for a quick steam results in veggies that have a nice light buttery glaze, without a whole lot of fat. You can use olive oil . . . but try the butter.

1½ tablespoons unsalted butter or olive oil

1 small shallot, chopped or thinly sliced, or ½ teaspoon minced garlic

½ pound haricots verts or green beans, trimmed (see Note)

½ pound sugar snap peas (see Note)

Kosher or coarse salt and freshly ground black pepper

1 tablespoon fresh lemon juice (optional)

1 teaspoon freshly grated lemon zest (optional)

1. Heat a large skillet over medium heat and add the butter or olive oil. Add the shallot or garlic and cook until tender, about 4 minutes for the shallot or 1 minute for the garlic.

2. Add the haricots verts and sugar snap peas to the skillet and season with salt and pepper to taste. Increase the heat to medium-high and cook, stirring occasionally, until the vegetables are nicely coated with the butter or oil, about 2 minutes.

3. Add 2 tablespoons of water, cover the skillet, and steam the vegetables until they are bright green and almost cooked through, 3 minutes longer. Remove the lid, stir the vegetables, and cook until the liquid has evaporated and the vegetables are cooked to your liking, 1 to 2 minutes.

4. Taste for seasoning, adding more salt and/or pepper if necessary. Toss the vegetables with the lemon juice and zest, if using, and serve.

Note: Make sure when you trim the green beans and sugar snaps that as you snap off the end you pull the string so that it comes up and off the length of the bean. This little step will reward you with no strings to get stuck in your teeth.

A small amount of butter turns into a wonderful glaze.

Cooking Tip: If you use the lemon juice, sprinkle it on just before you serve the veggies as sometimes fresh lemon juice can turn pretty green vegetables a less appealing shade of khaki.

What the Kids Can Do: The kids can snap off the ends of the peas and beans and pull off any strings.

Lazy Oven French
Toast (page 274)

Chapter 17

Weekend Brunches

The word *brunch* connotes many things that are the antithesis of the average mom's busy life. Brunch suggests a sense of leisure, of lingering over a meal, of relaxation. It also might possibly suggest a mimosa or a Bloody Mary. And it should—you deserve it. But most weekends that would entail going to flag football practice or art class slightly buzzed, and people do talk. Also, if you're the one doing the cooking for this lovely, laid-back meal, then something is not quite copacetic about the whole brunch concept.

> ### THE PARADOX
> *A relaxing brunch that you have to cook.*

Here are five recipes that will provide that sense of calm and well-being that should be connected to this meal, without making you insane while striving for it. The Lazy Oven French Toast comes together quickly the night before, gets slipped into the refrigerator, and then is baked, providing French toast for the masses. A good, simple pancake recipe is much more special than opening a box of mix. The frittata puts eggs center stage, without you taking orders like some short-order cook. And apple coffee cake and banana muffins or bread are simple and quick and smell fabulous coming out of the oven.

There are other breakfast options in the Quick and Easy Breakfast chapter (pages 3 to 17), and you might also consider the Potato Pancakes (page 255), Berries with Sweetened Yogurt (page 296) and Fruit Salad Kebabs (page 295). And a chocolate-covered strawberry (see page 292) to finish things off will make you look heroic.

Lazy Oven French Toast

Serves 6 to 8
Vegetarian

Basically a strata, this dish is composed of layers of eggs, milk, and bread, plus your choice of flavorings. Stratas can be sweet, enhanced with chopped dried fruit, nuts, chocolate, or booze (that's for another book, though), or savory, layered with cheese, ham, and so on. This one cooks up much like a French toast casserole. The title of the recipe implies that your oven is lazy, which of course is ridiculous. Rather, it's the perfect brunch dish for a lazy weekend morning because everything can be assembled the night before and transferred in the morning from the fridge to the oven.

Butter or nonstick cooking spray, for greasing the baking dish

4 cups milk (see Note)

6 large eggs

2 tablespoons granulated sugar

2 tablespoons maple syrup, plus more maple syrup for serving (optional)

I teaspoon pure vanilla extract

½ teaspoon ground cinnamon

½ teaspoon kosher or coarse salt

I large loaf challah bread, preferably slightly stale, sliced ¾ to I inch thick (see the Cooking Tip)

¾ cup whole raisins, chopped dried fruit, or chopped nuts (optional)

Fresh fruit such as berries, sliced peaches or pears, and/or confectioners' sugar, for serving

So much easier than individual slices of French toast.

1. Grease a 13 by 9-inch baking dish with butter or spray it with cooking spray.

2. Place the milk, eggs, sugar, maple syrup, vanilla, cinnamon, and salt in a medium-size bowl and whisk to mix well. Set the milk mixture aside.

3. Arrange half of the slices of bread in the prepared baking dish, cutting the bread so that it fits in a solid layer. Pour half of the milk mixture over the bread, then evenly distribute about half of any dried fruit or nuts, if using, on top.

4. Repeat, creating a second layer of bread and then pouring the rest of the milk mixture on top and distributing the rest of the fruit or nuts over the bread. Lightly press the bread down into the liquid.

5. Cover the baking dish with plastic wrap and refrigerate it overnight. The bread will have absorbed almost all of the milk mixture. Uncover the baking dish and if there are dryer looking pieces on top, take them off and carefully tuck them underneath the bread on the bottom so that the more milk-soaked pieces are now on top (this is messy but it all works out in the baking). Note that any dried fruit sitting on the top of the French toast will get pretty chewy when baked and nuts on top will get toasty; the fruit and nuts that are tucked into the French toast will be softer, so disperse the fruit and nuts as you see fit.

6. Preheat the oven to 425°F.

7. Bake the French toast, uncovered, until it is puffed and golden, 30 to 35 minutes.

8. Let the French toast sit for 5 minutes to firm up a bit, then cut it into squares and serve it hot with your choice of maple syrup, fresh fruit, and/or confectioners' sugar.

Note: This is luxurious made with whole milk, but 2 percent or 1 percent milk works fine. Conversely, for an even more decadent dish you can replace one of the cups of milk with a cup of cream or half-and-half if you like.

Cooking Tip: Use slightly stale bread for this recipe; because it is a bit dry, it will absorb the milk and egg custard better. If your bread is fresh, you can slice it and let it sit out for several hours or a day to dry slightly, or even toast it very lightly.

Make Ahead: The ultimate make ahead dish, a strata has to be prepared about eight hours before it's cooked. So an overnight rest in the fridge makes sense. Leftovers do reheat nicely in the microwave or oven.

What the Kids Can Do: They can help put together pretty much the whole French toast, although you'll have to decide if they are old enough to help slice the bread. Kids can also pick and choose whatever dried fruits or nuts they like to go in the casserole.

You-Are-the-Best-Mom-in-the-World Pancakes

Serves 4; makes about a dozen 3½-inch pancakes
A Fork in the Road Recipe
Vegetarian

There is something so comforting and happily indulgent about a weekend day that starts with pancakes. A boxed mix is oh so fine, but a pile of fluffy homemade pancakes is oh-so-much-finer. And here's the deal; that boxed mix is essentially just a blend of flour, leavening, sugar, and salt—you still have to add the oil or butter, eggs, and milk and then cook the pancakes. So if you're willing to take an extra couple of minutes and mix up the dry ingredients from your pantry, you can be the proud server of a platter of homemade flapjacks. My sister-in-law Lisa makes pancakes almost every weekend, which explains why there are about forty-five assorted and sundry teenage boys in her house Saturday mornings, besides the three that actually live there.

These pancakes are homey and fluffy and simple, just what you want yours to be. The recipe doubles and triples easily, which is a critical feature for a pancake recipe. Feel free to sprinkle blueberries or chocolate chips over the batter as soon as you ladle it into the skillet, especially if you're really working on that mom-of-the year thing.

What the Kids Can Do:
Kids can measure, dump, and mix the dry ingredients, crack the eggs, stir the pancake batter, and carefully sprinkle the blueberries or chocolate chips on top of the pancakes, if desired.

Fork in the Road

One batch of pancake batter plus one bowl of blueberries plus one little bowl of chocolate chips equals everyone getting an ideal pancake breakfast. Just ask people what they'd like and sprinkle it over the pancake batter once you've poured it into the skillet. You'll need about 1 cup of fresh blueberries and ½ cup of chocolate chips if you want to sprinkle the whole batch. And lest you forget, banana slices, and in the warmer months, fresh cut-up strawberries and peeled peaches are also glorious toppings.

I¼ cups all-purpose flour

I tablespoon granulated sugar

I tablespoon baking powder

½ teaspoon kosher or coarse salt

I large egg

I¼ cups milk, preferably whole

2 tablespoons vegetable oil, plus oil for cooking the pancakes

Maple syrup, softened butter, or jam or jelly, for serving

1. Place the flour, sugar, baking powder, and salt in a medium-size bowl and whisk until combined.

2. Place the egg, milk, and oil in a large bowl and beat until well blended. Add the flour mixture to the egg mixture and stir everything together until *just* blended. There will still be a significant number of little lumps in the batter but this is fine.

3. Heat a large skillet over medium heat and add about 1 teaspoon of oil. Swirl the skillet to make sure the bottom is covered with the oil. Add the batter by scant ¼ cups.

4.  You can continue with Step 5 or see the Fork in the Road suggestions for add-ins on the facing page.

5. Cook the pancakes until you see bubbles forming on the top and the edges start to look cooked, about 2 minutes. Using a spatula, flip the pancakes (they should be golden underneath) and cook them until the second side is golden brown, another 1 to 2 minutes. Adjust the heat as necessary and repeat, adding more oil as needed, until all of the batter has been used.

6. Serve the pancakes with maple syrup, butter, or jam or jelly.

One recipe, three variations, everyone's happy.

A wedge of frittata can be eaten out of hand any time, any place.

Vegetable Frittata

Serves 6
Vegetarian

A frittata is an Italian omelet to which the add-ins (potatoes, ham, cheese, veggies, rice, what have you) are beaten directly into the eggs. Generally it's cooked first on the stovetop, then finished under the broiler. Some people cook a frittata entirely on the stovetop, flipping it during the cooking process instead of transferring the unflipped frittata to the broiler. Some people are also circus acrobats or professional skydivers.

Frittatas are great warm, or at room temperature, happily hanging out for a couple of hours before being cut up and served. Ideal for brunch, they are a subtle way of saying "I'm not making individual omelets for all of you." A good potluck notion and, when cut into small squares, a lovely hors d'oeuvre.

You will need a skillet that can go from stovetop to oven and stand up to the heat of the broiler, and that means one without a plastic handle. If you have one that is ovensafe *and* nonstick, you are golden. Now, notice that the cheese choices are quite varied. Each will give you a distinctly different frittata. Start with a milder cheese you know your kids will like. The next frittata, maybe switch to a new cheese.

My kids picked at frittatas the first few times I served them. The first time they fully embraced frittatas was when I pulled out a plastic container of little frittata wedges at the park one day (these are quite portable) and within minutes a group of four kids had demolished them. Maybe it was the fresh air, maybe it was the unusual setting for such a snack, maybe it was that they were extremely hungry (reminder of critical mom tip: Try new foods when your kids are *starving*!), but whichever, it worked.

TABULA RASA

This is Latin for "blank slate" (two years of high school Latin, thank you), which is just to say that there are many, many possible combinations of ingredients for frittatas. It's a great way to use up that extra cup of cooked veggies from the night before. Substitute shallots or scallions or leeks for the onion. Use three quarters of a cup of cooked rice or plain pasta instead of the potatoes; just stir the cooked rice or pasta into the eggs and pour it all into the skillet. Asparagus, broccoli, mushrooms, olives, scallions, tomatoes, zucchini, spinach—if you root around in your refrigerator you can probably find about ten things that would be great frittata fillings. If you are thinking about interesting combos, and not worrying about picky eaters, you could mix a dollop of pesto or tapenade or sun-dried tomato paste into the eggs. Bacon, feta cheese, and scallions is a favorite combo in my house.

2 tablespoons (¼ stick) unsalted butter

I large waxy potato, such as white, red, or Yukon Gold, peeled, quartered, and thinly sliced

I onion, quartered and very thinly sliced

½ teaspoon dried thyme, oregano, or basil, or I teaspoon chopped fresh thyme, oregano, or basil

Kosher or coarse salt and freshly ground black pepper

IO large eggs

¼ cup coarsely chopped fresh Italian (flat-leaf) parsley or basil (optional)

½ cup shredded or crumbled cheese, such as cheddar, provolone, Monterey Jack, mozzarella, feta, Parmesan, or goat cheese

1. Preheat the broiler with the rack set about 4 inches away from the heat source.

2. Melt the butter over medium heat in a medium-size (10-inch) broiler-proof skillet. Add the potato, onion, and the ½ teaspoon of dried thyme, oregano, or basil, if using, and season with salt and pepper to taste. Cover the skillet and cook the potato and onion until they are beginning to become tender, about 10 minutes, stirring occasionally. Reduce the heat if it seems like the vegetables are starting to burn. Uncover the skillet and cook the vegetables until they are tender and turning golden, about 4 minutes longer.

3. Meanwhile, place the eggs, parsley, and 1 teaspoon of fresh thyme, oregano, or basil, if using, in a medium-size bowl and whisk to combine well. Season the egg mixture with salt and pepper to taste. When the vegetables are ready, pour the eggs into the skillet and stir to combine everything. Let the frittata cook until the eggs start to set on the bottom. Reduce the heat to medium-low and, using a spatula, gently lift the edge of the frittata so that the uncooked eggs run underneath those that are set on the bottom. Do this every couple of minutes until the frittata is pretty much set on the bottom but the top and middle are still a bit runny.

4. Sprinkle the cheese over the top of the frittata and place the skillet under the broiler. Broil the frittata until it is set, the cheese is melted, and the whole top is lightly golden, 2 to 4 minutes. Remove the skillet from the broiler and let

Cooking Tip: Frittatas are just as delicious served at room temperature as hot. So, if you are feeding a bigger group, whisk up two or more, making one quite simple and others much more adventurous.

Make Ahead: You can make a frittata a day ahead of time and store it well wrapped in the fridge. Serve it slightly chilled, at room temperature, or warm. To rewarm the frittata, unwrap it and heat it in a 350°F oven for ten minutes. You can also let it sit out covered at room temperature for up to six hours.

What the Kids Can Do: Kids can pick the add-ins and beat them into the eggs. If they are old enough they can help cook the frittata with supervision.

the frittata sit for a minute or two on a heatproof surface. Leave a dishtowel draped over the handle of the skillet to remind yourself that the handle is hot!

5. Run a spatula or knife around the edge of the skillet to loosen the frittata. You can cut it into wedges and serve it directly from the skillet. Or carefully slide the whole thing onto a serving plate, using a spatula to help guide the frittata out, then cut it into wedges.

Variation

Mini Frittatas

This is a kid-pleaser—frittatas in a muffin tin. It's a bit more work to pour the mixture into the individual cups, but you actually save the hands-on cooking time on top of the stove, freeing you up to slice cantaloupe, or yell at the kids to set the table, or carve small swans out of radishes for garnishes.

To make miniature frittatas, transfer the cooked vegetables to the bowl with the whisked egg mixture and stir to combine. Butter the cups of a regular-size 12-cup muffin tin. Fill the cups of the muffin tin halfway with the frittata mixture and bake in a preheated 350°F oven until cooked through, 10 to 15 minutes.

Obviously the sprinkled herbs are optional. ↓

Aaron E.'s Favorite Apple Coffee Cake

Makes one 9-inch square cake
Vegetarian

Charlie's friend Aaron E. is an excellent litmus test for identifying kid-friendly recipes because he is (and I say this with great affection) a typical picky kid. Now, because he has parents who are pretty sophisticated eaters, it's not like he's a just-plain-pasta kid. I have found that there is often a very eclectic selection of foods some pickier kids will like, for example: pizza, chicken nuggets, pasta, those king crab dumplings from that certain Japanese restaurant, mussels, and that thing their grandmother makes, the one with the prunes.

Anyway, Aaron E. asked me to try his favorite recipe, a coffee cake that he and his dad make. I tinkered with it a bit and it was supereasy and just what one would be overjoyed to see on a Sunday morning with a steaming cup of coffee (or a glass of milk) alongside. The cinnamon sugar topping really took me back; I made a Bisquick coffee cake with a similar topping every Sunday for a large chunk of my childhood, until my parents begged me to stop. This is also highly suitable as a dessert, a snack, or a bake sale item, not to mention a potluck offering.

HOW DO YOU LIKE THEM APPLES?

Firm apples that won't turn into mush when cooked work best in baked goods. How tart or sweet the apple is is up to you. When making an apple pie (see page 311) or applesauce, or anything with a large quantity of apples it's nice to mix a couple of kinds to get a multifaceted flavor, but in the case of a recipe like Aaron E.'s coffee cake you're only using one apple, so just pick one you know you like. And then, every time you make this you can try a different apple and give the coffee cake a slightly different personality.

Some good cooking apples are: Cortland—they have a red skin, bright white flesh, and are a bit tart • Empire—a mottled red in color, these are sweet-tart • Fuji—red, sweet, juicy, and firm • Golden Delicious—yellow, with pointy bumps on the bottom, these are sweet and mellow tasting • Granny Smith—green, sour, tart • Jonathan—mixed red and yellow in color, they're tart and crisp • McIntosh—red with some green coloration, mild and less firm • Rome—red a bit tart, and fairly crisp.

FOR THE CINNAMON SUGAR TOPPING

¼ cup granulated sugar

I teaspoon ground cinnamon

FOR THE COFFEE CAKE

8 tablespoons (I stick) unsalted butter, at room temperature, plus butter for greasing the baking pan

1¼ cups all-purpose flour

2 teaspoons baking powder

½ teaspoon kosher or coarse salt

⅓ cup granulated sugar

2 large eggs

I teaspoon pure vanilla extract

⅔ cup whole milk

I large apple (see How Do You Like Them Apples? this page), peeled, cored, and coarsely chopped

1. Make the cinnamon sugar topping: Place the sugar and cinnamon in a small bowl and stir to mix. Set the cinnamon sugar topping aside.

2. Make the coffee cake: Preheat the oven to 375°F. Grease a 9-inch square (or round) baking pan.

3. Place the flour, baking powder, and salt in a small bowl and whisk to mix. Set the flour mixture aside.

4. Place the sugar and butter in a medium-size bowl and, using an electric mixer, beat them until fluffy, about 3 minutes. Add the eggs one at a time, beating until each is incorporated, then add the vanilla. Add the flour mixture and the milk alternately, in about 2 batches of each, beating after each addition just until almost incorporated; at the end you still want to see streaks of flour and milk.

The light cinnamon sugar topping is the kicker.

5. Using a wooden spoon, fold in the apple until everything is just combined. Spoon the batter into the prepared pan and smooth the top. Sprinkle the cinnamon sugar topping over the top.

6. Bake the coffee cake until it is golden brown and a toothpick or wooden skewer inserted in the middle of the coffee cake comes out clean, about 30 minutes. Let the coffee cake cool in the pan on a wire rack. Serve the coffee cake warm or at room temperature, cut in squares or wedges.

Make Ahead: The coffee cake keeps at room temperature, wrapped, for a couple of days.

What the Kids Can Do: Kids can measure, dump, and mix the dry ingredients and crack the eggs. They can peel the apple and chop it if they are old enough to cut firm fruit with a sharp knife. And, kids can sprinkle the cinnamon sugar topping over the coffee cake.

Moist Banana Muffins

Makes 12 generous regular-size muffins
Vegetarian

Have bananas turning dark and spotted on your kitchen counter? Good for you. Don't toss them, don't hesitate, just grab flour, sugar, and eggs and you're making banana muffins. Homemade muffins really do come together very quickly, and it's hard to imagine a homier snack or treat or brunch offering. Let's face it, muffins are a very close cousin of cake, and cake is always welcome.

You can make these muffins with a standing mixer, but if you do, use the paddle attachment and *do not* overbeat. Overbeating quick bread batters results in tough breads and muffins. You want to still see faint streaks of flour and mashed banana.

Serve warm or at room temperature.

1¾ cups all-purpose flour

1 teaspoon baking soda

½ teaspoon kosher or coarse salt

8 tablespoons (1 stick) unsalted butter, at room temperature

¾ cup granulated sugar

2 large eggs

1 teaspoon pure vanilla extract

2 large very ripe bananas, peeled and mashed (about 1 cup)

½ cup buttermilk, heavy (whipping) cream, or sour cream

½ teaspoon grated orange zest, or ½ teaspoon ground cinnamon (optional)

⅓ cup mini chocolate chips (optional), for sprinkling on top

Cooking Tip: Paper muffin cup liners are very handy. They ensure muffins won't stick to the pan, which is very frustrating after all of your effort. They also make the muffins easier to transport and serve. And there's something to be said for the fact that some kids (not mine, of course, but I've heard stories) tend to want to touch a few muffins before landing on the one they feel is their destined muffin soul mate, and the paper liners make this a little less germy feeling.

1. Preheat the oven to 350°F. Pop paper liners in the cups of a regular-size 12-muffin tin.

2. Place the flour, baking soda, and salt in a small bowl and whisk to mix. Set the flour mixture aside.

3. Place the butter and sugar in a large mixing bowl and, using an electric mixer, beat them until light and fluffy, about 3 minutes. Add the eggs one at a time, then add the vanilla. Blend in the mashed bananas and buttermilk along with the orange zest or cinnamon, if using.

4. Using a wooden spoon, add the flour mixture to the banana mixture in batches, mixing until each addition is just incorporated. At the end the batter should be barely blended (it will be thick). Fill each muffin cup liner three quarters full of batter. Sprinkle mini chocolate chips evenly over the tops of the muffins, if using.

5. Bake the muffins until they spring back when pressed lightly in the center and a toothpick inserted into the center of a muffin comes out clean, 23 to 27 minutes. Let the muffins sit in the muffin tin on a wire rack for 5 minutes, then gently turn them out of the tin and let them cool upright on a wire rack.

Variation

Banana Bread

Preheat the oven to 350°F. Pour the batter into a 9 by 5-inch loaf pan that has been greased with butter or sprayed with nonstick cooking spray. Sprinkle the chocolate chips on top, if desired. Bake the banana bread until a toothpick or wooden skewer inserted into the loaf comes out clean, about 45 minutes. Let the banana bread cool in the pan on a wire rack for 10 minutes, then turn the loaf out of the pan and let it finish cooling upright on the wire rack.

Make Ahead: The banana muffins or bread will last in a tightly sealed container for up to three days without drying out much, thanks to the bananas and dairy. You can freeze muffins easily, which is very useful for weekday breakfasts and spur-of-the-moment snacks. Put them in a freezer-proof, zipper-top plastic bag, squeeze out any extra air, trying not to squeeze the muffins, and put them in the freezer. You can defrost the muffins at room temperature or in a microwave oven, or you can reheat them in a 375°F oven for fifteen minutes or so. Give a muffin a light squeeze or insert a toothpick into the center to see if it's fully thawed. Or eat one.

What the Kids Can Do: Kids can put the liners in the muffin tin and mash the bananas (if you have an old-fashioned potato masher this becomes much more fun; if not use a fork). They can measure the ingredients, crack the eggs, stir the batter, and then scoop it into the muffin tin and sprinkle chocolate chips on top, if desired.

MILK

SEMISWEET

Chapter 18

Simple Weeknight Desserts

It is quite obviously your call whether dessert makes a regular appearance in your home during the week. What you'll find here has less to do with the need for daily desserts than the need to have some dessert recipes that are fast and easy. That way on the days when you do want to serve dessert and have it not be a production (whether that is a Tuesday or a Saturday), you'll have some choices.

Two of the recipes are for ice cream toppings. They are quick enough to make during the week and if you have them on hand, a scoop of ice cream (or a piece of pound cake, or some cut-up fruit) becomes something even more decadent in the time it takes to drizzle over the sauce. Chocolate-Dipped Strawberries turn any day into Valentine's Day. Then the healthier options: self-explanatory Fruit Salad Kebabs and the simple and elegant Berries with Sweetened Yogurt.

Other options are banana muffins (see page 284), any of the sweets in the Bake Sale chapter (pages 321 to 333), Chocolate Pudding (page 318), or Gingersnaps (page 314).

Hot Fudge Sauce

Makes 2 cups
A Fork in the Road Recipe

Say when...

Sorry, I think I blacked out for a minute there. Look, whenever cream, chocolate, and butter meet, only good things can happen. In this case it's a thick sauce begging to be drizzled over ice cream, or maybe a slice of pound cake, or maybe your tongue. And it's as easy as turning on your stove. The chocolate sauce will stay perfectly fresh in your refrigerator for two weeks, and if you want to see a friend's eyes shine with admiration and unbridled affection, bring a mason jar of this next time you go visit.

You probably should save the expensive bittersweet chocolate for the grown-ups since most kids don't go for the sophisticated 72 percent cacao stuff, and they certainly don't care what region of Madagascar the cacao beans are from. I first opened a bag of Nestlé semisweet chocolate chips when I was a wee lass, embarking upon the timeless and unparalleled pleasure of making Toll House cookies, and to this day I remain a dedicated fan, both of the chips, which I use often, and the cookies (you'll find my version of their recipe on page 323). This fudge sauce uses a combination of semisweet and milk chocolate chips, for a balance of chocolatyness that isn't too intense nor too sweet. You can also use all milk chocolate if you're going for a very soft, gentle chocolate flavor.

1 to 1¼ cups heavy (whipping) cream (see Cooking Tip #2)

2 tablespoons (¼ stick) unsalted butter

¾ cup semisweet chocolate chips

¾ cup milk chocolate chips

2 tablespoons light corn syrup

1 teaspoon pure vanilla extract

¼ teaspoon kosher or coarse salt

Ice cream or pound cake, for serving

Cooking Tip #1: Heating liquid in a saucepan until little bubbles form along the perimeter of the liquid is called scalding, in case you've ever been perplexed by this word.

Cooking Tip #2: If you like a fudge sauce with a thinner consistency, then go for the larger quantity of cream. There are arguments to be made for both consistencies, and it's an argument most people enjoy best over a bowl of ice cream covered with hot fudge sauce.

What the Kids Can Do: Scoop out the ice cream or slice the pound cake and drizzle the fudge sauce on top.

1. Heat the cream and butter in a medium-size saucepan over low heat until the butter melts and the mixture is hot but only just beginning to simmer. You'll see little bubbles around the edge of the pan. With the pan still on the heat, add the chocolate chips and let them sit in the hot liquid for a minute or two, until they start to melt. Then stir the mixture occasionally just until it is smooth, about 4 minutes.

2. Remove the chocolate mixture from the heat and stir in the corn syrup, vanilla, and salt. The sauce can be used right away, hot or warm. It will be fairly thin but as it sits and cools the sauce will thicken.

3. ◀━━ You can continue with Step 4 or see the Fork in the Road suggestions for add-ins below.

4. Serve the fudge sauce over ice cream or slices of pound cake. (You can store the sauce, well covered, in the fridge for up to 2 weeks. It will be quite solid when it is cold but can be reheated over low heat or in the microwave at low power.)

◀━━ Fork in the Road

You can add many different flavorings to the chocolate sauce (although the booze options are just for you), or, divide the Hot Fudge Sauce into two cups, keep one plain and simple and doctor up the other cup with any of these:

¼ teaspoon of finely grated orange zest • ½ teaspoon of instant coffee • 1 tablespoon of peanut butter (trust me) • 1½ teaspoons of liqueur, such as Grand Marnier (an orange liqueur), Kahlúa (a coffee liqueur), Frangelico (a hazelnut liqueur) • 1½ teaspoons of any kind of rum, whiskey, or brandy

Caramel Sauce

Makes about 1½ cups sauce

There's something wonderfully old-fashioned about the flavor of caramel, the warm and tickly way it feels in your mouth and throat. If you have never made caramel before you will probably think this is a scary concept. Caramel is in fact nothing more than almost but not quite burnt sugar. It turns a bowl of ice cream into a party and is wonderful to put out in small bowls for little hands to dip apple slices into.

As Charlie would say, "That's what I'm talking about." ↓

I cup granulated sugar

I cup heavy (whipping) cream

¾ teaspoon pure vanilla extract

¼ teaspoon kosher or coarse salt

Ice cream or apple slices, for serving

1. Combine ¼ cup of water and the sugar in a small saucepan. Place over medium-low heat and heat until the sugar dissolves, picking up the pan by its handle and swishing the liquid in the pan gently from time to time (see Note). Do not stir the sugar water (this is hard, I know, being a person who feels the need to do something to the food that is cooking on the stove). When the sugar has dissolved, increase the heat to medium-high. Let the sugar water come to a boil and bubble away until it turns golden brown, gently swirling it from time to time, about 12 minutes. No stirring!

2. When the sugar water has reached a deep, rich, golden amber color, but absolutely before it starts to burn (the color develops quite quickly at the end and darkens a bit more after it comes off the heat; pay close attention), take the pan off the heat and slowly, gradually whisk in the heavy cream. This will cause the mixture to bubble up and sputter and maybe get lumpy for a minute; don't be scared. Whisk the caramel sauce until it is well combined and smooth, then add the vanilla and the salt. Let the caramel sauce cool; it will thicken considerably. Serve the ice cream in individual bowls topped with the caramel sauce. Or set out individual bowls of caramel sauce and a large bowl of apple slices and let everyone dip away.

Note: Um, melted sugar is hot. Like, hot hot. Like don't-learn-this-the-hard-way hot. You do *not* want this touching your skin, or the skin of anyone around you, so be sure to be of sound mind as you make caramel and tell the kids to go away; it's not the best thing to tackle if you're in a multitasking frame of mind.

Cooking Tip: There are two weird things about making caramel sauce. One is that you can't stir the sugar and water mixture while it is cooking, otherwise it will crystallize. Also, you have to let it get deeply golden in color, because that's how it becomes not just sugar and water but true caramel (it really smells like caramel when it's ready). The color will deepen just a bit after you remove the pan from the heat, so take it off the second you feel like the mixture is approaching the color you're looking for, knowing that the amount of time between just right and burnt is a matter of mere seconds.

Make Ahead: The caramel sauce can be refrigerated in a sealed plastic container or a glass jar for several days. Let it come to room temperature before using—it will be thick—or heat it gently in a microwave-safe container in the microwave, or in a saucepan over low heat, before serving.

What the Kids Can Do: Basically, kids can stay clear of the kitchen and think about what ice cream flavors they can scoop out for dessert.

Chocolate-Dipped Strawberries

Makes 25 to 30 strawberries

If you've ever pressed your nose up against the glass of a fancy chocolatier's window, lusting after the fat strawberries enrobed in chocolate, nestled in little ruffled paper negligees, then you will be heartened to see how easy they are to make at home. And if you want to go the extra step and drizzle some melted white chocolate over the strawberries, the result will be quite gorgeous. Oh, and do try the Chocolate-Covered Pretzels (an unusual dessert, a decadent snack) and succumb to the brilliance of salt and sweet vying for your attention.

> 1 package (about 12 ounces) milk chocolate or semisweet chocolate chips
>
> 2 pints strawberries (see Notes)
>
> Melted white chocolate (optional), for drizzling

And they come with their own handles!

1. Line a baking sheet with waxed paper or parchment paper. To melt the chocolate on the stovetop, you can either use a double boiler or place a small, preferably tall and slender, saucepan in a larger skillet. Fill the skillet with enough water to come about ½ inch up the outside of the saucepan. Put the chips in the saucepan and stir over medium heat until the chocolate is fully melted. You can also melt the chocolate in the microwave (see Notes).

2. Using tongs, or your fingers, quickly dip the strawberries in the melted chocolate, tilting the bowl so that the chocolate coats each berry two thirds to three quarters of the way up. Let the excess chocolate drip off. Place the dipped strawberries on the prepared baking sheet.

3. If you are using the melted white chocolate, dip a fork into the chocolate, and working with a back and forth motion,

drizzle it over the dipped portion of the strawberries. Let the chocolate harden, about 15 minutes. If the weather is warm and/or humid you may need to refrigerate the strawberries for a while.

Notes: Make sure the strawberries are very dry before dipping them in the chocolate or it won't stick.

Place the chocolate chips in a deep microwave-safe bowl and microwave them until melted, about 2 minutes, making sure to keep a close eye on them and taking the bowl out to give the chocolate a stir every 20 seconds or so. When the chips are all thoroughly melted, give the chocolate a final stir until everything is smooth.

Make Ahead: Chocolate-dipped strawberries will last in a covered container in the fridge for one day.

What the Kids Can Do: As long as they are old enough to understand and obey the dictum "Don't touch the hot melted chocolate, it will burn you," kids can help dip the strawberries.

Variation

Chocolate-Covered Pretzels

I'm evidently not the kind of mom who lets my kids have candy on a daily basis, although they would probably trade me in a heartbeat for one who would. This recipe variation appears in the weeknight dessert chapter because of its simplicity and speed, but should you decide to throw caution to the winds and put out small plates of sundry things for your kids to roll their pretzels in, you may consider this more of a non-school-night treat.

One 12-ounce bag of chocolate chips melted makes enough to coat one 10-ounce bag of pretzel rods. You can certainly enjoy them plain. But if you're planning ahead and feeling very generous toward your children you might give them some assorted toppings to play with, letting them customize their pretzels just so. Place any or all of the following on small plates: chopped nuts • colored sprinkles • sweetened flaked coconut • crushed cookies • miniature M&M's or other tiny chocolate candies.

Follow the instructions in Step 1 of Chocolate-Dipped Strawberries, then quickly dip the pretzels in the melted chocolate so that the chocolate coats each pretzel two thirds to three quarters of the way up. While the chocolate is still melted, roll the pretzels in the topping of your choice and place them on the baking sheet until the chocolate hardens.

During cooler months the chocolate-dipped pretzels can be stored at room temperature for up to four days in a container with layers of waxed paper or parchment paper to separate them. During warmer months they may be refrigerated for up to two days.

Who's fun mommy now?

Fruit salad +
a stick = fruit
salad kebabs.

Fruit Salad Kebabs

Serves 4 to 6

ORANGE YOU GLAD I DIDN'T SAY BANANA?

On a daily basis, one of the best things you can do to ensure your kids are eating well is to have lots of fruit around, lots and lots of it, so that grabbing a pear or an apple or a bunch of grapes or some strawberries becomes quite routine. Keep cut-up pineapple and melon in the fridge. Let your kids loose in the farmers' market or the produce aisle, and let them choose the fruits they are into at the moment. And keep the fruit visible and accessible. As in put a big basket of fruit on the counter, within reach, and let your kids know it's there for the grabbing. Refrigerated cut-up fruit should be on a shelf they can get to. And when you're looking for a day in, day out weeknight dessert with hardly any fuss or muss, you aren't ever going to do better than fruit.

This is just fruit salad with the added magical ingredient of a skewer (see page 237) because half of winning the battle with getting kids to eat something is often in the presentation. A bowl of fruit salad is perfectly attractive on its own, but when you skewer up patterns of brightly colored sweet fruit it becomes something special. And if you let your kids skewer up their own concoctions, it's a pretty sure bet they're going to eat them.

This fruit salad is great when you have a larger group of kids, who are old enough to handle a skewer (chopsticks are also an option, although they are a bit blunter, so bayoneting the fruit can be a bit more messy). Put the fruit in bowls, set out the skewers or chopsticks, and let everyone spear away.

The fruits here are just a list of suggestions; you'll use whatever you have, what you like, whatever is in season, whatever looks stab-able. Some of the fruit, such as cubed pears or sliced bananas, should be cut up at the last minute to avoid browning.

4 to 6 cups any combination of strawberries, grapes, pitted cherries, thickly sliced banana, and cubed apples, pears, pineapple, and/or melon, such as cantaloupe or honeydew

Sweetened yogurt (optional; see page 297), for serving

YOU'LL ALSO NEED

Four to six 12-inch skewers or eight to twelve 6- or 8-inch skewers

Put the prepared fruit on a platter or in individual bowls. Let everyone pick a combination of fruit to lance up on the skewers. Then, serve the skewers of fruit with sweetened yogurt for dipping, if desired.

What the Kids Can Do:
Choose their favorite fruits, cut them up (with supervision, using age-appropriate knives, sticking to the softer fruits if they are using blunter knives), and skewer everything up.

Berries with Sweetened Yogurt

Serves 4 to 6

A bowl of berries is nice, but a bowl of berries with sweetened yogurt is dessert. Even though this recipe is planted in the weeknight desserts chapter, it wouldn't exactly be out of place with Special Occasion Desserts, or even in the Potluck chapter. Thinking on it, who wouldn't be happy to see these berries for breakfast or brunch? My friend Mary Goodbody brought them for dessert one night and they have become a house standard ever since.

You can use any berry you like, or for the prettiest presentation and the most fanfare, offer an assortment (remember this recipe on the Fourth of July; think red and blue berries with white yogurt). At first, kids seem to stare at the white blob of yogurt on their plate. They dip one tine of their fork in gingerly, lick it, dip two tines in, lick that, and then ask for a big spoon.

A bit of sugar is optional in the berry mixture. The berries will taste wonderful on their lonesome, but, if you like, you can sprinkle some granulated sugar over them and let them marinate (or macerate, which is the fancier term meaning basically the same thing) for one to two hours in the fridge, or a half hour at room temperature, or (more likely) whatever time you have available. The berries will release some liquid and be snuggled in a sweetened juice that somehow elevates their berriness. They will however be softer, so you'll need to judge how that flies with your kids.

For a weeknight dinner you may not give two hoots about what the serving dish looks like, but if you're presenting this to company you probably do. There is no reason you can't use your nice serving bowls to mix the berries and the yogurt in, thus saving yourself the annoyance of washing two extra mixing bowls.

Cooking Tip #1: You can use I percent, 2 percent, or full-fat Greek yogurt. I guess you could use fat-free yogurt, but too much virtue is bad for a soul. Greek yogurt, now very widely available, is thicker, creamier, and richer than regular yogurts (see My Less Fat Greek Dressing on page 85).You can also serve these berries and sweetened yogurt with the Fudgy One-Pot Brownies on page 328.

Cooking Tip #2: Do you have a bottle of imitation vanilla extract in your pantry? Throw it out. It isn't a real ingredient; pure vanilla extract is.

Make Ahead: You can slice and/or macerate the berries an hour or two ahead of time, and you can also mix the sweetened yogurt up to four hours before serving.

What the Kids Can Do: Stir up the yogurt mixture, choose their favorite berries, slice any bigger berries using a kid-friendly knife, and gently toss the berries with sugar, if you are using it.

FOR THE BERRIES

6 cups berries of your choice, such as strawberries (cut in half or sliced, depending on size), raspberries, blueberries, or blackberries, or a mix of 2 or more

2 teaspoons granulated sugar (optional)

FOR THE SWEETENED YOGURT

2 cups Greek yogurt (see Cooking Tip #1)

1 to 2 tablespoons confectioners' sugar

1 teaspoon pure vanilla extract (see Cooking Tip #2)

1. Prepare the berries: Place the berries in a medium-size bowl and very gently toss them with the granulated sugar, if using. Refrigerate the berries for an hour or two or let them stand at room temperature if you'll be eating them within half an hour.

2. Make the sweetened yogurt: Place the yogurt, confectioners' sugar, and vanilla in a smaller bowl and mix until blended. Serve the yogurt with a spoon alongside the berries.

Pretty enough for your in-laws.

When was the last time you had
homemade pudding?

Chapter 19

Special Occasion Desserts

Sometimes life calls for—no—sometimes life *insists* upon a special dessert. Maybe it's because company is coming, maybe it's because you're celebrating something, maybe it's just because a homemade dessert says "Woo hoo!" like nothing else.

You will certainly notice that all of these desserts fit neatly into the category of homey. Even if it's a

THE DILEMMA

I know they won't leave till I serve them dessert.

special occasion, even if you are entertaining, there's not much of a chance that many of us are going to be spinning sugar or making whimsical edible figurines out of marzipan. These are just five desserts that say "I made you something special 'cause I think you're swell." They also all travel well, so they make great potluck contributions.

I'm not a cake baker by nature; cakes make me nervous because all of your eggs are literally and figuratively in one basket. You can't sample a cake ahead of time, like you can with a batch of brownies or cookies, unless you plan to serve a cake with a slice removed from it, so you have to hold your breath and be positive. With cookies, if one tray burns a bit, oh well, those are the cookies my family will be dunking in milk for the next week—not so much with a cake.

So, in this chapter you'll find recipes for one great, reliable chocolate cake and one great, reliable vanilla cake, with your choice of the two quintessential frosting flavors to mix and match. A lot of cakes came and went through my kitchen in the search for two very delicious basic cakes that you can call upon again and again and that don't rely on a degree in pastry making or chemistry to bake successfully. Then there is an apple pie that has practically been a member of our family for years—the kind of pie that you could imagine cooling on the windowsill of a Pennsylvania Dutch kitchen. Gingersnaps also take many of us back to a happy place, and when transformed into ice cream sandwiches become unforgettable. And lastly, there's a chocolate pudding that also speaks to all that is holy and comforting.

There's a maxim about entertaining that goes something along the lines of "The only parts of a dinner that people really remember are the appetizers and the dessert, so make sure the start and the end of the meal are fabulous." I don't know if that's completely true (if it is, I have wasted a lot of time and energy), but these desserts are geared toward leaving your friends and family with happy parting memories.

It's hard not to be happy around a bowl of pudding.

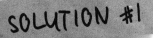

Birthday Chocolate Cake

Makes one 2-layer cake; serves 10 to 12

This layer cake relies on cocoa powder, not melted chocolate, for its good chocolaty flavor, which saves you washing a pan. The cake is light but immensely satisfying, and when it's topped by the chocolate buttercream frosting on page 306, you have a Norman Rockwell chocolate cake, one that begs for candles and a small round-cheeked child to blow them out. You can also choose to go with vanilla buttercream (see page 306), plain or tinted. Cake mixes are great (see Ain't Nothing Wrong with Cake Mixes on page 309), but sometimes you just have to go from scratch. If you'd rather make cupcakes, follow the instructions in the variation on page 305.

I cup (2 sticks) unsalted butter, at room temperature, plus butter for greasing the baking pans

2 cups cake flour (not self-rising), plus more for flouring the baking pans

⅔ cup unsweetened Dutch-processed cocoa powder

2 teaspoons baking powder

½ teaspoon kosher or coarse salt

2 cups granulated sugar

3 large eggs, at room temperature

2 teaspoons pure vanilla extract

½ cup sour cream, or another ½ cup whole milk

¾ cup whole milk

Easiest White or Chocolate Buttercream Frosting (page 306), at room temperature

1. Place a rack in the center of the oven and preheat the oven to 350°F. Place two pieces of waxed paper or parchment paper on top of each other. Set a deep (2-inch) 9-inch cake pan on top and trace the bottom of the pan on the paper.

BUTTERING, FLOURING, AND LINING THE PAN— A NECESSARY EVIL

I haven't been shy about expressing my love and admiration for nonstick cooking spray. I don't use aerosol deodorants or hair sprays because I am aware that they get blamed for holes in the ozone (though I also understand these issues have been somewhat addressed by the aerosol conglomerates), but I do love my nonstick spray. A few things to note.

Stick with (pun intended) sprays made with canola oil, not one of the flavored ones, or the butter or olive oil ones, which don't taste anything like good butter or olive oil and just impart an artificial taste into your food.

Nonstick cooking sprays are not for use on nonstick pans, especially when you are cooking at higher temperatures, as they will leave a stubborn residue on your cookware.

Baker's Joy is a spray that combines fat and flour, saving you the pesky task of buttering and flouring a pan. It really works. Other companies, like PAM, make a "baking spray" that is essentially the same thing.

Having said that, when you are baking a homemade cake I still think you have to perform the pesky chore of cutting out waxed paper or parchment paper circles to line the bottom of your cake pans, to make sure the cakes come out cleanly and in one piece. Just trace the bottom of the pan onto the paper, cut it out, spray the pan, place the circle in the bottom, then spray the circle of paper to coat it. The paper thing is annoying but not nearly as annoying as spending the time to bake a cake from scratch and flipping it out of the pan only to see a big chunk of cake stuck to the bottom of the pan.

Cut out two circles following the trace marks. Butter two deep 9-inch round cake pans, then place a paper circle inside each of the two pans. Butter the paper circles and add a bit of flour to each pan, knocking it around so it coats the bottom and side. Turn the pans upside down to tap out the excess flour. (Don't let the paper circles drop out.) You can also use Baker's Joy or another baking spray instead of the butter and flour (see Buttering, Flouring, and Lining the Pan: A Necessary Evil, page 303).

2. Combine the cake flour, cocoa powder, baking powder, and salt in a medium-size bowl.

3. Place the butter and sugar in a large mixing bowl and, using an electric mixer, beat them until light and fluffy, about 3 minutes. Scrape down the side of the bowl and add the eggs one at a time, beating well after each addition. Beat in the vanilla, blending until the mixture is smooth and glossy, about 2 minutes longer. Scrape down the side of the bowl again. Blend in the sour cream, if using, or the additional ½ cup milk. Add half of the flour mixture and mix at low speed until just almost blended. Add half of the ¾ cup of milk, beating until almost incorporated, then add the remaining flour mixture, blending until almost combined, followed by the remaining milk. Stop while you can still see streaks of flour and milk in the batter, scrape down the side of the bowl, and give a few final stirs with a wooden spoon or a rubber spatula, mixing until everything is just blended.

4. Divide the batter evenly between the two prepared cake pans, smoothing the tops so they are level. Place the cake pans in the oven side by side. Bake the cake layers until a toothpick or wooden skewer inserted near the center of the layers comes out clean, 32 to 36 minutes.

5. Let the cake layers cool in their pans on wire racks for 10 minutes, then invert them onto the racks, removing the pans and the paper circles. Gently turn the layers right side up and let them cool completely.

6. When the cake layers are completely cool, use a thin spatula or butter knife to spread a very thin layer of frosting over the top and side of each layer. Then let the layers sit until the frosting starts to dry and harden a bit, about 15 minutes. Don't worry if some crumbs are visible in this layer; you will be covering it with a nice thick layer

Make Ahead: The cake layers can be made two days ahead of time and, when completely cooled, wrapped well with plastic wrap and held at room temperature until you are ready to frost them.

What the Kids Can Do: They can measure the ingredients for the cake and work the mixer with supervision, if they are old enough. They may enjoy cutting out the circles of waxed paper or parchment paper to line the cake pans. They can help frost the cooled cakes and they can decorate them. For some suggestions on cake decorations, see Step Away from the Cake on page 307.

of frosting. (If it's hot out, or you want to speed up the process, put the layers, unstacked and uncovered, in the fridge for about 10 minutes.) The base layer of frosting seals in the crumbs and then allows you to spread on a thicker layer of frosting without having to worry too much about the crumbs from the layers surfacing as you frost the cake.

7. Spread a thick layer of frosting over the top of one of the cake layers. Place the other cake layer on top, then generously frost the side of the cake. Finally, frost the top of the cake. You can use the spatula or knife to smooth the side and top of the cake or swish and swirl so that nice little peaks and valleys of frosting are created, depending on what look you're going for.

Variation

Birthday Chocolate Cupcakes

Preheat the oven to 350°F. Line 24 medium-size cupcake cups with paper liners (you'll need two cupcake pans with 12 cups each). Fill each cupcake cup liner about two thirds full with the chocolate cake batter. Bake the cupcakes until a toothpick or wooden skewer inserted in the center comes out clean, 22 to 24 minutes. Let the cupcakes cool in the pans on wire racks for 10 minutes, then carefully remove them from the pans, arrange them upright on wire racks, and let them cool completely before frosting.

Happy Birthday to you.

Who needs cake?

Easiest White or Chocolate Buttercream Frosting

Makes enough to frost two 9-inch layers or 24 cupcakes

This is embarrassingly easy. Well, not embarrassingly; we have so many more things to be embarrassed about than how easy it is to make frosting. But you can be sure that people will ask you if you made this yourself, since frosting from a can is so prevalent these days, and you will be able to lower your eyes modestly and say "yes." And, psst, even if you are using a cake mix (see Ain't Nothing Wrong with Cake Mixes on page 309) for the cake or cupcakes, nothing transforms a boxed mix into something more special than homemade frosting.

There are absolutely no secrets or tricks here, no cooking, just a few ingredients that add up to a creamy, buttery frosting that requires one bowl and items you're likely to have in your kitchen at this very moment. The vanilla extract will turn the vanilla frosting a slightly creamy color, vs. straight white, and you can leave it out if you're looking for a bright white frosting, though it sure does add a good flavor. On a happy note, if you are going to tint the frosting with food coloring, the slight color that the vanilla extract adds will not be at all noticeable, so definitely use the vanilla if you are headed in that direction.

What the Kids Can Do: Kids can help measure and they can work the electric mixer if they are old enough. They can certainly weigh in on decisions pertaining to frosting colors.

Make Ahead: The frosting can be made a day ahead and kept at room temperature, covered with plastic wrap or in a plastic container, or you can make it several days ahead and refrigerate it, although you should let it come to room temperature before attempting to spread it on a cake. You will also want to beat the frosting with a spoon or an electric mixer after it does warm to room temperature, and maybe add a tablespoon or two more of milk, which will make it smoother and easier to spread.

5 cups confectioners' sugar

⅓ cup unsweetened Dutch-processed cocoa powder, if you are making chocolate buttercream (see Note)

Pinch of kosher or coarse salt

8 tablespoons (1 stick) unsalted butter, at room temperature

2 teaspoons pure vanilla extract (optional, but recommended)

About 9 tablespoons milk (preferably whole), half-and-half, or heavy (whipping) cream

Food coloring (optional)

1. Place the confectioners' sugar, cocoa powder (if you're making chocolate frosting), salt, and butter in a large mixing bowl and, using an electric mixer, beat them on the lowest speed, so the sugar doesn't poof out all over the counter, until just combined.

2. Add the vanilla and 5 tablespoons of the milk or cream (see Note). Keep blending until everything is smooth and creamy, about 3 minutes, increasing the mixer speed to medium, then to high once the liquid has been incorporated. Add more milk or cream 1 tablespoon at a time as needed to reach the desired consistency.

3. If you are making the vanilla frosting and wish to tint it a color, use the food coloring. You can divide the frosting into several bowls and tint each a different color if that fits into your decorating plans (see Step Away From the Cake on this page).

Note: If you are using the cocoa powder to make chocolate frosting, you should start with 7 tablespoons of milk or cream and you can add more depending on what consistency you are looking for.

Give the frosting a good stir right before you frost the cake.

STEP AWAY FROM THE CAKE

Unless your cake is destined for a formal occasion once it's frosted you may want to let the kids unleash their creative talent. You can put a small amount of frosting, either vanilla (plain or mixed with a few drops of food coloring) or chocolate, in a freezer-proof zipper-top bag. Cut the tiniest hole possible in one corner of the bag and let the kids write or squiggle all over the cake. If the cake is for a kids' party, you can use any kind of candy to decorate: M&M's, sprinkles, jelly beans, gumdrops, Skittles, gummy candies, licorice, whatever you want. And you can choose whether to supervise this closely or let your kids go at it and create the cake of their dreams, which may resemble an impressionist painting that only a dentist who doesn't take insurance could love.

Simple Vanilla Cake

Makes one 2-layer cake; serves 10 to 12

This is just a great, simple, buttery two-layer vanilla cake. It goes beautifully with either vanilla or chocolate buttercream frosting (see page 306), and you can serve the cake up in all of its plain, unadulterated glory or you and your kids can decorate it any way you see fit (see Step Away from the Cake, page 307). For instructions on how to turn the cake into cupcakes, see the variation on page 305.

I cup (2 sticks) unsalted butter, at room temperature, plus butter for greasing the baking pans

3 cups cake flour (not self-rising), plus more for flouring the baking pans

I tablespoon baking powder

½ teaspoon kosher or coarse salt

2¼ cups granulated sugar

5 large eggs, at room temperature

2 teaspoons pure vanilla extract

I cup whole milk

Easiest Vanilla or Chocolate Buttercream Frosting (page 306), at room temperature

1. Place a rack in the center of the oven and preheat the oven to 350°F. Place two pieces of waxed paper or parchment paper on top of each other. Set a deep (2-inch) 9-inch cake pan on top and trace the bottom of the pan on the paper. Cut out two circles following the trace marks. Butter two deep 9-inch round cake pans, then place a paper circle inside each of the two pans. Butter the paper circles and add a bit of flour to each pan, knocking it around so it coats the bottom and side. Turn the pans upside down to tap out the excess flour. (Don't let the paper circles drop out.) You can also use Baker's Joy or another baking spray instead of the butter and flour (see Buttering, Flouring, and Lining the Pan: A Necessary Evil, on page 303).

Make Ahead: The cake layers can be made two days ahead of time and, when completely cooled, wrapped well with plastic wrap and held at room temperature until you are ready to frost them.

What the Kids Can Do: They can measure the ingredients and work the mixer with supervision, if they are old enough. They might actually like the bothersome chore of cutting out waxed paper or parchment paper to line the cake pans. And of course when the cakes have cooled kids can help frost. Then comes the best part of all: decorating (see Step Away from the Cake, page 307).

2. Combine the cake flour, baking powder, and salt in a medium-size bowl.

3. Place the butter and sugar in a large mixing bowl and, using an electric mixer, beat them until light and fluffy, about 3 minutes. Scrape down the side of the bowl and add the eggs one at a time, beating well after each addition, then beat in the vanilla. Scrape down the side of the bowl again. Add half of the flour mixture and mix at low speed until just blended. Add the milk, blending just until it is almost incorporated, then add the remaining flour mixture, mixing at low speed just until everything is almost combined. Stop while you can still see streaks of flour in the batter, scrape down the side of the bowl, and give a few final stirs with a wooden spoon or a rubber spatula, mixing until everything is just blended.

4. Divide the batter evenly between the two prepared cake pans, smoothing the tops so they are level. Place the cake pans in the oven side by side. Bake the cake layers until a toothpick or wooden skewer inserted near the center of the layers comes out clean, about 35 minutes for the cakes.

AIN'T NOTHING WRONG WITH CAKE MIXES

I love cake mixes. There, I said it, and I'm not at all embarrassed. The talented Anne Byrn has made an entire career out of doctoring cake mixes so they don't taste like cake mixes (hence her nom de plume, The Cake Mix Doctor) and now even has her own line of excellent cake mixes. When I have to make three dozen cupcakes for a school function, like cupcake decorating for the spring festival, where nuanced flavor isn't exactly a top criteria and half of the cupcakes end up squished in backpacks, I'd no sooner make homemade cupcakes than individual crèmes brûlées or baklava.

However, for birthdays and other cake-oriented occasions, a homemade cake is in order, and while it would be ridiculous to say it's just as easy to make a cake from scratch, it's not molecular gastronomy either, and the difference is notable. Plus you get to be a hero when a child asks in a demanding and slightly incredulous tone, "Did you make this from scratch?"

← The Platonic ideal of cake.

5. Let the cake layers cool in their pans on wire racks for 10 minutes, then invert them onto racks, removing the pans and the paper circles. Gently turn the layers right side up and let them cool completely.

6. When the cake layers are completely cool, use a thin spatula or butter knife to spread a very thin layer of frosting over the top and side of each layer. Then let the layers sit until the frosting starts to dry and harden a bit, about 15 minutes. Don't worry if some crumbs are visible in this layer; you will be covering it with a nice thick layer of frosting. (If it's hot out, or you want to speed up the process, put the layers, unstacked and uncovered, in the fridge for about 10 minutes.) The base layer of frosting seals in the crumbs and then allows you to spread on a thicker layer of frosting without having to worry too much about the crumbs from the layers surfacing as you frost the cake.

7. Spread a thick layer of frosting over the top of one of the cake layers. Place the other cake layer on top, then generously frost the side of the cake. Finally, frost the top of the cake. You can use the spatula or knife to smooth the side and top of the cake or swish and swirl so that nice little peaks and valleys of frosting are created, depending on what look you're going for.

Variation

Simple Vanilla Cupcakes

Preheat the oven to 350°F. Line 24 medium-size cupcake cups with paper liners (you'll need two cupcake pans with 12 cups each). Fill each cupcake cup liner about two thirds full with the vanilla cake batter. Bake the cupcakes until a toothpick or wooden skewer inserted in the center comes out clean, 23 to 25 minutes. Let the cupcakes cool in the pans on wire racks for 10 minutes, then carefully remove them from the pans, arrange them upright on wire racks, and let them cool completely before frosting.

The Best Streusel Apple Pie Ever

Makes 1 deep-dish pie; serves 8 to 10

Prone to hyperbole? You bet I am. But this pie deserves as much hyperbolic praise as it can get. It is inspired by an apple pie from an old cookbook, Marcia Adams's *Cooking from Quilt Country.* The apples are blanketed and bound up with a custardy coating, and a thick layer of sweet, crumbly streusel topping makes this like an amazing apple crisp in a pie crust. The pie is great still warm from the oven, and a wedge for breakfast the next day is a gift.

FOR THE STREUSEL TOPPING

⅓ cup granulated sugar

¼ cup firmly packed light or dark brown sugar

½ cup plus 2 tablespoons all-purpose flour

I teaspoon ground cinnamon

½ teaspoon ground ginger

½ teaspoon kosher or coarse salt

8 tablespoons (I stick) cold unsalted butter, cut into small pieces

FOR THE PIE FILLING

6 large Granny Smith apples, or a mixture of Granny Smith and any other firm baking apple, peeled, cored, and sliced about ½-inch thick

I unbaked 9-inch deep-dish pie shell

I cup granulated sugar

3 tablespoons all-purpose flour

½ teaspoon ground cinnamon

¼ teaspoon ground cloves

I large egg

I cup heavy (whipping) cream

I teaspoon pure vanilla extract

Whipped cream (see the Cooking Tip on page 318) or vanilla ice cream (optional, but well worth it), for serving

---

REFRIGERATED PIE CRUSTS: A BRILLIANT INVENTION

You surely can make your own pie crust, you overachiever, you. I am usually quite lazy in this regard and partial to the rolled-up pie crusts you can find in the refrigerated section of the supermarket, usually somewhere near the biscuits sold in tubes and the flour tortillas. You can also use the frozen deep dish pie crusts that are already rolled out and fitted and crimped into their aluminum pie plates.

The smell of this pie baking could make you cry.

1. Preheat the oven to 350°F.

2. Make the streusel topping: Combine the ⅓ cup of granulated sugar, the brown sugar, ½ cup plus 2 tablespoons of flour, 1 teaspoon of cinnamon, the ginger, and salt in a food processor and give it a good whirl. Add the pieces of butter and pulse until the butter is incorporated and the mixture is crumbly. Do not overprocess; you don't want a paste (see Cooking Tip #1). Set the streusel topping aside.

3. Make the pie: Put the apples in the pie shell.

4. Combine the 1 cup of granulated sugar and the 3 tablespoons of flour, the ½ teaspoon of cinnamon, and the cloves in a small bowl.

5. Beat the egg in a large bowl, then add the cream and vanilla and blend well. Add the sugar mixture to the egg mixture and stir to blend. Pour the custard mixture over the apples; if the mixture comes more than three quarters of the way up the side of the crust, *stop pouring* so it won't bubble up and overflow.

6. Place the pie on a baking sheet in the oven (see Cooking Tip #2) and bake it for 20 minutes. Carefully remove the pie from the oven, making sure the custard mixture doesn't pour over the side. Evenly and carefully (take your time) distribute the streusel topping over the top of the pie. Carefully (again) return it to the oven and bake until the top is browned and a knife inserted into the pie ensures that the apples are cooked through, about 50 minutes longer.

7. Let the pie cool on a wire rack for at least 20 to 30 minutes, then serve it warm with whipped cream or vanilla ice cream, if desired (and who wouldn't desire that?).

Cooking Tip #1: If you don't have a food processor, or you aren't in the mood to whip it out, you can make the streusel topping by using your fingers to rub the butter into the dry ingredients until the topping is uniform and crumbly.

Cooking Tip #2: It is a good idea to put a baking sheet under the pie as it bakes, as the streusel topping can tend to bubble off the side a bit, and trust me when I tell you that your kitchen will get more than a little bit smoky if this happens.

Make Ahead: You can bake the whole pie a day ahead of time, even two if necessary, and keep it in the fridge, well wrapped. Either let the pie return to room temperature before serving or warm it in a preheated 300°F oven.

What the Kids Can Do: Measure the streusel ingredients and, if you choose to make the streusel topping by hand, kids can help with that or—with supervision— help pulse the streusel in the food processor. If they are old enough, they can peel the apples. They can make the custard and help whip the cream.

Gingersnaps

Makes about 3 dozen (3- to 3¹/₂-inch) cookies

Right up front you should know that this cookie dough has to be refrigerated for about 30 minutes before you roll the cookies into little balls. The dough is quite soft and so needs to firm up before you can shape it without making a huge, sticky mess. Plus the refrigeration time gives the flavors a chance to meld (see the Cooking Tip for Big Fat Chocolate Chunk Cookies on page 324).

There are two reasons these cookies are in the Special Occasion Desserts chapter and not the Bake Sale chapter. First, that chapter was full. There is clearly no reason under the sun that these gingersnaps would not be delightful bake sale fare.

And second, if you take a few extra minutes and a pint of ice cream you can make some of the world's most awesome ice cream sandwiches with these cookies. See page 316 for directions for making ice cream sandwiches.

Make Ahead: The gingersnaps keep well in a sealed container for up to five days. The cookie dough can be made up to four days in advance and refrigerated, covered.

What the Kids Can Do: Kids can measure and stir and use the mixer if they are old enough. They can roll the cookie dough into balls and then roll the balls in the sugar and lightly flatten them on the baking sheet. This provides a lovely teaching moment to talk about how to handle certain foods gently.

2 cups all-purpose flour

2 teaspoons ground ginger

I teaspoon ground cinnamon

¾ teaspoon ground cloves

I teaspoon kosher or coarse salt

I¹/₂ teaspoons baking soda

¾ cup (I¹/₂ sticks) unsalted butter, at room temperature

I cup firmly packed light or dark brown sugar

I large egg, at room temperature

¼ cup molasses

¾ cup granulated sugar, for rolling the cookies

1. Place the flour, ginger, cinnamon, cloves, salt, and baking soda in a medium-size bowl and stir to mix.

2. Place the butter and brown sugar in a large mixing bowl and, using an electric mixer, beat them on high speed until very light and fluffy, about 3 minutes. Scrape down the side of the bowl and add the eggs one at a time, continuing to beat on high speed until the mixture is very light and somewhat shiny, about 2 minutes. Reduce the mixer speed to medium, then blend in the molasses. Add the flour mixture in 3 batches, blending after each addition until well incorporated and scraping down the side of the bowl as needed. Cover the dough and refrigerate it for at least 30 minutes or up to 4 days.

3. Position two oven racks so that they divide the oven into thirds and preheat the oven to 350°F.

4. Place the granulated sugar in a shallow bowl. Pinch off little hunks of dough and use your hands to roll them into fat 1½-inch balls. Then, roll each ball in the sugar. Arrange the balls about 3 inches apart on ungreased baking sheets and press them with the palm of your hand to flatten them slightly. You'll probably fit 12 cookies on each baking sheet so this will take at least three baking sheets to bake all the cookies. You'll want to bake two sheets at a time, placing one on the top rack and one on the bottom. Refrigerate the remaining dough until you are ready to bake it.

5. Bake the gingersnaps until they are browned and cracked a bit on the top, 10 to 12 minutes. Peek partway through the baking time and rotate the baking sheets if the cookies seem to be cooking unevenly. Transfer the cookies to wire racks and let cool (or see the Bonus Solution for ice cream sandwiches, next page).

You can bake these chewy or crisp.

Ice Cream Sandwiches

Makes about 18 ice cream sandwiches

Gingersnaps make great ice cream sandwiches, perfect for a party. Vanilla ice cream is the clear front-runner for most people, especially little ones, but if you wanted to go a little more sophisticated you could try ginger ice cream, chocolate, butter pecan, dulce de leche, or some of the more exotic flavors on the market (cheesecake? pumpkin? caramel apple pie? maple? crème brûlée?).

    For the record, the Big Fat Chocolate Chunk Cookies (page 323) and the Chewy Sugar Cookies (page 326) also make fantastic ice cream sandwiches (see photo, right).

I batch Gingersnaps (page 314)

I pint ice cream of your choice, removed from the freezer for 15 minutes to soften slightly

1. Let the cookies cool, at least partway.

2. Scoop a generous 3 tablespoons of the softened ice cream onto the center of the flat bottom side of 1 cookie. Press the flat bottom side of a second cookie onto the ice cream so that the ice cream oozes out toward the edges of the cookies. Repeat with the remaining ice cream and cookies. That's it.

If you want something spectacular, two slightly warm cookies filled with cold ice cream is a sensory pleasure like few other things.

WHAT IS THE DIFFERENCE BETWEEN LIGHT AND DARK BROWN SUGAR?

The answer is stupidly simple: It's the amount of molasses that has been mixed in with the sugar. Dark brown sugar has more molasses, light brown sugar has less. If you like a more pronounced molasses flavor in your baked goods, go for the dark; if you prefer a subtler molasses flavor, hit the light brown sugar.

Make Ahead: If you want to make the ice cream sandwiches ahead, you can store them in the freezer on a baking sheet covered with plastic wrap. For longer storage place them in a sealed container and they can be frozen for up to 3 days. Let the ice cream sandwiches sit at room temperature for 15 minutes before serving so that the cookies get a bit warmer and the ice cream softens slightly.

← Gingersnaps

← Chewy
Sugar
Cookies

← Big Fat
Chocolate
Chunk
Cookies

Chocolate Pudding

Makes 8 servings, about ⅔ cup each
A Fork in the Road Recipe

Comfort in a cup . . . or a bowl . . . or a vat. Have you ever watched a kid (or, for the sake of discussion, yourself) scrape, scrape, scrape the corners of a bowl of pudding until you could practically put it back in the cabinet without needing to wash it? There's a reason that pudding has long been one of the most consoling and uplifting desserts around. The British actually call all desserts pudding, which shows you right there how elevated the status of actual pudding is in that culture.

You do not have to make the whipped cream, but the chocolate pudding is rich and the whipped cream balances it out gorgeously, decadently. And here's something somewhat surprising: That whipped cream that comes in a can? It's real whipped cream! It just has a blast of nitrous oxide in it, so it shoots out of the nozzle in a fluffy, whipped way. Not bad, in a pinch.

2 tablespoons unsweetened Dutch-processed cocoa powder

2 tablespoons cornstarch

⅔ cup granulated sugar

Pinch of kosher or coarse salt

I cup light or heavy (whipping) cream, at room temperature

3 large egg yolks, at room temperature

2 cups whole milk, at room temperature

4 to 6 ounces semisweet chocolate (see Note), chopped or in morsels

2 tablespoons (¼ stick) unsalted butter, at room temperature

I tablespoon pure vanilla extract

Copious amount of whipped cream, for serving (see the Cooking Tip)

Cooking Tip: To make whipped cream, pour 1½ cups of chilled heavy (whipping) cream into a large chilled bowl, preferably metal (either the bowl of a standing mixer or a mixing bowl, if you are using a hand mixer). Beat the cream at high speed until it starts to thicken, about 2 minutes, then add I teaspoon of pure vanilla extract and 3 tablespoons of either confectioners' or superfine sugar and continue to beat until soft peaks form, about 2 minutes longer. You'll have about 3 cups of whipped cream. Serve immediately or store it covered in the fridge for up to 6 hours.

Make Ahead: You can leave the pudding out for up to two hours if you want to serve it at room temperature. The pudding can also be made up to two days ahead of time and refrigerated. Serve it cold or allow it to return to room temperature before serving. The whipped cream can be made up to six hours ahead of time and refrigerated.

1. Combine the cocoa powder, cornstarch, sugar, and salt in a large saucepan over medium-high heat. Slowly whisk in the cream, then beat in the egg yolks and whisk in the milk. Let the mixture come to a brisk simmer, whisking almost constantly and making sure to keep scraping the sides and bottom of the saucepan. Let the mixture simmer until it starts to thicken, 1 to 2 minutes, then add the chocolate and stir until it melts. Reduce the heat to medium and continue to cook, whisking frequently, until the pudding is fairly thick (it will thicken much more upon cooling), about 2 minutes. Whisk in the butter and vanilla, until the butter is melted.

2. You can strain the pudding through a fine-mesh strainer if you're determined to rid the pudding of any lumps or bumps, or simply transfer the pudding into a big serving bowl or a bunch of individual serving dishes.

3. ⬅ You can continue with Step 4 or see the Fork in the Road suggestions for an adult variation on this page.

4. Press some plastic wrap directly on top of the pudding so it doesn't form a skin, unless you like the skin (like my mom does), in which case just cover it with plastic wrap but don't press it against the surface. Refrigerate the pudding until chilled, about 2 hours or more for a bigger bowl, at least 1 hour for smaller servings. If you like your pudding warm, you can let it sit at room temperature for about 20 to 30 minutes; don't bother to refrigerate it.

Note: Four ounces of chocolate yields a chocolate pudding that is softer in texture and flavor. Six ounces creates a thicker pudding with a fairly intense chocolate taste. If you want an even more bittersweet chocolate pudding, for a more grown-up ending to a meal, you can use bittersweet chocolate.

One spoon for each hand.

Fork in the Road

If you are serving the chocolate pudding in individual cups you can flavor those for the grown-ups with a liqueur. Fill half of the cups with the plain pudding, then stir a teaspoon of any of the following into the rest of the pot:

Cointreau or another orange liqueur • Frangelico or another nut liqueur • coffee liqueur, such as Godiva • an Irish cream liqueur, such as Carolans.

Once you've filled the remaining four cups, *remember which is which!* Like, use different colored cups.

If you think of it, the next time you make a batch of brownies or blondies, bake two. Once they're baked and cooled just cut one whole slab in half, wrap the pieces very well in plastic wrap or aluminum foil, slide them into a freezer-proof zipper-top bag, label and freeze.

You can either freeze baked cookies, after wrapping and sealing them very well, or you can freeze balls of the uncooked dough, which can be thawed at room temperature for thirty minutes, then popped onto baking sheets and baked. The next time your child tells you at ten P.M., "Oh, by the way, Mom, I told my coach you'd bake cookies for the bake sale tomorrow," you will be in good shape. Of course you can still sing a few bars of the "this is ridiculous, you need to be more responsible" song that seems to be a running soundtrack in all of our lives.

Chapter 20

Bake Sale

Those darn bake sales. They seem to pop up like weeds. My older son's school has a bake sale taking place about every other day, with various classes raising money for numerous causes, all of them worthy. You can bake or buy brownies to save the whales, send the chess team to the nationals, and support the theater program, all within one week.

And it's not just bake sales; it's harvest celebrations, birthdays in school, Halloween parties, teacher appreciation lunches, Valentine's Day treats, pot-lucks, the multicultural festival, and the need to say thank you to all kinds of people for all kinds of reasons that make me preheat my oven with regularity. If there aren't two sticks of butter softening on my kitchen counter I feel like I'm forgetting something.

> **THE LAST STRAW**
>
> *You signed me up to bake what?*

These are five trusty recipes that won't let you down. They're sturdy, portable, kid tested (and how, let me tell you), and ready to report for duty. Other recipes to check out are Simple Vanilla Cake (page 308), Birthday Chocolate Cake (page 303), both of which can be baked as cupcakes, Gingersnaps (page 314) and Chocolate-Covered Pretzels (page 293).

You can do half the Butterscotch Brownies (page 330) with chocolate chips, half with butterscotch chips.

I guess I have to eat the broken one . . .

Big Fat Chocolate Chunk Cookies

Makes about 3 dozen (3- to 3½-inch) cookies

A buttery cookie, studded with chocolate, crispy at the edge, chewy in the middle (or crisp all over, depending on how you bake them), the chocolate chip cookie is most people's cookie of choice.

Most chocolate chip cookie recipes resemble each other very closely, and after years of dedicated tinkering, selflessly testing batch after batch after batch, I have to say the recipe on the Nestlé package is pretty much on the money. This tweaked version has extra vanilla and owes much to an article in *The New York Times* written by David Leite that changed my cookie-baking life. It included excellent points about the use of salt (critical) and the optimal size of the cookie (big). The larger size allows for an evolution of textures from the crisp outside to the soft center, and the delightful transition between the two in the middle ring of the cookie. But the kicker was that making the dough ahead of time and letting it sit in the refrigerator for a day or two to develop its flavor is the key to a transcendent chocolate chip cookie (see the Cooking Tip, page 324).

Finally, I have drifted away from chocolate chips toward chunks. There is something about the way the dough balances with those bigger but slightly less frequent melty bites of chocolate that is sheer bliss. I mostly use Toll House for my chunks and my chips and they have never let me down, not once. But if you want to take the time to chop up bars of semisweet chocolate by hand, you will be rewarded with pretty, striated cookies with irregular bits of chocolate interspersed throughout the cookie dough. Don't be hesitant to scrape every bit of the chocolate shards into the batter; bigger pieces and little fragments together are what make these cool.

If cookies were to elect their king, it would undoubtedly be the chocolate chip cookie.

2 cups all-purpose flour

I teaspoon kosher or coarse salt

I teaspoon baking soda

I cup (2 sticks) unsalted butter, at room temperature

¾ cup firmly packed dark brown sugar

¾ cup granulated sugar

2 large eggs

2 teaspoons pure vanilla extract

2 cups (I2 ounces) semisweet chocolate chunks or hand-chopped chocolate bars (regular chips are also fine and dandy)

Poor Charlie had to test cookie after cookie.

Cooking Tip: In Ruth Wakefield's original recipe for Toll House cookies she recommended making the dough a day before you planned to bake the cookies. This piece of information isn't printed on Nestlé's Toll House chocolate morsel package. The reason for this omission, I imagine, is that when most of us get into cookie baking mode, it's with either an imminent deadline or a fierce hankering for immediate gratification, and refrigeration time isn't in the cards. Understood—there are times when cookie baking must happen now and quickly. *But,* if you do have a bit of advance notice, and can make the dough a day or two ahead of baking the cookies, you will notice a deeper, more caramely flavor in your cookies and a more satisfying consistency thanks to a drier dough. You may become a convert. It happened to me.

Make Ahead: The chocolate chip cookies will keep in a tightly sealed container for four to five days.

What the Kids Can Do: Measure, pour, crack eggs, scoop out balls of dough— all the usual baking tasks, including using the electric mixer if they are old enough.

1. Position two oven racks so that they divide the oven into thirds and preheat the oven to 375°F if you are planning to bake the cookies right away, otherwise preheat the oven 30 minutes before you want to bake them.

2. Place the flour, salt, and baking soda in a large bowl and whisk to mix. Set the flour mixture aside.

3. Place the butter, brown sugar, and granulated sugar in a large mixing bowl and, using an electric mixer, beat them on medium speed until creamy and well blended, about 3 minutes. Scrape down the side of the bowl and add the eggs one at a time, beating until each is incorporated. Blend in the vanilla.

4. Gradually add the flour mixture, mixing in each addition until incorporated. Stir in the chocolate chips using a spoon or a rubber spatula if you like your chips to be intact or continue using the electric mixer if you are interested in little bits of the chips breaking off and flecking the batter attractively. If you are not planning on baking the cookies immediately, press plastic wrap directly onto the dough in the bowl and refrigerate it for up to 4 days (the longer the dough sits, the richer and more developed the flavors will be).

5. When ready to bake, roll pieces of dough into 1½-inch balls and arrange them about 2½ inches apart on ungreased baking sheets. You'll probably fit 12 cookies on each baking sheet so this will take at least three baking sheets for all of the cookies. You'll want to bake two sheets at a time, placing one on the top rack and one on the bottom. Bake the cookies until nicely browned, 14 to 16 minutes. Peek partway through the baking time and rotate the baking sheets if the cookies seem to be cooking unevenly.

6. Remove the baking sheets from the oven and let the cookies sit on them for about 1 minute to firm up a bit. Using a spatula, transfer the cookies to wire racks to finish cooling. Serve the cookies warm or let them cool completely.

ONCE UPON A TIME, THE CHOCOLATE CHIP COOKIE WAS BORN

Chocolate chip cookies have a good story behind them. The tale goes that a woman named Ruth Wakefield, who owned the Toll House Inn with her husband in the 1920s, was making her popular chocolate cookies and realized that she didn't have her usual kind of chocolate. She substituted a chopped up bar of semisweet chocolate, only this chocolate didn't melt and blend right into the batter like she expected, it just softened slightly, staying in little pieces that dotted the cookies. The cookies became famous, and sales of the semisweet chocolate bar, given to her by a certain gentleman named Andrew Nestle, skyrocketed. Andrew Nestle got Ruth's permission to print the Toll House recipe on his company's packaging—in exchange for a lifetime supply of chocolate. (It's evident that Ruth Wakefield could have used an agent.) The cookie's fame continued to soar and in 1939 history was made when the Nestlé company created chocolate chips, calling them chocolate morsels, and chocolate chip cookies became the most popular cookie in the United States.

Chewy Sugar Cookies

Makes about 3 dozen (3-inch) cookies

I had forgotten all about sugar cookies—modest, unshow-offy sugar cookies—until our neighbor Donna showed up with a platter of them for dessert one night. Placed alongside some fancier offerings, they were the first to go, and the kids in particular went bonkers over them. They're bake sale naturals.

The baking time is important, because it's a key factor in producing a chewier cookie vs. a crunchier one. You may have to play around a bit to determine what amount of time results in your perfect cookie. This is a pleasant chore.

2¼ cups all-purpose flour

I teaspoon baking soda

¾ teaspoon baking powder

½ teaspoon salt

I cup (2 sticks) unsalted butter, at room temperature

¾ cup granulated sugar, plus ½ cup for rolling out the cookies (optional)

½ cup confectioners' sugar (see Note)

2 large eggs

2 teaspoons pure vanilla extract

Unpretentious and delicious.

1. Position two oven racks so that they divide the oven into thirds and preheat the oven to 375°F.

2. Place the flour, baking soda, baking powder, and salt in a medium-size mixing bowl and whisk to mix. Set the flour mixture aside.

3. Place the butter, 3/4 cup of the granulated sugar, and the confectioners' sugar in a large mixing bowl and, using an electric mixer, beat them on medium speed until light and fluffy, about 2 minutes. Scrape down the side of the bowl and add the eggs one at a time, beating until each is incorporated. Add the vanilla and mix until the batter is very light and smooth, about 2 minutes longer. Gradually add the flour mixture, mixing each addition until blended.

4. Place the remaining 1/2 cup of granulated sugar, if using, in a shallow bowl. Roll pieces of dough into 1 1/2-inch balls; they'll be sticky and soft and don't have to be perfectly round at all (see Cooking Tip #1). Roll each ball of dough in the sugar (see Cooking Tip #2), then arrange them about 3 inches apart on ungreased baking sheets. You'll probably fit 12 cookies on each baking sheet so it will take at least three baking sheets for all of the cookies. You'll want to bake two sheets at a time, placing one on the top rack and one on the bottom. After you have placed all of the balls on the baking sheets, using your palm, gently press down on each ball until it is about 1/3-inch thick (this is enjoyable to do, very satisfying somehow).

5. Bake the cookies for 11 to 14 minutes, depending on how chewy or crisp you like them. I like them chewy, hence the name of the recipe, so I bake them for the shorter time. The cookies will still be very pale when they are done, so don't think you should be waiting for them to turn golden brown.

6. Remove the baking sheets from the oven and let the cookies sit on them for about 1 minute to firm up a bit. Using a spatula, transfer the cookies to wire racks to finish cooling.

Note: If you prefer or if you don't have confectioners' sugar on hand, you can use an additional 1/2 cup of granulated sugar in place of the confectioners' sugar.

Cooking Tip #1: If the cookie dough is very soft, you can refrigerate it for 20 to 30 minutes so that it firms up a bit and is easier to handle.

Cooking Tip #2: You don't have to roll the little balls of dough in granulated sugar. This adds that extra something, and children find it entertaining to do, but if you're not in the mood, just skip it. The balls of dough will be a bit sticky when you press them flat, so instead of using your palm you may want to butter the bottom of a glass and use that to press the cookies down.

You can play around with colored sugars to dress up the cookies for various occasions—green and red for Christmas, blue and white for Hanukkah, black or orange or some of each for Halloween, pink or blue for a baby shower, brown for Groundhog Day . . . maybe not.

Make Ahead: These will keep in a tightly sealed container for three to four days.

What the Kids Can Do: The kids will enjoy measuring, pouring, cracking eggs—all the usual cookie baking chores, including using the electric mixer if they are old enough. And they can roll the cookie balls, coat them with sugar, and flatten them slightly before baking.

Fudgy One-Pot Brownies

Makes 12 huge or 24 reasonably sized brownies

It had been dawning on me that the surest way to achieve brownie nirvana, the kind of fudgy chocolatiness that wimpy people say is *too* chocolaty (and then go on to polish off another brownie or two), is best achieved by combining cocoa powder and melted chocolate. During this period of intense brownie contemplation I had lunch with Melissa Clark, food writer and mom to young Dahlia, and mentioned my brownie quest. She thought she had a recipe somewhere with dueling chocolates, and she e-mailed it to me that afternoon. I tinkered with it a bit, determined to decode a perfect brownie that could be mixed right in the saucepan. This is the one-pot result. Fifteen minutes of hands-on time, max, and well worth every minute.

I am also ridiculously pleased to say that this recipe shaves off two more common brownie-making steps. Often a recipe will tell you to chop the chocolate before melting it. Here you just make sure to melt it with the butter over low heat, and the chocolate will dissolve gently into the butter, without scorching. Also, you can skip the whole double boiler thing if you keep the heat low enough, don't stray too far, and stir frequently. This saves you washing a chopping board, a knife (or a food processor bowl and blade), and the second double boiler pan. You will want to celebrate this with a brownie.

Cooking Tip: A bit of bad news, I'm afraid. You really need to let these brownies cool completely before you cut them or they will cut messily and not hold their shape very well. It's best to leave the house to avoid temptation. But, hey, they're for a bake sale. You weren't going to actually eat one? Oh, okay, that'll cost you $1.00. By the way, the brownies are *so* much better, both in terms of taste and consistency, when they are completely cool—in fact they're even better the next day, firm and amazingly moist inside, with that gorgeous lightly crackled top crust.

Make Ahead: I have heard that these brownies can be stored in a tightly sealed container for up to five days, but this may be just a rumor.

What the Kids Can Do: They can measure, mix, dump, stir, pour, stand around saying "Are they cool yet? Are they cool yet? How about now? Are they cool now?"

I cup (2 sticks) unsalted butter, plus butter for greasing the baking pan (optional)

Nonstick cooking spray (optional)

3 ounces unsweetened chocolate

½ cup unsweetened Dutch-processed cocoa powder

2½ cups granulated sugar

½ teaspoon kosher or coarse salt

I tablespoon pure vanilla extract

3 large eggs

1½ cups all-purpose flour

1. Preheat the oven to 350°F. Generously butter a 13 by 9-inch baking pan or spray it with nonstick cooking spray.

2. Place the butter and chocolate in a medium-size saucepan over low heat and let melt together, stirring until smooth. Remove the saucepan from the heat and stir in the cocoa powder, sugar, and salt, then blend in the vanilla. Beat in the eggs one at a time, stirring to mix quickly so they don't have a chance to cook at all before they are blended in. Blend in the flour.

3. Scrape the thick batter into the prepared baking pan and smooth the top with a spatula. Bake until the edges just begin to pull away from the sides of the pan and a wooden skewer or toothpick inserted into the middle comes out clean, 25 to 30 minutes.

4. Let the brownies cool in the pan on a wire rack. When completely cool, cut them into 12 or 24 squares.

Save me a corner.

Butterscotch Brownies (aka Blondies)

Makes 12 huge or 24 reasonably sized squares

Jack seems to be quality control testing this batch.

Hard as it may be for some of us to believe, sometimes people—both big people and little people—aren't in the mood for chocolate. That's okay; there's nothing wrong. These bar cookies, also known as blondies, have all of the satisfying texture and heft of a brownie plus a wonderful old-fashioned butterscotch flavor, courtesy of the brown sugar, butter, and generous dose of vanilla. You will likely be able to whip up a batch without leaving your home, since the ingredients are very straightforward pantry items. And unless one of your kids chooses that very moment to distract you, you will be able to get the pan in the oven in ten to fifteen minutes.

If you're looking to be the school hero, you can make a batch of these *and* a batch of the equally easy Fudgy One-Pot Brownies (page 328) and put them together on the bake sale table. You know what else looks pretty? Stack a blondie on top of a brownie, slide both of them into one of those small clear-plastic party goody bags, and tie the top with ribbon. This combo would also make a pretty compelling parting gift if you were hosting a baby shower or some such. Or you could just stack a blondie on top of a brownie and eat them.

¾ cup (1½ sticks) unsalted butter, plus butter for greasing the baking pan (optional)

Nonstick cooking spray (optional)

1¾ cups packed light or dark brown sugar

2 teaspoons pure vanilla extract

2 large eggs

1¾ cups all-purpose flour

¾ teaspoon baking soda

½ teaspoon kosher or coarse salt

1 cup semisweet chocolate chips, butterscotch chips, or chopped nuts, such as walnuts or cashews (optional; see Note)

1. Preheat the oven to 350°F. Butter a 13 by 9-inch baking pan or spray it with nonstick cooking spray.

2. Place the butter in a medium-size saucepan and melt it over low heat. Remove the saucepan from the heat, add the brown sugar, and stir until blended, then let cool for at least 5 minutes. Add the vanilla followed by the eggs, one at a time, stirring to mix quickly until well combined, so the eggs don't cook in the still slightly warm brown sugar mixture.

3. Combine the flour, baking soda, and salt in a small bowl. Add the flour mixture to the saucepan and stir until combined. Stir in the chips or nuts, if using. Scrape the batter into the prepared baking pan and smooth the top with a spatula. Bake until a wooden skewer or a toothpick inserted in the middle comes out clean, 24 to 28 minutes.

4. Let the blondies cool in the pan on a wire rack. When cool, cut them into 12 or 24 squares.

Note: You can mix semisweet chocolate and butterscotch chips or add enough chopped nuts to equal one cup if you're feeling really frisky.

ALLERGIES

We all know a person or two (me, for example) with allergies, and because nut allergies are so prevalent among kids, it's often good to steer clear of them (the nuts, not the kids). However, if you know your audience, and love nuts, go right ahead and nut these puppies up. I often make blondies with chocolate chips and/or butterscotch chips baked in (which does make them a bit sweeter), but they are also excellent unembellished; they'll work every which way you like them.

Cooking Tip: If you like your blondies pretty moist and a little sticky, bake them for the shorter length of time. If you prefer them more fully cooked and a bit more cakelike, then leave them in for longer.

Make Ahead: The blondies can keep in a tightly sealed container for up to four days.

What the Kids Can Do: Like most baking recipes, this one has loads of opportunities for measuring and dumping and egg cracking.

Chocolate Peanut Butter Squares

Makes 25 squares

I really hope that this isn't the first recipe you flip to in this book, not because it isn't good (oh, it's good) but because it's so decadent that if this is your first impression of what I am feeding my family you will probably call the authorities. In short, this is rich, fattening, and a total indulgence—meant to be served in very small portions on rare occasions or as a no-fail deal maker at bake sales.

There are certain foods that have an immense "first bite" potency, as in the first bite is so amazing that about 47 percent (give or take) of the pleasure of that particular food resides in that initial mouthful. Reese's Peanut Butter Cups embody that quality for me, not that I'm not happy to keep going, mind you. This is an easy and homey version of that enduring, mouthwatering candy, and you will want to cut them into small squares since they are rich, rich, rich. The variation offers a chance to make adorable individual portions in little ruffled cups, should you be in the market for that kind of thing. I will warn you, this version is a bit of a pain in the rear.

6 tablespoons (¾ stick) unsalted butter, at room temperature, plus butter for greasing the baking pan (optional)

Nonstick cooking spray (optional)

¼ cup firmly packed dark brown sugar

1¼ cups confectioners' sugar

¾ cup creamy peanut butter

¼ cup graham cracker crumbs (see Note)

2 cups (12 ounces) semisweet or milk chocolate chips, or a combination of the two

That whole chocolate-and-peanut-butter concept is pretty compelling.

Make Ahead: You can make the Chocolate Peanut Butter Squares up to one week in advance. Keep them tightly sealed in the fridge and let them come to room temperature before serving.

What the Kids Can Do: Pounding graham crackers into crumbs is great fun. They can do all of the basic measuring and press the peanut butter mixture into the pan.

1. Lightly butter a 9-inch-square baking pan or spray it with nonstick cooking spray (or use a nonstick pan).

2. Place the brown sugar, confectioners' sugar, peanut butter, graham cracker crumbs, and 5 tablespoons of the butter in a medium-size bowl and beat with an electric mixer until well combined but still a bit crumbly, about 1 minute (it won't get totally smooth; that's okay). Press the peanut butter mixture evenly into the prepared baking pan in a thin layer, about ¼ inch thick.

3. Place the chocolate and the remaining 1 tablespoon of butter in a small saucepan over very low heat and melt, stirring frequently until smooth, about 7 minutes. You can also do this in the microwave, stirring every 20 seconds or so, until smooth, 2 to 3 minutes in all. Let the chocolate mixture cool briefly, then while still hot, using a rubber spatula, gently spread it over the peanut butter layer. Refrigerate, covered with plastic wrap, until the chocolate has firmed up, about 1 hour. Cut into 36 small (roughly 1½-inch) squares.

Note: You can either buy graham cracker crumbs or make your own by putting graham crackers into a zipper-top bag and pounding it gently with a rolling pin or the bottom of a pan or a can of beans or anything sturdy with some weight to it. Four graham cracker squares make about ¼ cup of crumbs.

Variation

Chocolate Peanut Butter Cups

These are adorable, but definitely a bit fussy to make. You will need to use 3 cups of chocolate chips instead of 2. Before beginning the recipe, line 36 mini muffin tins with mini paper liners. After you have made the peanut butter mixture as described in Step 2 and melted the chocolate, put about a teaspoon of melted chocolate in each liner, making sure it covers the bottom of the cup. Then pinch off about a teaspoon of the peanut butter mixture, flatten it into a nickel-size disk (it does not need to be neat at all, this is the filling), and top the chocolate with the peanut butter circle. Spoon another 1 to 2 teaspoons of melted chocolate on top until the peanut butter filling is not visible; as you work you may need to rewarm the chocolate, which will thicken as it sits. Refrigerate the chocolate peanut butter cups for 1 hour to set.

In the 1970s when my sister and I were little, my mother had fully bought into the health food thing, making us peanut butter and jelly sandwiches with homemade peanut butter that had to be vigorously stirred to reincorporate the oil that had separated to the top, eighteen-grain bread, and jelly that was essentially fruit that someone had briefly stepped on. I remember how heavy the sandwiches were, outweighed only by Mom's wheat germ pancakes. I looked longingly at my friends' sandwiches, with squishy white bread, pale creamy peanut butter, and grape jelly smooth as silk. They had little bags of chips, even candy in their lunches—on a weekday! For lunch! We occasionally got a piece of rectangular sesame candy or a bumpy fruit roll, then called fruit "leather," which could not have been more aptly named.

True story—for Halloween, this is what my mother handed out as treats for many years: a marshmallow impaled on a toothpick with either two dried apricots or two dried prunes, one on each side, wrapped in plastic wrap. I swear to you. Later she decided that she had had enough bean sprouts and moved on to ethnic foods like paella and *choucroute*. By the time we were older, she was elbow deep in our Halloween bags, digging for mini Snickers. Now those bran-infused times seem like a distant carob-colored memory (but if you'd like a recipe for granola, see page 12).

What You May Be Looking For

DINNER IN UNDER AN HOUR

MAKE-AHEAD DISHES

Breakfast and Brunch

Lunch

Snacks and Appetizers

Soups

VEGETARIAN DISHES

PORTABLE DISHES

MEAT DISHES

FORK IN THE ROAD

FOR THE PICKY EATER

Breakfast and Brunch

Lunch

Snacks

Appetizers, Soups, and Salads

Main Courses

Sides

Desserts

Menus

Resources

Amazon

www.amazon.com

A one-stop shopping go-to source for lots of specialty ingredients, and they carry (or present purveryors who carry) a large assortment of French Le Puy and Umbrian/Italian lentils, as well as all kinds of Asian and Hispanic/Mexican ingredients as well.

Asiafoodgrocer.com is another good source for Asian ingredients.

Kalustyan's

www.kalustyans.com

A great online source for spices, herbs, seeds, chiles, and many other specialty items. They carry raw, shelled pumpkin seeds (also shelled pepitas), handy for making the House Pumpkin Seeds (page 40), when you are not concurrently carving a Jack-o'-Lantern.

Penzey's

www.penzeys.com

There are lots of good herb and spice lines, and some stores have great in-house lines of spices, too, but one excellent one-stop shopping website with tons of choices is Penzey's. They have brick-and-mortar stores, too.

Conversion Tables

Approximate Equivalents

I STICK BUTTER = 8 tbs= 4 oz= ½ cup

I CUP ALL-PURPOSE PRESIFTED FLOUR OR DRIED BREAD CRUMBS = 5 oz

I CUP GRANULATED SUGAR = 8 oz

I CUP (PACKED) BROWN SUGAR = 6 oz

I CUP CONFECTIONERS' SUGAR = 4½ oz

I CUP HONEY OR SYRUP = 12 oz

I CUP GRATED CHEESE = 4 oz

I CUP DRIED BEANS = 6 oz

I LARGE EGG = about 2 oz or about 3 tbs

I EGG YOLK = about I tbs

I EGG WHITE = about 2 tbs

Please note that all conversions are approximate but close enough to be useful when converting from one system to another.

Weight Conversion

U.S./U.K.	METRIC	U.S./U.K.	METRIC
½ oz	15 g	7 oz	200 g
I oz	30 g	8 oz	250 g
I½ oz	45 g	9 oz	275 g
2 oz	60 g	I0 oz	300 g
2½ oz	75 g	II oz	325 g
3 oz	90 g	I2 oz	350 g
3½ oz	100 g	I3 oz	375 g
4 oz	125 g	I4 oz	400 g
5 oz	150 g	I5 oz	450 g
6 oz	175 g	I lb	500 g

Liquid Conversion

U.S.	IMPERIAL	METRIC
2 tbs	I fl oz	30 ml
3 tbs	I½ fl oz	45 ml
¼ cup	2 fl oz	60 ml
⅓ cup	2½ fl oz	75 ml
⅓ cup + I tbs	3 fl oz	90 ml
⅓ cup + 2 tbs	3½ fl oz	100 ml
½ cup	4 fl oz	125 ml
⅔ cup	5 fl oz	150 ml
½ cup	6 fl oz	175 ml
½ cup + 2 tbs	7 fl oz	200 ml
I cup	8 fl oz	250 ml
I cup + 2 tbs	9 fl oz	275 ml
I¼ cups	I0 fl oz	300 ml
I⅓ cups	II fl oz	325 ml
I½ cups	I2 fl oz	350 ml
I⅔ cups	I3 fl oz	375 ml
I¾ cups	I4 fl oz	400 ml
I¾ cups + 2 tbs	I5 fl oz	450 ml
2 cups (I pint)	I6 fl oz	500 ml
2½ cups	20 fl oz (I pint)	600 ml
3¾ cups	I½ pints	900 ml
4 cups	I¾ pints	I liter

Oven Temperatures

°F	GAS MARK	°C	°F	GAS MARK	°C
250	½	120	400	6	200
275	I	140	425	7	220
300	2	150	450	8	230
325	3	160	475	9	240
350	4	180	500	I0	260
375	5	190			

Note: Reduce the temperature by 20°C (68°F) for fan-assisted ovens.

Index

manhole eggs, 8–9

mini frittatas, 281

moist banana muffins, 284–85

oatmeal your way, 16–17

potato pancakes, 255–57

scrambled eggs, many ways, 5–7

vegetable frittata, 279–81

you-are-the-best-mom-in-the-world pancakes, 276–77

Brie cheese:

adding to macaroni and cheese, 169

the great grilled cheese sandwich, 20–21

Broccoli:

adding to English muffin pizzas, 11

adding to frittata, 279

adding to grilled pizzas, 189

adding to meat loaf, 157

adding to quesadillas, 201

adding to sesame noodles, 184

cheesy rice with, 246–47

florets, storing, xxiv

green eggs, 7

Japanese restaurant salad, 86–87

or cauliflower, roasted, with (or without) olive vinaigrette, 264–65

simplest chicken or shrimp kebabs, 237–39

tofu-veggie stir-fry, 194–95

vegetable bin stone soup, 79–81

Broiled miso cod fingers, 146–47

Broth:

canned or boxed, buying, xxiv

low-sodium, xxiv

using bouillon cubes for, 69

Brownies:

butterscotch (aka blondies), 330–31

carryover cooking, note about, 136

fudgy one-pot, 328–29

Brown sugar, types of, 316

Bruschetta:

compared with crostini, 53

tomato, 52–53

Butter, for recipes, xxii

Buttercream frosting, easiest white or chocolate, 306–7

Buttermilk:

lower-fat ranch dressing, 85

ranch dip for veggies, 85

ranch dressing, 85

Butterscotch brownies (aka blondies), 330–31

C

Caesar salad dressing, 90–91

Caesar salad with garlicky croutons, 89–91

Cajun rub, 103

Cake mixes, baking with, 309

Cakes:

birthday chocolate, 303–5

birthday chocolate cupcakes, 305

coffee, Aaron E.'s favorite apple, 282–83

letting kids decorate, 307

simple vanilla, 308–10

simple vanilla cupcakes, 310

Capers:

about, 233

chicken piccata-ed or plain, 233–35

roasted asparagus, 262–63

Caramel sauce, 290–91

Carbohydrates, note about, 255

Carrot(s):

adding to cheesy rice, 247

adding to meat loaf, 157

adding to sesame noodles, 184

-ginger dressing, Japanese, 87

Japanese restaurant salad, 86–87

kitchen sink chopped salad, 92–93

peeled and cut, storing, xxiv

tofu-veggie stir-fry, 194–95

vegetable bin stone soup, 79–81

Cauliflower:

adding to cheesy rice, 247

and cheddar soup, 74–77

or broccoli, roasted, with (or without) olive vinaigrette, 264–65

simplest chicken or shrimp kebabs, 237–39

vegetable bin stone soup, 79–81

Celery:

adding to meat loaf, 157

vegetable bin stone soup, 79–81

Charlie and Jack's "sub" sandwiches, 23

Charlie's olive percenter, 5